Contributions to Management Science
www.springer.com/series/1505

Jane E. Klobas · Paul D. Jackson
(Editors)

Becoming Virtual

Knowledge Management
and Transformation
of the Distributed Organization

160401

With 25 Figures and 20 Tables

Physica-Verlag
A Springer Company

Professor Jane E. Klobas
UWA Business School
University of Western Australia
35 Stirling Highway
Crawley, WA 6009
Australia
jane.klobas@uwa.edu.au
and

Carlo F. Dondena Centre
for Research in Social Dynamics
Università Bocconi
Via Sarfatti 25
20136 Milano
Italy
jane.klobas@unibocconi.it

Dr. Paul D. Jackson
School of Management
Edith Cowan University
100 Joondalup Drive
Joondalup, WA 6026
Australia
p.jackson@ecu.edu.au

Library of Congress Control Number: 2007934382

ISSN 1431-1941

ISBN 978-3-7908-1957-1 Physica-Verlag Heidelberg New York

Physica-Verlag is a part of Springer Science+Business Media

springer.com

© Physica-Verlag Heidelberg 2008

Production: LE-TEX Jelonek, Schmidt & Vöckler GbR, Leipzig
Cover-design: WMX Design GmbH, Heidelberg

SPIN 12036219   134/3180YL - 5 4 3 2 1 0   Printed on acid-free paper

Preface

The editors and research team would like to thank the management and staff of TPC, who must remain anonymous. Without their enthusiastic involvement, openness and patience, this project would not have been possible. We hope that the outcomes are useful to them and any others wishing to understand the complexities and implications of becoming virtual.

June 2007   Jane Klobas
                                                            Paul Jackson

Contents

Contributors

Dr. Gaela Bernini

Department of Management, Economics and Industrial Engineering, Politecnico of Milan, P.za Leonardo da Vinci 32, 20133 Milan, Italy, gaela.bernini@polimi.it

Dr. Hosein Gharavi

School of Business, American University in Dubai, PO Box 28282, Dubai, United Arab Emirates, hgharavi@aud.edu

Dr. Paul Jackson

School of Management, Edith Cowan University, 100 Joondalup Drive, Joondalup 6026, Western Australia, p.jackson@ecu.edu.au

Dr. Ivan Jensen

University College Copenhagen and MetaManagement, Hultmannsvej 5A, 2900 Hellerup, Denmark, ij@metamanagement.dk

Louise Kjaer, MSc

Consultant, Frederiksdalsvej 200, 2830 Virum, Denmark, louisekjaer@gmail.com

Prof. Jane Klobas

Carlo F. Dondena Centre for Research on Social Dynamics, Università Bocconi, via Sarfatti 25, 20136 Milan, Italy and UWA Business School, University of Western Australia, PO Box 1164, Nedlands 6909, Western Australia, jane.klobas@unibocconi.it, jane.klobas@uwa.edu.au

Dr. Stefano Renzi

Istituto di Metodi Quantitativi, Università Bocconi, via Sarfatti 25, 20136 Milan, Italy, stefano.renzi@unibocconi.it

Abbreviations

CoP	Community of Practice
DF	Dialogue Forum (Unit 2's electronic discussion forum)
DIP	Development Information Portal (Unit 2's intranet)
HO	Head Office
ICT	Information and Communications Technology
IS	Information Systems
IT	Information Technology
OC	Organizational Commitment
OM	Organizational Memory
OS	Outside Head Office
PP	Project Portal
SU	Social Uncertainty
TMS	Transactive Memory Systems
TPB	Theory of Planned Behavior
TPC	Unit 2's parent company ("The Parent Company")
Unit 2	The International Development Unit of TPC

Introduction

Jane Klobas and Paul Jackson

The past two decades have seen a growing diversity of organizational form as organizations use new technologies to reconfigure work, distributing it more than ever across distant locations, different time zones and even diverse organizations. Companies have been able to place their staff with customers. Production and service work can be moved to low cost countries or people's homes, or subcontracted to more qualified firms or individuals. Teams of empowered and motivated specialists can be drawn from around the world, using information and communications technologies (ICT) to communicate and share knowledge. A shirt can be designed in Italy, made in China and sold in Australia. The world is said to be increasingly "virtual", a condition in which organizational solidity is only apparent: the reality is one of high performing, dynamic networks which connect staff, enterprises, processes and expertise, where the drive to produce or compete has displaced the need for permanency and structure.

ICT offers distributed organizations the chance to become virtual organizations, organizations that use computer-based networks (in particular, the Internet) to capitalize on the advantages of actual differences in time zones, locations and contractual relationships between individuals and groups; communications, work processes and organizational culture are as natural in the distributed form as if the organization were virtually working together in a single location. Virtualization might be a deliberate and premeditated organizational response to these opportunities or an emergent phenomenon that develops *ad hoc* as individuals and groups use tools such as hand-held communication devices or wikis (tools that allow joint authorship of public and private Web pages) to support their work.

Indeed, there are many forms of virtual organization, the most effective of them "singularly focused on creating, nurturing, and deploying key intellectual and knowledge assets while sourcing tangible, physical assets in a complex network of relationships" [19:1]. The key to effective virtual organizations is their responsiveness, flexibility and ability to configure knowledge and capital assets based upon changing needs.

Telework is a basic form of virtual work that involves working at a location other than the employer's office or plant, often at home [10; 13; 17]. Telework can meet the personal needs and preferences of employees who choose when and where they work. At the same time, employers may save office space and have access to a wider pool of talent from which to select, including people who cannot easily reach a central office. Problems experienced with telework include isolation, greater vulnerability of staff and performance measurement.

Mobile virtual work generally continues to revolve around a head office, but certain staff are given technology and resources that enable them to perform tasks that were previously performed in the office while traveling [1; 6]. Typical examples are: sales personnel who can visit customers, check inventory, raise queries and place orders while still at a customer site and then move directly to the next customer; and service and maintenance workers who install or maintain gas and electricity services and use ICT tools to download orders and locate infrastructure such as underground pipes.

Customer frontline work is the placement of staff at a customer site [7]. This enables more informed provision of client services. However, it may blur the structural lines between organizations when frontline workers develop a sense of loyalty and common purpose with the customer rather than their employer.

A *virtual team* is a team brought together with no consideration for physical location [9; 11; 12; 16]. Virtual teams may be enduring, e.g., the international sales team for a particular product, or project-based. Computer systems (usually via the Internet) provide support for communication, collaboration, knowledge sharing and storage.

The *virtual supply chain* is a materials supply system which functions on the Internet using a network of often anonymous suppliers who respond to requests for supplies via an e-business hub or other Web-enabled system [5; 14; 20]. Indeed, there are now firms that no longer produce anything, but rely on computer-mediated, just-in-time e-commerce supplies in order to service customers. In its extreme form, the firm supplies a known brand, organizes suppliers and controls the customer relationship functions, with no inventory and little direct labor.

Finally, the *virtual corporation* is one which exploits the virtual form at the inter-organizational level. It is an organizational response to market demands and opportunities and consists of transient consortia or associations of organizations, each of which provides specific capabilities to meet a specific – often sudden – requirement [8; 18; 19]. In this form, an association of firms or parts of firms can rapidly present a "virtual shop front" of skills and experience which no single company could acquire with sufficient speed to respond to sophisticated customer needs or large, complicated projects.

New forms of virtualization are emerging as technology develops and new social institutions evolve. Many of these new forms are forms of ICT-enabled "networked enterprise",

the organizational form built around business projects resulting from the cooperation between different components of different forms, networking amongst themselves for the duration of a given business project, and reconfiguring their networks for the implementation of each project ... the network is the enterprise" [4:67]

Some forms build on networks of individuals. "Networked collective intelligence" [15] is the ICT-enabled collaborative development of knowledge resources by networks of individuals. Such networks have created the online encyclopedia, Wikipedia, and the computer operating system, Linux, and added reviews and ratings to books and resources sold online by Amazon.com. NASA's Clickworkers extend the boundaries of the organization to include networked, remote individuals who volunteer to identify Mars craters.

Any organization might use one, some, or all of these forms of organizing – and, potentially, other forms yet to develop – to improve the way it works and to increase its range of opportunities. The exact form of virtuality will depend on market demands, operational needs and preferences and new technologies and will change as markets and the business environment change [2].

But distributing work across locations, time zones and other individuals and organizations involves risk, of breakdowns, interruptions, or discontinuities on one or more dimensions of time, space, work practice or culture [21]. Virtualization may bring higher rewards for staff, but also higher expectations and an extended working day [7]. Poor coordination, stalled progress, difficulties in problem resolution, miscommunication and loss of cohesion are among the challenges that may have to be overcome. It is not enough for an organization to have a vision of a virtual form, but also the capabilities to transform itself, to become virtual. In a 2007 Global Survey, the international management consulting firm, McKinsey & Company, asked companies that have invested in modern communications technologies what they would have done differently to make their investment more effective: 42% would first have strengthened their capabilities [3].

In this book, we are interested in planned strategies for virtualization. How can managers envision the new organizational form, understand their progress and overcome the challenges they will inevitably encounter? We propose that indicators – which may themselves change over time – can be used to describe an envisioned virtual organization. A set of necessary capabilities can be identified and used to gauge the organization's capability to become virtual. These capabilities include leadership and vision, the design of virtual work and certain characteristics of employees as well as ICT.

The book is the result of a research project that planned to track a knowledge intensive organization on its journey from being distributed, with professional staff working largely alone in more than a dozen countries, to being virtual, using the Internet and new information systems to improve knowledge sharing and build culture. A research team made up of experts in knowledge management, online learning, psychology, strategy and ICT tracked an international development firm's capability for virtualization, along with its progress toward its envisioned virtual form, for eighteen months. Each expert contributed theory and methods from their own field, allowing the organization and its progress to be examined from multiple points of view. Drawing on the different fields, we developed indicators of virtuality and capability. Our tracking of capabilities suggested that only minimal change would occur, and our observations confirmed this was the case – but, in observing the organization over time, we were also able to develop a deeper understanding of the capabilities necessary for transformation.

We also gained a number of insights into the theory and practice of knowledge management in distributed and virtual organizations. These include observations about social uncertainty in distributed organizations and the place of knowledge transfer in social uncertainty, the potential incompatibility between creating strong communities of practice and achieving organizational goals for social cohesion and commitment, and the role of transactive "knowledge directories" in knowledge transfer and storage. We developed methods for mapping organizational memory and studying adoption of ICT that can be completed relatively quickly and at low cost.

This book introduces the theories and techniques used in our research in such a way that they can be applied in other organizations. We illustrate their application from our experience in the case study organization which, as a large global consulting business, can stand as proxy for many service-oriented knowledge-based firms. The methods and tools can be used by academics, managers, business students and consultants in future studies of virtualization and to examine specific aspects of knowledge management and systems for transfer of unstructured knowledge.

The first section introduces models and methods for envisioning the particular form of virtual organization that an organization might adopt to meet its strategic needs and monitoring progress toward achieving that form. Chap. 1, *Aligning Goals, Virtuality and Capability: A Virtual Alignment Model*, considers the background to virtualization. It introduces the dimensions along which an organization may be virtual and identifies necessary capabilities for virtualization. The chapter presents a model of how strategic goals for virtualization, current state of virtuality and capabilities for virtualization can be compared. We call this the Virtual Alignment Model (VAM); it identifies where alignment has been achieved or the organization is exposed to risk, and predicts future progress toward the envisioned virtual form. Techniques for envisioning the virtual form a specific organization might take, identifying indicators of virtuality, monitoring and measuring progress toward the envisioned form and monitoring capabilities are introduced in Chap. 2, *Envisioning and Monitoring the Process of Becoming Virtual*. We describe the methodology we used to uncover the case study organization's vision of the virtual organization and develop indicators of the current state of virtuality along with "dashboards" that summarizes status and capabilities along multiple indicators. This chapter also introduces our research project with a brief introduction to the case study organization and the research methodology. Chap. 3, *The Challenge of Becoming Virtual*, describes the case study organization and its needs in more detail. It gives background material on the industry, the business context and the major protagonists. This chapter can be used by teachers as a business case study.

The second section of the book focuses on planning and evaluating a range of knowledge management initiatives for virtualization. Chap. 4, *Social Uncertainty in Virtual Organizations: A Preliminary Ontology of the Constituent Elements*, considers the argument for focusing on knowledge sharing as a key pillar of the virtualization process. Distributed organizations risk high social uncertainty as a result of low frequency of communication among organizational members. Adoption of technologies to improve knowledge sharing should reduce social uncertainty. This, in turn, should have other benefits for the organization because social uncertainty is believed to be associated with important aspects of organizational culture including trust, commitment and sense of belonging. In this chapter, Ivan Jensen and Paul Jackson introduce a model of social uncertainty and discuss the theoretical relationship between social uncertainty, knowledge sharing, knowledge transfer and organizational culture. In Chap. 5, *When Communities of Practice Fail: Community Ties and Organizational Commitment*, Gaela Bernini and Jane Klobas consider the risks associated with one strategy for improving the sharing of unstructured knowledge in organizations, development of Internet-mediated communities of practice. They ask if this is an appropriate strategy for an organization that wants to strengthen organizational commitment. The chapter describes a method for comparing the strength of communities of practice with organizational commitment, reports on the relationship between the two, and concludes that communities of practice present risks to organizations to which organizational commitment is important.

New knowledge management initiatives should be aligned with the organization's structures and processes for knowledge transfer. The next two chapters introduce techniques for uncovering existing structures and processes. Chap. 6, *An Exploratory Survey of the Structure and Components of Organizational Memory* (Paul Jackson), describes a simple technique for mapping organizational memory and identifying knowledge structures. The technique is particularly appropriate when the purpose is to obtain an overview to support a broader organizational knowledge management initiative rather than uncover the detail required for building a formal knowledge management system. But it is not enough to understand the structure of organizational memory. We also need to know how it functions. Recent research on group memory suggests that memory is transactive, i.e. shared among members in a dynamic way. In Chap. 7, *The Organization as a Transactive Memory System*, Paul Jackson and Jane Klobas introduce a method for identifying and evaluating the organization's transactive memory and a model from which the types of information system that would improve transactive memory can be identified.

The last two chapters in this section consider two common issues in virtual organizations. Chap. 8, *Evaluating Adoption of Knowledge Management Initiatives* (Stefano Renzi, Jane Klobas and Paul Jackson), describes a model and method for evaluating users' attitudes to and adoption of knowledge management initiatives while Chap. 9, *Monitoring, Control and the Performance of Virtual Work*, considers the issue of control of the actions of distributed staff. In Chap. 9, Paul Jackson, Jane Klobas and Hosein Gharavi conclude that monitoring and information systems play a limited role in the power and control structures of distributed professional organizations. Management influence over knowledge worker performance and productivity should be seen as an assembly of various types of direct and indirect constraint which can be configured to achieve required results.

The final section of the book brings together the models and methods from section 1 and observations from section 2 to explain lack of transformation in the case study organization. It commences with Chap. 10, *The Challenge of Becoming Virtual (Part 2)*, a narrative description of the case study organization's pursuit of virtualization. This chapter is a continuation of the story begun in Chap. 3 and can be combined with that chapter to provide students with an extended case study. Chap. 11, *Reflections from the Frontline – Journey of a Knowledge Manager*, written by the organization's knowledge manager, Louise Kjaer, reflects on lessons from the organization's approach to virtualization. Chap. 12, *The Forensics of a Challenged Initiative* presents the results of the research team's causal analysis of virtualization in the organization. It presents explanations for the observed lack of change in the organization in terms of the capabilities identified in earlier chapters and identifies additional capabilities that appeared to be lacking. Chap. 13, *Tools and Capabilities for Becoming Virtual*, draws lessons for organizations planning to pursue knowledge management initiatives to transform distributed organizations. Among other things, we conclude that it is not sufficient to focus on developing and implementing knowledge management systems. Other key virtualization factors which, at first glance, are neither obvious nor glamorous, are nonetheless necessary for transformation to virtual organization.

References

1. Andriessen JHE, Vartiainen M (2006) Emerging mobile virtual work. In: Andriessen JHE, Vartiainen M (eds) Mobile virtual work. Springer Verlag, Berlin, pp 3–12
2. Becker WM, Freeman VM (2006) Going from global trends to corporate strategy. McKinsey Quarterly 3. Retrieved 27 May 2007 from http://www.mckinseyquarterly.com/article_abstract.aspx?ar=1830
3. Bughin J, Manyika J (2007, March) How businesses are using Web 2.0: a McKinsey global survey. McKinsey Quarterly. Retrieved 27 May 2007 from http://www.mckinseyquarterly.com/article_page.aspx?ar=1913
4. Castells M (2001) The Internet galaxy. Oxford University Press, Oxford
5. Chandrashekar A, Schary PB (1999) Toward the virtual supply chain: the convergence of IT and organization. The International Journal of Logistics Management 10:27–40
6. Corso M, Martini A, Pellegrini L (2006) Knowledge sharing in mobile work. In: JHE, Vartiainen M (eds) Mobile virtual work. Springer Verlag, Berlin, pp 291–318
7. Crandall NF, Wallace MJ (1998) Work and rewards in the virtual workplace. AMACOM, New York
8. Davidow WH, Malone MS (1993) The virtual corporation: structuring and revitalizing the corporation for the 21st century. HarperBusiness, New York
9. Duarte DL, Snyder NT (1999) Mastering virtual teams: strategies, tools and techniques that succeed. Jossey-Bass, San Francisco
10. Fritz MBW, Narasimhan S, Rhee H-S (1998) Communication and coordination in the virtual office. Journal of Management Information Systems 14:7–28
11. Haywood M (1998) Managing virtual teams: practical techniques for high-technology project managers. Artech House, Boston

12. Henry H, Hartzler M (1998) Tools for virtual teams: a team fitness companion. American Society for Quality, Milwaukee
13. Jackson PJ (1999) Introduction. In: Jackson PJ (ed), Virtual working: social and organisational dynamics. Routledge, London, pp 1–16
14. Klobas JE (1998) The virtual supply chain: a view of information flows, business structures and business opportunities. Business Information Review 15: 185–192
15. Linden A, Fenn J, Drakos N (2005, 23 September) Networked collective intelligence represents a new paradigm of work. Gartner Research Report G00131007. Gartner Inc, Stamford, CT
16. Lipnack J, Stamps J (1997) Virtual teams: reaching across space, time and organizations with technology. John Wiley and Sons, New York
17. Suomi R, Pekkola J (1999) Management rationalities and virtual working. In: Jackson PJ (ed) Virtual working: social and organisational dynamics. Routledge, London, pp 121–130
18. Travica B (2005) Virtual organization and electronic commerce. Database 36:45–68
19. Venkatraman N, Henderson JC (1998, Fall) Real strategies for virtual organizing. Sloan Management Review 40:33-48.
20. Wagner C et al (2004, February) Europe, competing: market prospects, business needs and technological trends for virtual, smart organisations in Europe, MG-195-EC, Report for the European Commission, Information Society. Rand Europe. Retrieved 27 May 2007 from http://www.rand.org/pubs/monographs/2004/RAND_MG195.pdf
21. Watson-Manheim MB, Chudoba KM, Crowston K (2002) Discontinuities and continuities: a new way to understand virtual work. Information Technology & People 15:191–209

Part 1
Envisioning and Planning for Virtualization

1 Aligning Goals, Virtuality and Capability: A Virtual Alignment Model[1]

Paul Jackson and Jane Klobas

1.1 Introduction

Given the many forms that a virtual organization might take, a critical first step in becoming virtual is to understand the form of virtual organization that is desired or envisaged. Once the desired form is defined, it is necessary to find out how close to, or distant from, that form the organization currently is, and to develop a strategy for moving from the current to the envisioned form. But, a strategy will only work if the organization has the capabilities necessary for transformation.

In this chapter, we demonstrate how the vision of the virtual organization, the current state of virtuality and capabilities for virtualization are inter-related. We describe a model that brings information about these three key elements together in such a way that an organization can use it to evaluate the alignment of the organization's goals, state and capabilities for virtualization and predict what might occur if alignment is not reached. We call this the Virtual Alignment Model (VAM).

1.2 Vision and Goals

In envisioning the future virtual organization, an important first consideration is the motivation for virtualization. This is a strategic question which requires consideration of the environment within which the organization is

---

[1] Portions of Chapters 1 and 2 are drawn from Jackson PD, Klobas JE (forthcoming) Strategies for Virtual Work. In Putnik GD, Cunha MM (eds) Encyclopedia of Networked and Virtual Organizations. IGI Press, Hershey, PA. Copyright IGI Global. Permission granted.

operating and changes to that environment, as well as internal challenges, needs and goals. Virtualizing an organization may be a strategy designed to solve problems of customer service, competitiveness, efficiency, and employee satisfaction. It may open up new markets, increase the availability of firm competencies and make the organization more responsive.

Once the drivers for virtualization have been articulated, it should be possible to begin to envision the transformed organization. Virtuality may be defined along several dimensions: physical, structural, legal, temporal and psychological.

The *physical* dimension is the most readily identified and defined. The staff of a virtual organization are usually geographically distributed from one another, but to what extent? Will the transformed organization be centered around a head office, be an international network of semi-autonomous entities, be a loose form in which individual staff in different geographical locations join together in different configurations for different projects, or some hybrid of these and other forms? If it is a head office based organization, what percentage of staff is likely to be based in head office and what percentage based outside or traveling?

The *structural* dimension may drive or follow from the physical dimension. Apart from those aspects of structure that are aligned with geographical distribution, structural considerations include the nature of staff relationships with the organization and the form of staff groupings, such as departments, teams, projects, matrix reporting and so on. To what extent will virtuality extend to the relationship between staff and the organization? What percentage of staff is likely to be permanent, what percentage on a retainer awaiting assignment to a task or project, and what percentage employed on a fixed term contractual basis? Will the organization introduce a flatter hierarchy, with greater self-management, or will work be project-based?

The *legal* dimension reflects those dimensions of structure which are influenced by regulations and legal agreements. A team-based approach is purely structural, but a team-based approach across different firms may require contracts and binding legal commitments. A full-time permanent member of staff embodies a structural arrangement with a different legal dimension to a part-time contractor. We need to ask questions such as: what is the contractual basis of the relationships between the staff and the organization, what obligations exist between partners in transient, multinational consortia bidding for large contracts, and between the different geographically distributed elements of a single organization?

The *temporal* dimension is usually associated with the physical dimension: when people are geographically distributed, they work across different time zones. But the temporal dimension can also apply to people working at different times in the same time zone: this refers not just to formal shift work, but also to the extent that the virtual organization might support different individual preferences for working at different times of day (or night) or on different days of the week, and with different rhythms.

The *psychological* dimension is often neglected in discussions of virtual work, but is an important aspect of the virtual organization. Thus, a virtual organization might be defined in psychological terms as an organization whose staff consider themselves part of one organization regardless of where and when they work or what structural or contractual relationship they have with the organization. We might say that the staff of a virtual organization share a "virtual mindset". Other aspects of the psychological dimension might include shared commitment to a set of common values and behavioral norms – for example, an organization might consider virtualization a strategy that helps maintain a policy of not giving bribes for services in any country anywhere – or a sense of belonging or commitment to the organization, or trust.

We describe a methodology for envisioning the form of virtual organization that a particular organization might seek in Chap. 2.

1.3 State of Virtuality

Once the desired form of virtual organization has been envisaged and described, it is possible to evaluate the extent to which the organization has achieved the desired form. This state of virtuality can be described or measured at any point in time and compared to the desired state. In addition, it can be compared to past states so that change can be monitored.

A number of survey instruments have been developed to measure virtuality [3; 5; 13] but these are static and proceed from a fixed notion of what virtuality is. Because we take the view that virtuality is highly fluid and contextual, we propose a contingent approach, tailored to the vision of each organization. In Chap. 2, we describe a methodology for determining what the specific indicators might be in a given organization and introduce common indicators for common dimensions of virtuality while in this chapter, we restrict discussion to how they work in monitoring virtualization.

Indicators of virtuality might be developed to reflect both vision and status on one or several dimensions. An example is given in Fig. 1.1, which provides a graphical representation of an indicator designed to demonstrate desired level of virtuality (marked by the diamond) and current level (marked by the dot). This type of indicator includes a description for different levels of virtuality and allows the organization to compare current status with vision at a glance.

NONE	BASIC	OPTIMIZING
Single office No working from home at all and no travel for most staff	Some working from home Some workers in partner offices Workers come to office at least weekly	Workers often at home or on the road Hiring not limited by location Virtual workspace supplied

Fig. 1.1. Comparing vision (diamond) and status (dot) for the indicator, Telecommuting

A set of indicators can be combined and reported in summary form on a dashboard. Like the dashboard of a motor vehicle, a performance dashboard can be used to provide a rapid, visual overview of current status compared with a benchmark (in this case, the envisaged level of virtuality) on a set of key indicators [9].

A dashboard that summarizes current and envisioned level of virtuality would require a scale. We adapted Haywood's existing four point scale to evaluate the functioning of virtual teams [11] into a five point scale for measuring the functioning of a virtual organization. The additional point on the scale acknowledges that, in some cases, an organization may have taken no action. The points on our scale are:

- *None*. No action or no sign of virtual activity.
- *Ad hoc*. Virtual working is effective only in head office or among senior staff or both
- *Basic*. Virtual work may be cumbersome and based on non-virtual processes, nevertheless some advantages are gained. The performance of collocated and distant staff is similar, but difficulties are still faced as a result of working virtually.
- *Standardized*. Virtual work processes are considered to be normal and the benefits of operating as a virtual organization outweigh the problems.
- *Optimizing*. All staff work effectively any time any place and improvements to the organization can be gained by standard methods for organizational improvement such as business process re-engineering and the adoption of new technologies.

Anchored indicators of the kind presented in Fig. 1.1 would underlie each of the summaries in a dashboard. For example, the ratio of contract staff to permanent staff could be used to measure the indicator, *Virtual staff*. The organization might define the *Optimizing* ratio as three contract staff members for every permanent staff member. A current ratio of 2.5:1 may be considered close to this and rated as *Standardized* to indicate that the organization was operating effectively on this dimension but some improvements could be made.

1.4 Capabilities

Capabilities enable an organization to close the gap between a desired and an actual state of virtuality and operate effectively in the chosen virtual mode. To be effective, virtual organizing requires capabilities beyond those of the non-virtual organization. If these capabilities are not present, they will need to be developed. Most obviously, technology is a critical enabler. But other factors are also indispensable and must be addressed. To raise a capability to an adequate level may itself be a significant undertaking, requiring managerial, technical or operational skills. The published literature identifies five capabilities: leadership, design of work processes, employee capabilities, ICT infrastructure, and business case.

- **Leadership** fosters a sense of collaboration, direction, cohesion and purpose, all of which are at risk in the face of the disjointedness and discontinuity which can be associated with virtual work. In the case of virtual knowledge workers, leaders have certain attributes which attract them and gain their commitment. Trust and empowerment will create the "volunteer" environment and sense of accountability with which knowledge workers flourish, while authoritarian, command and control styles will generally fail to generate the dynamics of knowledge creation. The development of a new organizational form requires effective and transparent change management. The leader [1; 4; 8; 15–17]:

  - has attributes which motivate and inspire knowledge workers
  - continuously communicates and reinforces a consistent message
  - makes the transformation meaningful
  - implements effective change management
  - builds a committed and effective management team
  - builds an environment of high trust
  - empowers staff and limits the extent of the command and control management style

- **Design of work processes**. Virtual work process design usually requires particular attention due to the difficulties of separation in time and space between staff and managers. Clear process definition, well defined interfaces at points of handover or dependency, clear roles, responsibilities, outputs and definitions of quality and completeness all gain greater importance, not only to reduce the incidence of problems, but also to gain the greatest leverage from work distribution. Virtual work should therefore [7; 10; 12; 14]:
  - be well designed and logical so that anomalies and exceptions are minimized
  - be well documented and the documentation available to all participants
  - allocate clearly defined roles and responsibilities
  - be role orientated with regard to business process, not based on person-related job description
  - have clear decision criteria and escalation procedures
  - clearly define task interdependencies and handover points
  - define timelines and milestones, quality criteria and so on
  - be process-driven rather than functionally orientated
  - use self-managing teams and matrix flexibility

- **Employee capabilities**. The capabilities required by virtual staff include competencies in technology and the ability to work alone and unsupervised, be autonomous and flexible, self-starting and self-reliant. Specific aspects of employee capability include:
  - a high level of the required skills and competencies
  - the availability of training and advice when required to bridge any gap between competence and task requirements
  - transparent and reasonable measurement of employee performance
  - fostering of collaboration through communities and mentors
  - induction which is explicitly planned for virtual work
  - being a team player

- **ICT**. The technology tools made available to staff to operate in virtual mode must provide the relevant functionality and have the necessary attributes to support effective virtual work. Aspects such as functionality, performance, reliability and usability of both the underlying infrastructure and the specific computer applications are important. Technology requirements are that [2; 10; 12; 18; 21]:
  - an adequately performing and functional infrastructure is present
  - software and communication tools are available for collaboration
  - tools are available for supporting work processes

- knowledge-based systems are available to build knowledge over distance as part of workflow
- the workplace is reflected in the functionality of the technology
- real time information is available irrespective of location

- **Business case**. Most businesses are resource constrained and competition between departments and groups means that a sound financial or material advantage must usually be demonstrated for a proposed course of action. The business case for virtualization needs to show that sufficient economic capability is present and there will be a return on investment of some kind, either in cost savings, improved customer service, shortened cycle times and so on. The business case for virtualization should [7; 20]:

  - be well thought through and understood
  - result in a clear allocation of sufficient resources
  - demonstrate a link between economic requirements, business drivers and capabilities
  - demonstrate that the costs and benefits are understood
  - demonstrate commitment to high performance rather than cost cutting
  - contain careful project planning, milestones and schedules

1.5 The Virtual Alignment Model (VAM)

Information about the envisioned form of virtualization, the current state, and capabilities for operating virtually, taken together, can be used to evaluate the organization's progress toward the desired levels of virtual work and the need for action. Table 1.1 demonstrates how this might be done using what we call the Virtual Alignment Model (VAM). Knowing that vision, state and capabilities are aligned suggests that no specific action needs to be taken, but any discrepancy suggests that the organization may be exposed and need to take action to improve capability or reduce the cost of capability which they do not need.

The VAM is a simple method for estimating the degree of action which is required by the company. The model emphasizes firstly that there must be alignment between how virtual an organization wishes to be and how virtual it is. In order to ascertain this, a problem statement or a vision is required; for example, "our salespeople spend too much time in the office – they must get out among the customers more". To then assess the gap between vision and reality, some basic measures are required, for example, what percentage of the week do the salespeople spend in the office? A

Table 1.1. Virtual Alignment Model (VAM)

Envisioned level of virtuality	Current level of virtuality	Capabilities for being virtual	Observations
Optimizing	Optimizing	Optimizing	An ideal state of alignment, where the resources for operating virtually are at the service of a virtualized workforce.
None/Basic	Optimizing	Optimizing	There may be over-expenditure and resources committed to maintaining an unnecessary preparedness for virtual operations. Further, there is possible strategic exposure from being too virtual.
None/Basic	None/Basic	Optimizing	There is possibly over-expenditure and resources committed to maintaining an unnecessary preparedness for virtual operations.
Optimizing	None/Basic	Optimizing	The strategic need for virtual work is not being met and the infrastructure is not being sufficiently utilized. There is work to do to become virtual.
None/Basic	None/Basic	None/Basic	An ideal state of alignment, where there is low resource commitment and no superfluous virtuality.
Optimizing	None/Basic	None/Basic	Major effort is required to provide the necessary capabilities for virtualization and transform the business to the level strategically required.
None/Basic	Optimizing	None/Basic	Low preparedness and low requirement. Exposure from overreach.
Optimizing	Optimizing	None/Basic	Exposure through an ill-prepared and inefficient context for virtuality.

target might be set for half a day only in the office. Subsequently, one can examine the capabilities required to achieve this goal effectively and not reduce other important aspects of work: do the sales staff require mobile sales and order equipment, are they motivated by this form of work, will we need regular in-house meetings to re-enforce sales strategies and swap experiences?

The more complicated the form of virtuality required, the more varied and sophisticated will be the measurements and capabilities. Fig. 1.2 summarizes the VAM approach and the key questions an organization needs to ask itself as it seeks to understand whether virtuality is an appropriate response to the challenges it confronts.

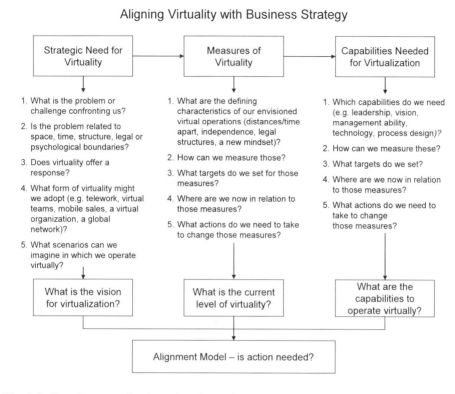

Fig. 1.2. Questions to ask when planning to become virtual

The VAM framework is both descriptive and analytical. It enables description of the organization at a point in time. It can be used to assess the extent of alignment between the envisioned form of virtualization, the current state of virtualization, and the capabilities required to move from current to envisioned state. Of course, the process of virtualization is dynamic; as the organizational state of virtualization changes, as its markets change, and as it changes in response to other internal and external changes, the vision for virtualization will change. The framework therefore provides a tool for capturing vision, state and capabilities at a given point in time. Used to record these dimensions at a series of intervals, this framework can be used to map changes in an organization as its understanding of and need for virtualization, its form of virtualization, and its capabilities to operate virtually evolve over time.

References

1. Aiken CB, Keller SP (2007, February) The CEO's role in leading transformation. McKinsey Quarterly. Retrieved 27 May 2007 from http://www. mckinseyquarterly.com/article_page.aspx?ar=1912
2. Alavi M, Tiwana A (2002) Knowledge integration in virtual teams: the potential role of KMS. Journal of the American Society for Information Science and Technology 53:1029–1037
3. Aris J (1999) Exploiting the wired-up world. Business Strategy Review 10:47–52
4. Bal J, Teo PK (2000) Implementing virtual teamworking, part 1: a best practice review. Logistics Information Management 13:346–352
5. Bauer R, Koszegi ST (2002) Measuring the degree of virtualization. Electronic Journal of Organizational Virtualness 5:22–46
6. Brown JS, Duguid P (2000) The social life of information. Harvard Business School Press, Boston
7. Crandall NF, Wallace MJ (1998) Work & rewards in the virtual workplace. AMACOM, New York
8. Drucker P (1999) Management challenges for the 21st century. Butterworth-Heinemann, Oxford
9. Eckerson WW (2006) Performance dashboards: measuring, monitoring, and managing your business. Wiley, Hoboken, NJ
10. Fritz MBW, Narasimhan S, Rhee H-S Communication and coordination in the virtual office. Journal of Management Information Systems 14:7–28
11. Haywood M (1998) Managing virtual teams: practical techniques for high-technology project managers. Artech House, Boston
12. Malhotra A, Majchrzak A, Carman R, Lott V (2001) Radical innovation without collocation: a case study at Boeing-Rocketdyne. MIS Quarterly 25:229–249
13. McConnell I (2000, August) Risk e-business: seizing the opportunity of global e-readiness. Retrieved 27 May 2007 from http://www.mcconnellinternational.com/ereadiness/EReadinessReport.htm
14. Nemiro JE (2000) The glue that binds creative virtual teams. In: Malhotra Y (ed) Knowledge management and virtual organizations. Idea Group Publishing, Hershey, PA, pp 101–123
15. Pan SL, Scarbrough H (1999) Knowledge management in practice: an exploratory case study. Technology Analysis and Strategic Management 11:359–374
16. Pfeffer J (1981) Management as symbolic action: the creation and maintenance of organizational paradigms. In: Cummings LL, Staw BM (eds) Research in organizational behavior. JAI, Greenwich, CT, vol 3, pp 1–52
17. Senge P (1990, Fall) The leader's new work: building learning organizations, Sloan Management Review 32:7–23

18. Steel GW (2003) Virtual project management: the new frontier. INDECO Ltd. Retrieved 12 November 2003 from http://www.indeco.co.uk/docs/Virtual%20Project%20Management%20march%202002.pdf
19. Venkatraman N, Henderson JC (1998, Fall) Real strategies for virtual organizing. Sloan Management Review 40:33–48
20. Warner W, Witzel M (2004) Managing in virtual organizations. Thomson Learning, London
21. Yap AY, Bjorn-Andersen N (2002) Capturing tacit mental models with 3D technologies: enhancing knowledge-sharing in virtual organizations. Electronic Journal of Organizational Virtualness 4:18–63

2 Envisioning and Monitoring the Process of Becoming Virtual

Paul Jackson and Jane Klobas

2.1 Introduction

In Chap. 1, we introduced the virtual alignment model and described its three elements: goals, status, and capability, and how they work together. In this chapter, we examine how an organization might establish a vision, identify indicators to monitor status and progress toward the vision, and measure progress and capability.

2.2 Envisioning the Virtual Organization

The vision of a virtual organization is a vision of what the organization will *be*, what it will be like and how it will feel to be a member of the organization. The process of envisaging is therefore a planning process, but one which has a very specific purpose and which needs to be addressed explicitly, whether as a stand-alone activity or as a purpose-specific activity within a larger planning and strategy setting process. Like all planning activities, it may be possible to involve a wide range of staff from different parts of the organization and at different levels, but the senior managers who will take leadership and guide the organization toward achieving the vision have a key role to play. In this section, we describe how a management workshop can be used to envision the virtual organization and identify indicators of progress toward virtuality.

Before embarking on a workshop that explicitly seeks to evoke the vision of the future organization, a good understanding of the motivation for virtualization is required. Existing market analyses, strategic plans and other documentation for organizational planning may already contain information about why virtualization is a desired strategy, but much of the information will be held tacitly in the heads of the managers who have conceived of the strategy. In our research, we gathered information about why virtualization might be an appropriate strategy, the goals of virtualization and problems anticipated in achieving a virtual form in a series of planning meetings attended by the organization's Director and the two senior managers reporting to him. In addition, we reviewed annual reports, business plans and strategies and the organization's Web site. We used the information we obtained to design a half-day management workshop which was attended by all members of the management team: the three senior managers and six market area managers. The workshop consisted of three activities: the shape of virtualization, goals for virtualization, and imagining the virtual organization. The activities are summarized here, while a more detailed outline is provided in Appendix 7.

2.2.1 The Shape of Virtualization

The aim of the first exercise is to develop a formal definition of virtualization as it is interpreted by the organization, along with an initial vision of what form virtualization might take. Participants are first asked to complete the sentence, "Virtualization in [organization name] is ..." Each participant is then asked to take the perspective of a different group of members of the organization (e.g., CEO, Department Manager, Project Manager, Administrative staff member, Union representative, contract consultant) and, playing the role they have been assigned, to envision the virtual organization in more detail. Questions that they might be asked include:

- What does virtualization mean to me in my job?
- What work is done virtually to make my job different to now?
- What must be done face-to-face?
- Who communicates with whom and how?
- What is the effect of virtualization on me (in my role) and the people I deal with?

In our research, this exercise in role play was very successful in breaking down reservations and reducing tension. Jokes were made when staff hammed up their positions and yet many insights were generated through questions asked of these roles by other roles. For example, the "Project Manager" said:

It doesn't matter what happens with virtualization: the role stays the same. Quality has to be ensured, the job needs to be done and we need good references from the clients.

The "CEO" then asked the "Project Manager":

I am worried about the threat to quality. I must provide the tools and the training – do we need new policies for the local mix of people on projects?

2.2.2 Goals for Virtualization

The second exercise aims to develop goal statements for virtualization in the organization in the form, "The objective of the virtualization process is TO achieve business goal xyz BY providing certain resources, capabilities and conditions". In our workshop, we first used brainstorming to identify the business goals (the "to …" part of the statement). Participants were then guided to tell us how they would measure achievement of each of the goals. The measures were later translated into indicators of virtuality in the organization.

Next, we asked participants to identify the resources and capabilities that would be necessary to achieve each business goal (the "by …" part of the statement) and to indicate to what extent those resources and capabilities already existed in the organization. This information provided us with the information needed to check that the capabilities listed in Chap. 1 was appropriate, and sufficient, for the organization. It also provided us with an initial assessment of the organization's capability for becoming virtual.

2.2.3 Imagining the Virtual Organization

In the third exercise, participants are assigned an organizational vignette to read and comment upon. The vignettes are designed to elicit more detailed information about the organization's capability for becoming virtual. We created one vignette for each capability described in Chap. 1, for example, the vignette that appears in Fig. 2.1 addresses the dimension of employee capabilities for virtual work. The full set of vignettes is included in Appendix 7.

In our research, this exercise revealed misgivings which transcended operational risk, and thus elicited information about emotional and psychological issues important to the virtualization process. These issues have not previously been included in the literature of virtual organizations.

Employees

Your company wins a lot of business and you need to expand quickly. You need new project managers and administrative staff. You advertise and the best candidates live overseas. You interview them through videoconferencing, employ them and commence induction through the Internet. They are assigned to projects and some travel to their site for months at a time and have their base at home. Every six months they come to Head Office and you meet them at six monthly intervals thereafter. They rarely meet other staff, even when they are in Head Office. You find it hard to assess their performance and contribution. Similarly, some tell you at intervals they don't feel valued by the organization and wonder how their great efforts are to be recognized if you don't even really understand how hard they are working and how difficult it is to overcome working alone and without someone to talk to. Meanwhile, the staff who are mostly at the office wonder what on earth the remote people are up to...

How do you feel about this?
Describe the particular problems in this scenario and how you would deal with them.
Do you have the people management processes to deal with this? What is missing?

Fig. 2.1. Sample virtualization vignette for employee capabilities

2.3 From Vision to Goals, Capabilities and Indicators

Workshop participants' contributions to all activities can be used to develop a description of the envisioned virtual organization. Specific goals for virtualization can be derived from the vision, and methods for monitoring achievement of those goals can be developed. In addition, the contributions can be used to identify organization-specific capabilities for being virtual, in addition to the generic capabilities described in Chap. 1, and to gain an initial impression of the extent to which the organization has the necessary capabilities.

To do this for our research, we audio-recorded and made notes of the contributions and remarks made by participants during the workshop. We pooled the data from all three exercises along with the preparatory material and some follow-up interviews, and then sorted them inductively into the dimensions of the VAM framework (vision, status and capability) using software that supports visual mapping of ideas and text. The workshop participants' own words were used to identify the vision and dimensions of virtuality and capability. We then prepared indicators of virtuality derived from the dimensions and developed a scheme for monitoring progress on each dimension.

2.4 Goals for Virtualization

Because each organization's goals for virtualization are different, we will not attempt to describe a common set of goals. Instead, we will describe here the vision and goals that emerged from our workshop.

The participants were introduced to the envisioned form of virtualization by Unit 2's Director. He expressed it in terms of the "Global Network Organization", which had the following characteristics:

There will be an increase in the dispersal and distribution of all permanent, contract and retainer staff. In this environment, a coherent and consistent view of the organization will be maintained, manifested in shared methods, values and work practices. This way of working will be facilitated by information and communications tools, such as the Internet, VOIP and intranets. New forms of workflow and management will evolve to meet new needs, and the organization will continue to be an attractive place to work and participate. Virtualization needs to be cost effective, and might even be a new form of service offering to clients.

This vision of organizational transformation, while containing the usual criteria of virtuality such as physical distance or dispersal, remote work and the use of ICT, was characterized by a significant new dimension, that of *virtual mindset*: that the staff had to discard the notion that travel, odd working hours and office absence were somehow anomalies. With this vision in mind, the following outcomes of virtualization were identified by participants:

- To be more flexible and responsive to the market in terms of competence, countries and clients.
- To broaden a sense of belonging to the organization and increase the stock of shared values and goals.
- To attract and retain the best people wherever they are.

We used the words used by participants as they expressed these goals to develop a set of statements that could be used to operationalize the goals for monitoring and measurement. These statements are expressed as indicators of virtualization in Tables 2.1a and 21b where they are divided into two groups. Table 2.1a contains indicators that can be measured using information and data available from the organization. We have called these indicators descriptive indicators. Table 2.1b contains indicators that can only be measured by asking members of the organization for the opinions or impressions. We call these psychological and cultural indicators. Within each of these major groupings, the indicators were further grouped into dimensions.

Table 2.1a. Goals for virtualization: Descriptive indicators

Dimension	Indicators
Dispersal of staff	- Days out of the office/total working days - Proportion of staff outside Head Office (HO) - Percentage of time spent traveling - Proportion of staff whose communication patterns demonstrate they are "connected" to a community of colleagues in the organization
ICT	- Installed ICT to support virtual work - Number of staff using each specific functionality of installed ICT (e.g. forums, VOIP, repository)
Workflow and management	- Procedures explicitly incorporate staff outside HO - Management practices explicitly include staff both inside and outside HO
Cost effective	- Square meters of office space per employee
Offer new services to clients	- Number of clients to whom virtual organization solutions are provided

2.5 Current Level of Virtuality

The impression conveyed by the participants in our workshop was that the organization already operated in a highly distributed mode (perhaps even virtual). Managers traveled for about 100 days per year, most projects were overseas, employees had been hired without being seen, administrative employees answered their e-mails at weekends and frontline staff were working increasingly as part of customer teams. However, the use of ICT to support collaboration and communication was low, due in part to remoteness, but also to restrictions imposed by the corporate information technology (IT) strategy. Further, staff had not internalized virtualization as the status quo; it remained something separate or "added on to" current operations.

But, these were all impressions obtained from senior managers. A more accurate and reliable indication of the extent to which the current state of the organization reflected the organization's goals for being virtual would require more systematic study. We therefore needed to translate the goals and indicators into a form that enabled the organization, or external consultants or researchers, to monitor progress. Beginning with the indicators in Tables 2.1a and 2.1b, we identified those for which data really were

Table 2.1b. Goals for virtualization: Psychological and cultural indicators

Shared understanding: A coherent and consistent view of the organization, sense of belonging, shared values and goals	- We act in accordance with [organization name]'s expressed corporate values - There is a good cooperative spirit in [organization] - I feel a part of the [organization] culture - I like to do things the [organization] way - I work to meet [organization]'s quality demands - I know what is going on in [organization] - I get quick replies to my questions - Sense of belonging and organizational identity
Attractive place to work and participate	- I feel a strong loyalty to [organization] - I have the contacts I need to be appointed to my next project for [organization] - The administrative framework is in place to ensure fair handling of my appointment - I have the skills I need to represent [organization] effectively to clients - I am pleased with the contribution I am making to [organization] - This organization is a good place for me to work
ICT and information	- Technology accessibility - Technology acceptance - Access to information needed to the job - Knowledge management
Virtual mindset Operations	- Doing things virtually is business as usual - Perceived ability to be more flexible and responsive to the market in terms of competence, countries and clients - Perceived ability to attract and retain the best people wherever they are

available in the organization. We re-examined the dimensions and indicators and sorted into logical sets that fit with the organization's way of speaking about business goals and organizational issues. Next, we used psychometric principles to develop, from the indicators, a survey instrument to measure organizational members' opinions, perceptions and positions on each of the dimensions. The survey would be supplemented by interviews with management and other members of the organization, in all locations. It would be distributed as an attachment to a standard e-mail message, in order to reach organizational members with poor Internet access.

The final set of dimensions and indicators is provided in Appendix 1. They are divided into two groups, virtuality and organizational. The virtuality dimensions are those that are specific to being a virtual organization, while the organizational dimensions reflect aspects of the organization that may be endangered or enhanced by being virtual. The dimensions and their definitions are summarized in Tables 2.2a (virtuality) and 2.2b (organizational).

Table 2.2a. Virtuality dimensions

Dimension	Definition
Virtual staff	The proportion of contract to permanent staff
Dispersal of staff	The extent to which staff are physically dispersed across different locations
Tools (ICT) for virtual work and communication	The extent to which ICT is used to support work, communication, and maintenance of organizational culture
Processes for virtual work and communication	The extent to which work methods, practices and work flow support virtual work and communication among dispersed staff
Virtual mindset	The extent to which staff think of the organization as a whole regardless of place of work and time zone (as distinct from thinking of the organization in terms of those people most closely collocated to them).
Innovation in client service	The ability to offer new services, based on virtual working, to clients

Table 2.2b. Organizational dimensions for measurement of state of being virtual

Dimension	Definition
Shared values	The extent to which values are shared among all staff, regardless of geographical location
Shared understanding	The extent to which staff have a shared understanding of the nature of the organization
Identity	The extent to which staff have a sense of belonging to the organization
Trust	The extent to which staff have positive expectations of the intentions or behavior of others irrespective of their ability to monitor or control them
Staff satisfaction	Satisfaction with working in the organization
Economic effectiveness	Changes associated with the move to a virtual organization are cost effective

To be a virtual organization, the organization needs to simultaneously meet its goals on all of these dimensions. In other words, the respective dimensions are necessary, but individually insufficient, indicators of the state of virtuality. Simultaneously monitoring the number and variety of dimensions, along with probable differences in level of virtuality on the dimensions at any one time, and anticipated change in level of virtuality on each dimension over time, requires a tool such as a dashboard. Fig. 2.2 contains the dashboard developed to monitor the organization on the dimensions shown in Table 2.2. The virtuality dimensions appear in the top part of the dashboard while the organizational dimensions appear in the lower section.

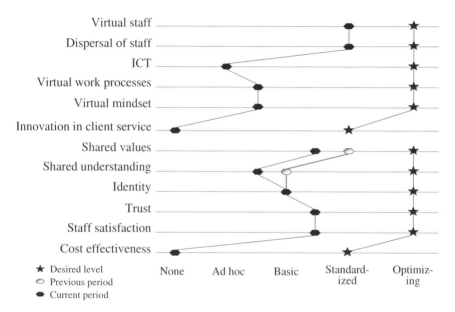

Fig. 2.2. Dashboard for monitoring state of virtuality in relation to goals

2.6 Capabilities for Being Virtual

The workshop has the potential to confirm the relevance of the capabilities for being virtual described in Chap. 1 and to identify any additional capabilities that might be specific to the organization. In the case of the workshop described here, it became clear that, although the literature treated them together, it was more satisfactory to treat vision and leadership separately. In addition, while working with members of the management team, we became aware that different managers had different levels of interesting in and capability for virtual work and managing in a virtual organization. We therefore added management capability to the set of necessary capabilities for becoming virtual. Apart from these additions, our scheme for monitoring capabilities was based on the literature. We summarized capability at different periods of time using the capabilities dashboard in Fig. 2.3.

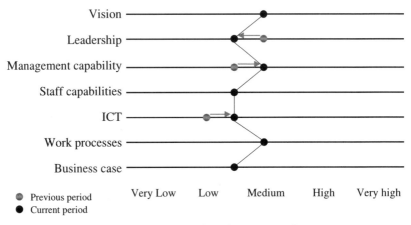

Fig. 2.3. Capabilities dashboard, showing change over time

2.7 The Research Project

The Virtual Alignment Model, described in Chap. 1, and the methods for envisioning and monitoring the process of becoming virtual, described in this chapter, were used to study virtualization in the international development unit of a Northern European consulting firm, The Parent Company (TPC). The director of the Unit ("Unit 2") was aware that, as the global and distributed characteristics of its operations became more pronounced, a change in operational paradigm was required. No longer could the head office (HO) be assumed to be "home", as remote work was becoming everyday for many staff. Staff and management were increasingly absent from the office, but operational and cultural habits reflected an office culture. Managers delegated much of their authority when not in the office, and yet were traveling for over 100 days per year. Meetings continued to take place (with pastries supplied) in progressively empty rooms. The Director declared that a mindset was required in which it did not matter where staff were located or where they lived: "home office" would be in "cyberspace". The Unit was already highly distributed geographically and across time zones, but this new vision depended on ICT, including new knowledge management systems, to transform the organization from being simply distributed to being virtual.

The research was a form of dialogical action research [1] in which the researchers spent one week in the organization at four six-monthly intervals: as the virtualization strategy was implemented, after the first six months, after twelve months and after eighteen months. During each of these visits, we used interviews, group meetings and a questionnaire to measure the organization's capability for virtualization and their progress toward their envisioned virtual form. We did not take direct action to influence the virtualization process, but we participated in discussions with managers and organizational members which almost certainly indirectly affected actions the members of the organization took.

Each visit, we interviewed the Director of the organization, asking him what action he had taken to lead the organization toward its envisioned virtual form during the preceding six months. In these interviews, we gave the Director a list of the capabilities for virtualization described in this chapter and asked him to comment on any action he had taken in relation to each of them.

We conducted an additional 25 to 35 interviews during each visit as part of our analysis of the state of virtuality and capabilities for virtualization. We established a quota for interviewees in different categories, making sure we spoke with managers and consultants based both in and outside of head office as well as administrative and ICT support staff. The interviewees were volunteers or members of staff who responded to a direct request for contribution. At each visit, a seminar was also held with a different group of staff to address a specific issue, such as acceptance of new information technologies or managers' perceptions of and attitudes toward the virtual organization.

After consultation about the best way in which to reach staff in remote locations with low bandwidth Internet connections, the questionnaire surveys were prepared in a word processor and distributed as e-mail attachments from the address of the administrative officer assisting senior members of the management team. Despite this approach, not all remote staff were contactable. In addition, it was not possible to know who, or how many staff were on leave at any one time and not reading their mail. We estimate that the questionnaires reached between 80 and 95 staff at different times and that between 45% and 55% of eligible staff responded to each of the first three surveys. The final survey took a different form and is described in Chap. 10.

During each visit to the organization, we presented the results of our earlier analyses in a face-to-face meeting with staff in Head Office (HO). The presentations were also made available on the organization's intranet and notices were sent to all members of the organization to advise them of their availability. We encouraged, and received, both group and individual feedback on these presentations. During the visits, we also met separately with members of the management team and specifically asked them questions about the accuracy of our assessments.

The analyses formed a kind of matrix in which information collected from each of the researchers' different points of view contributed to understanding of strategies and outcomes. Fig. 2.4 illustrates how the data were brought together. At the top of the cube are the specific research interests of each of the researchers. The front of the cube is the VAM. To the left of the VAM, is a column that shows how we collected descriptive information about the organization and its context throughout the project in order to be able to interpret and explain what we observed. The cube is completed by cells showing how the researchers visited the organization periodically and provided feedback after each visit.

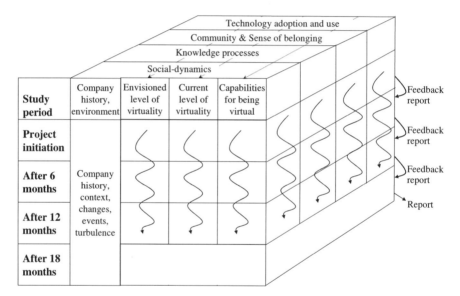

Fig. 2.4. The research project architecture

Chap. 3 describes the first stages of the organization's virtualization initiative in the form of a case study. We have disguised the real names of the organization and the participants, but the rest of the detail is true.

Reference

1.   Martensson P, Lee AS (2004) Dialogical action research at OMEGA Corporation. MIS Quarterly 28:507–537

3 The Challenge of Becoming Virtual

Jane Klobas and Stefano Renzi

3.1 Introduction

On a cold and damp late autumn afternoon, Peter Fischer looked out from his sixth floor window to the city a few kilometers to the south. He was thinking about what he had just heard. A research group had just presented him with their preliminary observations on the preparedness of his organization to deal with the challenges of working as a virtual organization. Two months earlier, Fischer had shared his vision of the organization as a "Global Network Organization (GNO)" with his staff:

> There will be an increase in the dispersal and distribution of all permanent, contract and retainer staff. In this environment, a coherent and consistent view of the organization will be maintained, manifested in shared methods, values and work practices. This way of working will be facilitated by information and communications tools, such as the Internet, VOIP[1] and intranets. New forms of workflow and management will evolve to meet new needs, and the organization will continue to be an attractive place to work and participate. Virtualization needs to be cost effective, and might even be a new form of service offering to clients.

The researchers reported that, while many elements of the GNO were already in place – the organization had consulting staff working effectively in 23 countries from Europe to Africa and from South America to South East Asia – there was still much to do. For several years, Fischer had worked to introduce information technologies to improve communications and develop a sense of community among his widely dispersed staff, but the research group indicated that technology and technology management were not yet strong enough to support his vision. The staff were strongly committed to the company, but some remained skeptical that the GNO was the right way to go.

---

[1] Voice Over IP, the provision of telephone services over the Internet.

Fischer wondered if he was doing all that could be done within the constraints of working as a division of a larger company. Were there other options? How urgent and important was it to make changes to information technology and its management in his unit? What other issues did he still need to address?

3.2 The Organization

Fischer is Director of the International Development Unit of an international engineering, environmental science and economics consulting firm based in Northern Europe. We will call the firm TPC ("The Parent Company"). TPC has around 3,400 employees of whom 2,000 work in Head Office (HO) and 1,400 abroad.

TPC is divided into ten units, nine units serving different industry sectors, and a Central Services Unit which provides administrative and technology services to the entire organization. Fig. 3.1 contains the organization chart.

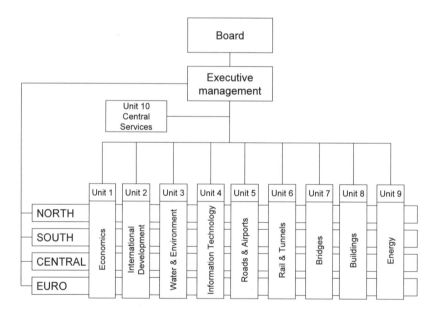

Fig. 3.1. TPC organization structure

In addition to projects in developed countries, the organization consults to governments and aid organizations in developing countries. The International Development Unit (Unit 2) is the primary organizational group that handles projects in developing countries.

Unit 2 aims to be a key player in providing development aid and assistance in the developing regions of the world. Its mission is poverty alleviation and sustainability. Drawing on resources from across the company, Unit 2 engages in consulting projects in water, urban, rural and natural resources management, and in social and institutional development.

Unit 2 has the structure of a network organization that operates globally. The six primary structural elements of the organization are:

- **Projects**. Members of staff and external experts come together to work on development consulting projects that range from a few days to three or more years. In December 2004, project teams were working in the 21 countries listed in Table 3.1. The project teams were staffed by 19 permanent consultants and over 100 international, local and regional experts working on short- or long-term contract.

Table 3.1. Unit 2 project locations, December 2004

No office	Company office	Unit 2 office
Argentina, Nicaragua, Finland, Czech Republic, Kyrgyz Republic, Benin, Botswana, Burkina Faso, Ghana, Mozambique, Niger, South Africa Egypt, Cambodia, Indonesia, Malaysia, Thailand	Tanzania	Uganda, Zambia, Vietnam

- **Market Areas**, each of which has a manager responsible for identifying market opportunities and attracting projects, and to whom project managers report on the progress of projects attached to the Market Area. The six market areas are: Water Sector Development, Urban Development, Agriculture and Natural Resources, Rural Development, Francophone West Africa, and Social and Institutional Development.
- **Two Department Managers**, who share responsibility for human resource development for all Unit 2 staff, but otherwise have separate responsibilities for management and development of the Unit. Jan Hendrickson is responsible for Resource Management while Louise Kjaer has been responsible for Knowledge Management and Development since late November 2004. Table 3.2 summarizes the responsibilities in each manager's portfolio.
- **HO administrative staff**, who support all other staff of the Unit, and execute many of the functions detailed under the responsibilities of the Department Manager for Knowledge Management and Development.

Table 3.2. Responsibilities of Unit 2 Department managers

Manager, Resource Management	Manager, Knowledge Management & Development
Shared responsibility: Human Resource Development	
Head of Department for all consultants	Head of Department for administrative staff and the training group
Staffing proposals and jobs	Business system and processes
Prognosis – forecasts and opportunities	Databank of external specialists
Briefing & debriefing – retaining/ sharing experience	Project support
	Proposal secretariat
Quality assurance (QA) audits	Marketing material and intelligence
	ICT development
	Project management skills & tools
	E-solutions
	Best practices
	Development fora for market areas
	Development projects
	Communication and dialogue
	Retainers[2]
	Offices abroad
	Overseas project staff
	Internal and external networks
	Virtual culture and framework
	Training
	Project-related human resource development courses

- **The Director**, Peter Fischer, who has overall responsibility for Unit 2, including strategy development, business development, the organization of Unit 2 and synergies with the TPC group, action plans, budgeting and financial management.
- **The Management Team**, which consists of the six Market Area Managers, the two Department Managers, and the Director.

Fig. 3.2 provides an overview of the Unit's structure. The columns marked "Project Manager" show how each project manager may at any time manage a portfolio of projects across a number of market Areas. There are also two senior specialists available to all projects.

---

[2] Retainers are contract staff who are on-call for projects that arise during the contract period, as distinct from project staff, who are appointed for the duration of a specific project.

Director, Unit 2 Strategy, business development, organization, intra-organizational synergies, budgeting						
Department Managers **Resources** – HR development, project staffing, proposals, forecasts **Knowledge** – Knowledge management, business systems, training, communication						
Market Area Managers	Project Manager	Project Manager	Project Manager	Project Manager	Project Manager	...
Water Sector Development	*project*			*project*		
Urban Development	*project*					
Rural Development & Natural Resources Management			*project*		*project*	
Social & Institutional Development	*project*			*project*		
Francophone West Africa		*project*				
Senior Specialists						

Fig. 3.2. International Development Unit (Unit 2) organization structure

In December 2004, the Unit had 84 permanent staff. Based at HO were the nine members of the management team, 17 administrative staff and 36 consultants. Three administrative staff and 19 consultants were based outside HO.

3.3 Market

The International Development Unit's clients were primarily donors of aid to developing countries, and the company held a dominant position in the market as a recipient of development aid contracts. Table 3.3 shows its position in relation to its national competitors for the year to December 2004.

Table 3.3. Top ten national contractors for development aid

Company	No. of long-term contracts	No. of short-term contracts	Total value of contracts (million US dollars)
TPC[3]	28	71	25.18
Company 2	14	29	11.61
Company 3	6	10	6.67
Company 4	6	17	5.32
Company 5	1	0	3.67
Company 6	11	0	3.33
Company 7	0	33	2.75
Company 8	0	38	2.54
Company 9	1	16	2.47
Company 10	1	16	2.23

During the past few years, the method for allocation of development funding has changed. In the past, it was usually allocated by donors from their head offices in the large capital cities of developed countries. Now, however, most development aid is allocated either from, or in conjunction with, agencies from the recipient countries. Thus, aid destined for projects in Tanzania is now allocated by the national Consulate in Dar es Salaam, rather than via government offices in the capital city where TPC's HO is headquartered. In some cases, the contractor is chosen not only by representatives of the donor country or organization but also by representatives of the recipient country's government.

Another change in the granting of development aid has been the untying of aid. While aid contracts used often to be contracts that tied the provision of goods and services to organizations from the donor country (e.g. contracts for projects funded by the national government would go to those companies) or to specific countries, aid is increasingly partially or largely untied. This means there is greater international competition for aid contracts. It also provides opportunities for companies based in a specific country to bid for contracts that were previously closed to them.

These changes have necessitated a change in the marketing and project management of international aid projects. Members of the Management Team now spend much more time in the field than in the past. During the year to December 2004, each of the Market Area managers spent around 150 days in the field, or about 50% of the available working days of the year. Other members of the Management Team were often absent. On average, 22% of HO permanent staff were outside of HO at any one time.

---

[3] Almost all of TPC's development aid work was done by Unit 2.

3.4 Unit 2 Staff and the GNO

Unit 2 staff are highly educated: many have doctorates, and most have Masters degrees. They are also strongly committed to Unit 2's mission of alleviating poverty and developing sustainability. They are independent thinkers and are strongly committed to the company and their work for the organization.

In early December 2004, soon after Kjaer's appointment as Department Manager with responsibility for knowledge management, 51 Unit 2 staff participated in a survey of their response to the notion of the GNO. All expected Unit 2 to have some of the characteristics of the GNO within the next two years. While many saw advantages, most also identified challenges to be addressed.

Given the market conditions, many staff accepted that a more dispersed organization was a necessity. One said,

> This type of organization is essential if Unit 2 is to survive.

Other staff noted additional advantages, even if there are some disadvantages:

> There are both pros and cons. Sometimes it's difficult to share information/knowledge with those who are not in headquarters. On the other hand, it is sometimes an advantage that people who work in countries that are behind us in time can work on a task we can send them when we go home, or we can send someone who is in front of us something and they can deliver it for us instead of e.g. having to send it by courier, thus saving days. The same time differences, though, can make it difficult to talk directly on the phone.

One staff member, was however, critical of the notion,

> The concept of the virtual organization is mainly with the management, who have not at all managed to convey the message to staff.

There was an expectation that some additional human resource development would be required if the GNO was become a reality:

> How will the human resources be prepared (in terms of improved knowledge and skills) in order to reach/accomplish the ... goals in various [places of work]. Will any specific training be provided? Who and how will this be done?

There was a strong sense among the staff that, while information technology (IT) may be useful to support communication between face-to-face meetings, it was still important for members of the Unit's staff to meet face-to-face. Several staff suggested to the research team that all Unit staff meet face-to-face once a year. One noted,

I can't but agree with the idea [of the Unit as a GNO], but sometimes there should be personal contact by means of short, tiring, but fruitful conferences/gatherings with a purpose. A visit once a year is not a luxury.

There is a strong project culture within Unit 2, and the work processes to support project operations are well developed. The staff recognized that this was a strength, while suggesting that more needed to be done to develop a shared organizational culture. One staff member commented,

I think that an organization that is as dispersed as you describe would have to embrace and celebrate a broad diversity of cultures, ideologies and nationalities, and so far this does not seem to be the case.

Another said,

I think you need to differentiate between the working culture in terms of shared values, feeling of belonging etc. etc. and the more process related aspects of work in Unit 2. In terms of process, I imagine that we will progressively become more virtual in the sense that we can conduct our work in an increasingly dispersed fashion provided that the technology is available. We may be highly challenged, however, to maintain a corporate culture that is more than superficial.

The strongest criticism of the notion of the GNO came from those staff working outside HO who had poor access to IT. The most critical said

We do not have the fancy software you mention, and most of us abroad are connected by modem, so it wouldn't work anyway. Furthermore, management puts very little effort into making the existing communication links work properly.

and

I think that the outlined scenario depends on the communication system around the world that isn't very developed and it will probably take many years before it will meet (some of) the European standards. When it comes to African countries, virtuality is a fantasy!

3.5 Strategic Challenges for the Coming Year

Also in December 2004, Peter Fischer prepared a list of strategic challenges for Unit 2 in 2005. Many of these challenges directly reflected changes in international processes for funding development aid projects. These challenges, in Fischer's own words, included:

- Maintaining our leading position with the national aid funding agency
- Diversification of client base is an imperative for growth
- Exploiting the ongoing untying of aid to further penetrate the Northern European market

- Developing a larger portfolio with the European Union
- Grasping the opportunities generated by decentralization of aid management.

Other challenges addressed the consequences of the changes in the market for management of Unit 2. These challenges were directly related with developing the GNO and echo those identified by the staff. They included:

- Reorient unit competencies to meet the change in demand of skills and services
- Recruit and retain staff for international activities
- Develop culture, processes and framework to sustain a progressing GNO.

A final challenge related to the position of the Unit within its parent organization:

- Synergies – tapping the potential of being big [i.e., part of a larger organization].

3.6 Information Technology

Northern European countries are among the world's leading users of IT. By world standards, TPC is a sophisticated user of IT. Among the installed corporate systems in December 2004 were SAP R3 (for financial and enterprise resource management) and EMC's Documentum (used to manage the company's Web site and as a Project Portal (PP) designed to allow sharing of documents between parties involved in projects, whether they were part of the company or not).

Technology services are provided to all units of the company by the IT Services Department which sits in the Central Services Unit (Unit 10). The IT Services Department manages corporate systems and provides day-to-day end-user support. Its structure is shown in Fig. 3.3.

3.6.1 Information Technology Management

Each Unit in TPC has its own IT Manager and IT Coordinator. The IT Managers act as the primary conduit between the Units and the IT Services Department. The Unit IT Managers are responsible for implementing the company's IT strategies in their Unit, monitoring the progress of IT projects that affect the Unit, and providing feedback from the Unit and its users to the IT Services Department. While most Units have IT Managers

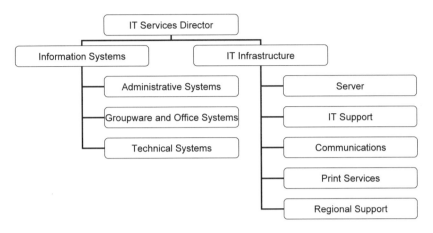

Fig. 3.3. The IT Services Department (Unit 10)

who are not IT experts, two Units share an IT expert who plays the role of IT Manager for both of them.

The IT Manager for Unit 2 was Louise Kjaer. Both Kjaer and her predecessor were social scientists with no formal background in IT or IT management. Peter Fischer viewed this as an important strength: the Unit 2 IT Manager was a person in touch with the needs of the Unit rather than a technologist who could be seduced by technology.

Kjaer was assisted in her role as IT Manager by the IT Coordinator, Krista Berger, who provided front-line user support, ordered hardware and assisted new staff to use IT and applications. In this role, she supported not just Unit 2 staff within HO but also those who worked in and traveled to remote locations. This was a more substantial role than that played by the IT Coordinator in other units, who was primarily responsible for ordering hardware.

Unit 2 also had an Assistant Web Manager, a part-time student who updated the Unit's intranet, known as the Development Information Portal (DIP). She worked within the structure of the site to load information and files which were usually sent to her by e-mail from Unit 2 managers and, occasionally, staff.

In addition to the permanent IT management structure described above, the company's Unit Directors met periodically to establish goals for IT initiatives. In late November 2004, they met to establish priorities for 2005. The top four ranked projects were:

1. Improvements to project management systems
2. IT for the global workplace
3. Resources for capacity planning

4. Modernization of the TPC home page and Internet site

Peter Fischer pushed particularly for the second of these projects, IT for the global workplace, because he saw this area as essential for Unit 2 to succeed as a GNO. He was also aware of weaknesses in the current systems.

3.6.2 Information Technology Infrastructure

Indeed, the IT capabilities necessary to support organizations that are dispersed across time and space are substantial. The necessary networking infrastructure to support the GNO included not just facilities at HO but facilities for users at each of TPC's locations and the infrastructure to connect HO reliably and securely with each remote user and to connect remote users with one another, all at sufficient bandwidth to support the necessary transactions and communications.

Then there are the software tools needed to support communication and collaboration. When the necessary communication is purely transactional, e-mail and similar tools may suffice, but Peter Fischer and the Unit 2 Management Team wanted to support more than transactions; they wanted to use communication and collaboration software to develop and maintain a sense of belonging to TPC and Unit 2 among dispersed staff as well as staff in HO. This required tools that enable more information transfer and richer interaction than access to the accounting system or occasional e-mail communication. Systems needed to support the sharing of corporate values as much as the sharing of the knowledge of staff across the Unit.

3.6.3 Network Infrastructure

The high level of dispersal of Unit 2 staff and the frequency with which HO staff were traveling meant that, more than any other part of the company, Unit 2 had special needs for information systems that enabled both business operations and communication and development and maintenance of a sense of belonging to the organization. But the corporate IT infrastructure was not yet well adapted to these needs.

The corporate IT infrastructure that supported traveling staff and staff working at subsidiary offices appears in Appendix 10. Most corporate systems lie inside the firewall and are inaccessible to users from outside unless they are able to activate the Virtual Private Network (VPN) that ensures secure access across the firewall. The company's intranet lies inside the firewall. The PP and the TPC Web site are in the Demilitarized Zone

(DMZ), an area outside the firewall that acts as an intermediary for access to information. Publicly available information from the TPC Web site is made available to all inquirers. The PP is made available to authorized inquirers with a username and password.

Requests for information held on the intranet inside the firewall are only satisfied if the user has activated a VPN connection. It was not possible to access the PP when VPN was open, so PP users had to close any open VPN connection before entering the PP.

Email may be accessed in one of two ways: with a VPN connection, from the corporate mail server using Microsoft Outlook or, when it is not possible to activate a VPN connection, from a webmail server in the DMZ. However, only browsers capable of activating a 128-bit SSL (Secure Socket Layer) can access the webmail server. Because webmail access requires a 128-bit SSL connection, it is available only from PC's or Internet cafes that had installed compatible browser. Yet, many staff worked in or traveled to remote locations in parts of the world where Internet access was poor. In many of these locations, Internet access could only be obtained through locally maintained PC's or Internet cafes that did not have browsers capable of making a 128-bit SSL connection. When connections could be made, there was often insufficient bandwidth to support effective communication with organizational systems, or the cost of keeping a line open to view email through a browser or download graphics or files was prohibitive, or both.

Even staff working on corporate PC's in countries with well developed IT infrastructure reported problems with network access. For security purposes, VPN passwords are changed regularly. Remote staff reported that, for effective access to corporate systems, the VPN password must be synchronized with the password on the user's computer, but they did not find this easy to manage without visiting technical staff in HO. Furthermore, administrative staff and consultants who visited TPC offices outside of HO reported that the realty of operations in the remote sites meant that systems did not work as seamlessly as they anticipated before arriving. The IT Services Department was convinced that training was the solution to these problems, while Unit 2 staff felt that the problem was more structural.

IT infrastructure includes common services available to staff such as backup and support. Backup services were available to staff in HO who may copy their data to a LAN drive. No backup services were provided to remote and traveling staff. User support was available only during HO working hours (8am to 5pm Central European Time). There was an introductory video to use of IT systems, but it was available only in the language of HO.

3.6.4 Systems for Communication and Collaboration

The company-wide standard for e-mail was Microsoft Outlook. Outlook was also used to manage calendars, including the calendars of traveling staff. Staff without VPN access could not use the company's Outlook system. One problem with use of Outlook was that the Internet browser must be connected to the mail servers in HO throughout the e-mail session. On low bandwidth connections, or with large files, mail access was slow and could be expensive. Remote users also had problems when connections dropped out.

Meetings that required the participation of people based both at HO and in remote locations were managed through conference calls, almost all of which were telephone conferences (teleconferences). Although videoconferencing had been considered, the company decided that teleconferences were effective for their needs and the additional investment in expensive videoconferencing equipment was not warranted.

The company had an intranet which provided news, information, reference files (including the database of contacts, staff and qualifications), and forecasting applications. The intranet was available to staff at HO and those who had VPN access to HO systems.

The PP was used by groups who wanted to share documents related to a specific project with all authorized people associated with the project. Project spaces could be established for both formal (funded) projects and informal projects among groups who had a need or desire to share information.

Unit 2's solution to the remote access problems among their own staff was to develop a PP which they called the Unit 2 "intranet" or, more frequently as time went on, the "Development Information Portal" (DIP). (The name was the result of a staff competition to name the resource.) Unit 2 staff logged in to the DIP from the PP's home page using Internet Explorer (the PP did not run on other browsers). The home page of the DIP had a simple interface with minimal graphics. A menu bar listed the functions available at the top of the screen, while the available news, reports and other documents are listed in the body of the page.

The DIP had become particularly important in the second half of 2004 because Fischer had decided that, in order to encourage Unit 2 staff to think and work as a virtual organization, Departmental meetings would no longer be held in HO. Information that would normally have been communicated at these meetings was to be distributed on the DIP.

In December 2004, up to half of Unit 2's staff based outside HO and about one third of the staff within HO consulted the DIP. About half of those staff consulted the DIP weekly and most of the other users consulted it at least once a month. Almost all users said that they used it to keep up to date with what was happening in the Unit rather than to obtain news about clients or markets. For example, a consultant working outside HO said, "This is the only way to get updates on what happens in Unit 2" while a member of HO staff said "I would not otherwise get this information". Several HO staff remarked that it was easy to use, while staff outside HO found it more difficult to access and navigate, particularly when they were working from slow connections.

Staff based both at HO and outside noted that there was poor access from many locations. Comments included: "can't get access in the countries where I'm working", "slow, unreliable Internet connections [when traveling]", "our network [outside HO] is too slow to surf and download data", "very poor local ISP and telecommunication network", "the Project Portal is not available here in Ghana on Ghana Telecom", "telephone charges in Uganda are high", and "urgent information gets to me on mail, which is faster to access on a slow connection in Sahara or Mongolia!"

While the DIP had solved some of Unit 2's information access problems, it was therefore not a perfect solution. Furthermore, Unit 2's use of the PP instead of the corporate intranet had some wider corporate implications. Some information posted to the DIP duplicated information already available on the corporate intranet. Information that was posted only to the DIP (e.g. client and market information) was only available to the wider company if a member of Unit 2 staff thought to also post it to the corporate intranet. This created some tension between Unit 2 and the rest of the company.

There was another problem: the company is Northern European and much of its material was written in the national language of HO. Unit 2, more than any other Unit, employed staff of many nationalities. English and French were the common languages of Unit 2. Even if all Unit 2 staff were able to access the intranet, they would be able to understand little of the material that it contains. While the DIP was an English language site, some material drawn from within HO was available only in the local language and therefore not accessible to all staff. Unit 2 management was aware of this problem and worked to ensure as much material as possible, such as the reports of weekly staff meetings, was published on the DIP in English. (Use of English was not a problem for the local staff, all of whom are fluent in English.)

For the 18 months prior to December 2004, Unit 2 had hoped to activate a discussion forum as part of the DIP, but technical problems with secure access had prevented its activation. The forum was conceived as a way to improve communication among staff working in diverse locations who shared an interest in a topic, project, country, etc. The hopes were that it would become a tool to support communities of practice. One possible use, for example, would be to provide a forum for new staff who are recruited outside HO to learn about TPC and Unit 2 and develop a sense of belonging through electronic discussions with staff who have been in the organization for a longer period of time. Unit 10 had promised a technical solution for the problem by mid-2005. In the meantime, the principal tools available to staff in diverse locations who wanted to communicate with one another were the telephone and e-mail.

Some Unit 2 staff had experimented with Skype to enable more frequent voice conversations. This had been successful for communication with staff located in countries with well developed IT infrastructure and in those offices in other countries that had relatively high bandwidth Internet connections, but it had not proved successful for traveling staff or staff in the field who relied on dial-up connections. Staff who relied on dial-up connections pointed out that they may as well talk on the phone once the connection was made! Despite its promise, Skype was not widely used in Unit 2.

A simple solution for enhancing the quality of communication between HO and staff remote from HO was the use of digital cameras to take photographs of events in HO. The idea was to improve the sense of "social presence", going beyond the simple exchange of business news and information by publishing photographs of people, events and even objects that have some social or cultural significance for staff of the Unit. The photographs were available from the DIP.

3.7 Possible Solutions

The Director of the IT Services Department believed that the most significant IT issues facing the company were associated with re-engineering business processes and changing people's behavior rather than with the IT infrastructure. The Department was therefore putting much of its development effort into new systems.

Corporate projects in December 2004 included specification of the "2nd Generation Net" to be used as "a medium for broadcasting and communication, a portal for information and tools, a tool for production and collaboration, a market place for business and transactions, and a learning place with dialogues and development" and investigation of software to support computer supported collaborative work (CSCW). Unit 2 was one of the two units that agreed to participate in a trial of new CSCW software to be held later in 2005.

Staff working in the field pointed out, however, that one of their greatest difficulties was simply obtaining access to the Internet or to HO systems over the low-bandwidth Internet connections available to them. Their problems were at the level of network infrastructure rather than the higher level of the systems that one might use once one has access to the network. One possibility that was occasionally considered was the provision of satellite access via an Internet Service Provider. The availability of satellite services had increased greatly in recent years while costs had decreased significantly. Most of the areas in which Unit 2 worked in Africa were covered by relatively low cost satellite access, but satellite access does require some technical skills (to position the satellite dish) and is subject to government restrictions in some countries.

Overall, Unit 2 staff thought of themselves as technology leaders within the company. The needs of their geographically dispersed group meant that they sought solutions to problems before they arose in the company as a whole. They perceived the solutions that they implemented to be innovative solutions. While they acknowledged that the IT Services Department was open to innovation, Unit 2 management and IT staff would have preferred faster resolution of the problems that they faced. They were conscious that the IT Services Department saw access, communication and collaboration issues from the inside looking out whereas Unit 2 staff saw these issues from outside HO looking in. Peter Fischer said,

> I have to drive this so that IT is established from outside HO looking in, but why should I have to be the one driving this thrust? I need ideas, challenges, choices. I have to be very pushy.

The IT Services Department responded in part to these criticisms by recommending increased training for Unit 2 staff. The IT Services Director said

> One obstacle is also training of the people: they have to learn to work in a different way. This is a big bottleneck.

Unit 2 staff recognized the need for more information and training, particularly for new technology such as Skype, and younger members of staff also noted that use of Internet-based systems is more of a habit for them than for older staff.

As Louise Kjaer stepped into her new position as Department Manager with responsibility for, among other things, Knowledge Management and the Virtual Organization, she was aware of these issues through having worked as assistant to Peter Fischer during the previous six months. But she was new to the organization and there was much to learn. She began her new job with enthusiasm, a sense of optimism and commitment to making the GNO work. Soon after, she received information about Unit 2's state of virtuality and capabilities for virtualization, gathered by a research team almost simultaneously with her appointment as Department Manager.

3.8 Toward Virtualization: Baseline Measurements

In December 2004, the researchers held interviews and seminars with more than 30 staff and surveyed permanent and contract staff based both within and outside HO. The survey questions were those developed to measure the indicators of virtuality and capabilities described in Chap. 2 and included in Appendices 1 and 4. Fifty-one (51) staff and contractors responded to the survey (a response rate of around 55%).

A dashboard was used to record the Unit's vision for virtualization and the extent to which the Unit had reached its goals. On the dashboard (Fig. 3.4) stars represent the desired level of virtuality on each dimension identified as important for Unit 2 while the sliders represent the level of virtuality in December 2004. Appendix 2 contains detail of the analyses on each dimension of virtuality.

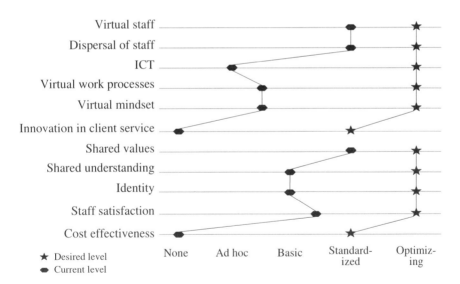

Fig. 3.4. Virtuality dashboard, December 2004

Unit 2's capabilities for virtualization were also summarized on a dashboard (Fig. 3.5). Capabilities were about the mid-point of the scale and below the desired levels of High to Very High on all dimensions. More details are given in Appendix 5.

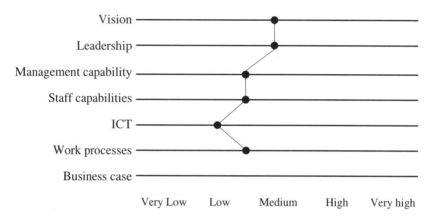

Fig. 3.5. Capabilities for virtualization, December 2004

The researchers concluded:

The limitations in capabilities suggest that there will be little progress toward virtualization during the next six months. Advances in ICT infrastructure in particular, but also management and staff development, processes for virtual work and communication, and sharing the vision with permanent consultants will be necessary before significant progress can be made.

Part 2
New Insights into Knowledge Management and Virtualization

4 Social Uncertainty in Virtual Organizations: A Preliminary Ontology of the Constituent Elements

Ivan Jensen and Paul Jackson

4.1 Introduction

In this chapter, we inductively develop a theory of the constituent elements of social uncertainty, based on the results of investigating Unit 2. We posit that social uncertainty is a sociological construct describing the interpersonal, social space which contains shared meanings and which enables the actions of others to be anticipated and understood. Theory formation is driven by the tenet that social uncertainty leads to withdrawal or avoidance behavior which has a deleterious effect upon knowledge creation and sharing. The theory predicts that, with the organization as the level of analysis, social uncertainty is constituted by four conceptual elements: concurrence, coherence, cognition and conformance. The theory is expressed in formal, symbolic notation to aid its experimental verification. The results from the research project provide face validity of the theory.

Whatever the world is now, it is definitely not what it was – and the change from now to next seems to take place at an accelerating rate [3; 9; 13; 22; 23; 28–30]. In the words of Tom Peters "(the) world is going bonkers. And it is going to get more bonkers; bonkers squared in a few years with bonkers cubed on the way" [24]. The way we perceive this change – its extent, rate, desirability and how profoundly it affects us – varies tremendously from person to person. One consequence of rapid and significant change, however, is undisputed: it leads to a loss of predictability. This reduced predictability, or uncertainty, is the result of incomplete knowledge and, in turn, leads to the perception that the future is fraught with risk [10].

While longitudinally following Unit 2's engagement in a process of strategically anchored virtualization, we became increasingly aware of some of the forces that influence actors in a field which is incrementally being stripped of its bricks-and-mortar structure and predictability. We posit that human beings generally strive to avoid or reduce unpredictability and uncertainty and that the need to do so is a deeply rooted driving force, both individually and collectively. Because we locate ourselves as agents and objects within the causality of social space, social uncertainty is related to our understanding of self and identity [14]. We predict that the need to manage social uncertainty will become more pronounced, as relentlessly increasing rates of change drive us towards volatile, complex and virtual environments. "All that is solid melts into air", as hierarchies collapse, organizational boundaries become porous and firms develop novel and ephemeral forms and structures. The corollary to this axiom is that organizational leaders who are confronted with discontinuity and instability need conceptual tools with which to first understand the influences upon social uncertainty and secondly to develop appropriate managerial responses.

This paper inductively develops a conceptual understanding of social uncertainty within organizations. We used an iterative and recursive approach to identify elements which appear to influence levels of social uncertainty within Unit 2. This represents an ontological approach at the organizational level of analysis. We attempt to isolate factors which influence social uncertainty as well as compounding and reciprocal relations between them. However tempting it might be, we do not in this paper deal with purely structural aspects of social uncertainty [2; 31; 32], but restrict ourselves to reflect upon those issues of human interaction and agency that we see as relevant for social uncertainty.

In this chapter we first explain the construct of social uncertainty. We proceed to explain the constituent factors which emerged during the research project and refer to the organizational literature where appropriate. We summarize these in symbolic notation within a formula in order to facilitate a detailed analysis of the constituent elements as a means of inviting a more precise, and potentially useful, dialogue. We then present the case study data which supported theory formulation. We end the chapter by reflecting upon the organizational importance of social uncertainty and the potential of this work to contribute to practical management.

4.2 Background

Webster's unabridged dictionary defines uncertainty as

the state of being uncertain, doubt, hesitancy … vague or indistinct, not perfectly apprehended … ambiguous, unreliable, undependable, dependent upon chance ... unforeseeable outcome or affect ... That which is uncertain is doubtful or problematical; it often involves danger through an inability to predict or place confidence in the unknown.

Uncertainty is thus caused by incomplete knowledge, as discussed by Galbraith [8] in a task-related, organizational context; conversely, certainty is related to complete knowledge. Uncertainty is an important concept because of its relation to loss of predictability and perceptions of risk [10].

Social uncertainty, then, is uncertainty related to or located in the *social* field, where losses of predictability, hesitancy, vagueness, ambiguity or lack of confidence are reflexive characteristics of social actors in a community. It should be noted that social uncertainty is predominantly a cognitive concept, caused by incomplete knowledge about the social field, which may well be but is not necessarily associated with any emotional manifestations. Social uncertainty describes a characteristic of the interpersonal social arena, where meanings and interpretations may not be clearly shared or even known, and the predictability of the behavior of others is therefore low. Complete social certainty comes when the social landscape is predictable, even though the behavior of any specific individual within that field may not be. When the meaning structures of all participants within a particular social landscape are known to me, then I have social certainty. I may not like these meanings, and they may cause me personal uncertainty and stress, but I am socially certain – there is no incomplete knowledge regarding the social action of others. It should be noted that individual tolerance of social uncertainty is highly variable [6].

Social uncertainty is, we assume, related to but distinct from social complexity [21]. Social complexity, e.g. determined by size, hierarchical stratification, functional sub groupings, task, competence or cultural differences, does not directly determine the level of social uncertainty experienced by the members of the organization. Where social complexity is high and the rate of change is zero or low – what we call *static complexity* – we anticipate that social uncertainty is low. Where social complexity is high and the rate of change is increasing – what we call *dynamic complexity* – we expect social uncertainty to increase as a function of the rate of change.

Our unit of analysis is the organization and we seek to understand the impact of social uncertainty upon organizations, rather than at the interpersonal level. We take Scott's definition of an organization as an open system:

organizations are systems of interdependent activities linking shifting coalitions of participants; the systems are embedded in – dependent upon continuing exchanges with and constituted by – the environments in which they operate [25:25]

Thus, some of the social uncertainty within organizations may originate in their environment.

We also take Scott & Christensen's further development of these ideas and see an organization as a collection of normative, cognitive and regulative systems and processes [26]. As we will argue below, however, the social landscape of present day organizations must also somehow relate to dispersion/collocation of their members.

Social uncertainty will influence the effectiveness of an organization [34]; when levels of social uncertainty increase, members collectively react to actively reduce or avoid that uncertainty. This will cause participants to spend more time making sense and evaluating risks [32]. Managers, who need to maintain productive momentum, must anticipate and minimize the impact of these diversions. Even at the organizational level, higher social uncertainty may well lead to anxiety which, if prolonged, inevitably induces stress and somatic or psychological dysfunction or overt disease. Managers therefore have both an operational and an ethical obligation to attend to social uncertainty and its consequences. Uncertainty reduction can be achieved through implicit or explicit manipulation of the constituent variables. Where this is not possible, uncertainty avoidance is typically attempted through a move (metaphorically or factually) away from the larger, high social uncertainty context towards sequentially smaller constellations of actors with a lower social uncertainty (larger or smaller groups, triads, dyads, or, ultimately, monads). In an organizational context, such constellations may include teams, networks, communities of practice, groups, etc.

A certain amount of social uncertainty may be a necessary condition for desired outcomes such as an innovation or high performance. In the face of complete information, writes Stacey, the consequence is the maintenance of the status quo through "ordinary management". Conversely, incomplete information requires "extraordinary management" [29]. For every organization at any point in time there is thus a level of social uncertainty which represents an optimum equilibrium between innovation, openness, order and self-assurance, rigidity, impenetrability, chaos and anxiety or even withdrawal of commitment. The point is not to eradicate the latter, but to find a point in the scale which represents optimal positioning for the particular requirements of an organization. The conceptual framework developed in this paper will help managers to make more informed decisions about the social landscape of their organizations.

In order to gain intellectual control over the factors which influence or are associated with social uncertainty, we reduce the participating variables to abstractions from which background noise has been filtered and which are condensed to give a distinct idea of their role and impact. The formulation should be able to be understood and interpreted at a glance. Therefore in the tradition of Lewin [19], we present our framework in formal, symbolic notation. The result of the formula is a social uncertainty index which is determined by the contributing variables and their interaction. The symbolic form is dense and generative, permitting the derivation of heuristics and quantifiable hypotheses. To take a simple example, the variable Trust is inversely related to social uncertainty: the higher the trust, the lower the social uncertainty. This may be a useful rule of thumb to guide management behavior, or may generate further hypotheses in association with other variables such as "the effect of reduction in trust on social uncertainty can be ameliorated through an increase in management control and authority". In the following sections we first define each contributing factor as a variable and declare the relationship of the variables to social uncertainty before combining them into an overall formula.

4.3 Theory Development

The following constructs have been derived from the authors' observations and reflections during our study of Unit 2. This chapter draws on data collected by the entire research team; structured interviews, surveys, workshops and workplace observation were used to collect a wide range of data over the 18 month period. The survey included two sets of items of particular relevance to understanding social uncertainty: the Twenty Statements Test (TST) [17] and a trust questionnaire. The TST generates statements about individual identity in the form "I am …" These statements can be classified as referring to individual identity (e.g., "I am a man"), relational identity (e.g., "I am a mother" expresses relationship with a child) or collective identity (e.g., "I am a member of Unit 2"). The trust items appear in Appendix 1. We conducted more than 60 semi-structured interviews specifically to explore the question of social uncertainty. Qualitative data analysis was conducted inductively and iteratively, following principles of the hermeneutic circle [15].

The individual variables of the conceptual framework we present are ontologically distinct but partially interdependent in organizations. Some of the variables are easily quantifiable whereas others can only be measured or visualized qualitatively or by proxy.

4.3.1 Dispersion Index

The dispersion index, DI, measures the degree of physical separation between members of the organization, simply expressed as the sum of the spatial distances. Physical separation generally decreases the regularity and richness of communication and interaction. The higher the dispersion index, the greater the social uncertainty. We use Eq. 4.1 to denote the sum of the spatial distances between individuals i and j.

$$\sum_1^N DI_{ij} \qquad (4.1)$$

4.3.2 Collocation Index

The collocation index measures the proportion of time spent by members of the organization in face-to-face contact. Face-to-face contact improves the construction of common mental models, the building of trust, the clarity of communication and helps reduce ambiguity. The greater the collocation index, the lower the social uncertainty of the organization. We use Eq. 4.2 to denote total time spent by individuals in the same place, expressed as a proportion of the total available work time.

$$\sum_1^N CI_{ij} \qquad (4.2)$$

4.3.3 Individual Identity

Individual identity (I_i) is a complex and controversial construct with some theorists such as Goffman [11], asserting there is in fact no such thing as a "real self". We take a pragmatic view that identity is a valid construct which is related to and drives attitudes, traits and behavior. Sedikides and Brewer write:

persons seek to achieve self-definition and self-interpretation (i.e. identity) in three fundamental ways: (a) in terms of their unique traits (b) in terms of dyadic relationships, and (c) in terms of group membership [27:1]

The greater the strength of individual identity, the lower the commitment of group members to group identity and the concomitant standardized behavioral patterns: this increases social uncertainty [18; 33]. We use Eq. 4.3 to denote the summation of the relative strengths of individual identity components across organizational members, e.g. as measured by the proportion of statements from the TST that are coded as "individual".

$$\sum_1^N I_i \tag{4.3}$$

4.3.4 Collective Ontology; Sharedness and Stability

This variable describes the degree to which an organization's members have a coherent and shared ontology, or common view of the organization and its underpinning social reality [12]. The more shared this view, the lower the social uncertainty [4]. However, the rate at which this understanding changes over time will also influence social uncertainty: the greater the rate of change, the higher the levels of uncertainty. It is possible that the mechanism through which a collective ontology is created and maintained is equivalent to that of "social categorization" [14]; i.e., striving to maximize the distance between self and out-group prototype(s) while, at the same time, minimizing the distance between self and in-group prototype(s). The representation of collective ontology is as denoted in Eq. 4.4. The rate of change in this shared ontology is represented in Eq. 4.5

$$O_c \tag{4.4}$$

$$\frac{dO_c}{dt} \tag{4.5}$$

4.3.5 Epistemology: Ratio of Information to Knowledge

These variables are necessary to capture the complex relationship between the information which is available to an organization and the explanatory power of the knowledge within the organization to give structure to that information [7]. The greater the ratio of knowledge to information (analogous to the "abstraction" and "codification" of Boisot [5]) the easier it is for an organization to make sense of its environment and the available data, and therefore the lower the social uncertainty. The notation is in Eq. 4.6.

$$\frac{INF}{KN} \tag{4.6}$$

4.3.6 Available and Requisite Variety

The principle of requisite variety, V, states that there must be as much diversity or complexity inside an organization as in its environment for the organization to be able to deal with complexity [1; 33]. When there is adequate available variety, i.e., when available variety is greater than or equal to required variety, organizational responsiveness and self-determination and will therefore reduce social uncertainty. An unfavorable ratio between information and knowledge (which leads to high social uncertainty) can be attenuated by high requisite variety. That is to say, where an organization has sufficient internal mechanisms to identify, process and react to relevant social stimuli, this will enhance confidence and certainty in the organization's ability to cope. The ratio between the available and the requisite variety is as in Eq. 4.7.

$$\frac{V_{avail}}{V_{req}} \tag{4.7}$$

4.3.7 Authority and Formal Legitimation

Authority and Formal Legitimation, S, describes the clarity and acceptance of modes of influence and control within an organization. These are usually, but not always, embodied within managerial or supervisory functions. Where power structures are not explicit or legitimated, there will be greater social uncertainty. In the formula this is indicated by the expression (1 - S), which may vary between 0 (crystalline order) and 1 (total anarchy).

4.3.8 Trust

Webster's unabridged dictionary defines trust (T) as "a reliance on the integrity, strength, ability, surety, etc. of a person or thing … trust implies instinctive unquestioning belief in and reliance upon something". In keeping with this, Luhmann [20] defines trust as a mechanism for the reduction of social complexity, which in turn reduces the cognitive load needed for constant checking, control and monitoring. The greater the trust existing in an organization, the lower will be the need for time and energy to be expended in pursuit of more complete information [16]. The summation of trust between individuals i and j is as denoted in Eq. 4.8.

$$\sum_1^N T_{ij} \tag{4.8}$$

4.4 The Formula for Social Uncertainty

Social Uncertainty (SU), we postulate, is a function of the behavior and interaction of the constituent variables described in the previous sections. We grouped together those variables which appear to amplify or attenuate one another. This adds to the conceptual clarity of the equation and suggests four major categories of influence upon social uncertainty.

- **Concurrence** – the spatial distance between organization members as expressed by the ratio between dispersion and collocation.
- **Coherence** – the consistency in perceptions and self-perceptions between members of an organization as expressed by the prominence of individual identity components and consistency of worldview.
- **Cognition** – the information processing level of the organization as expressed by the ratio of information to knowledge. This is relative to the organization's capability to ingest and process information to the level required (requisite variety).
- **Conformance** – the degree to which behaviors are legitimated, assertions are accepted on trust, and individuals subject themselves to the requirements of the organization as expressed by the ratio between authority and trust.

The stronger each of these characteristics, the lower will be the social uncertainty. The variables are, however, somewhat interdependent and may well influence, and be influenced by, variables in any of the other categories. For example, while high trust reduces the need for explicit power structures, it will also reduce the demand for exhaustive or complete knowledge. In its abbreviated form, the formula for social uncertainty is in Eq. 4.9.

$$SU = \mathbf{F}\left[Concurrence, Coherence, Cognition, Conformance\right] \qquad (4.9)$$

Eq. 4.10 describes in extended form the formula for social uncertainty.

$$SU = \mathbf{F}\left[\left(\frac{\sum_1^N DI_{ij}}{\sum_1^N CI_{ij}}\right)\left(\frac{\sum_1^N I_i}{O_c}\right)\left(\frac{\frac{INF}{KN}}{\frac{V_{avail}}{V_{req}}}\right)\left(\frac{1-S}{\sum_1^N T_{ij}}\right)\right]^N \frac{dO_c}{dt} \qquad (4.10)$$

Eq. 4.10 contains a power term (Eq. 4.11). The power term reflects our belief that social uncertainty increases as a non-trivial function of both the number of actors in the organization (*N*) and the rate of change of the shared ontology (Eq. 4.5). If, for example, the organization is large and the rate of change is negligible, i.e., Eq. 4.5 is close to zero, then social uncertainty will be very low. An illustration of this constellation could be a peacetime Army. When, on the other hand, the rate of change of the shared ontology is high due to internal and/or external influences then social uncertainty will increase very significantly. This constellation can be found, e.g., with start-up companies, in mergers, with significant changes in strategy, or potentially disruptive or destructive perturbations in an organization's markets or environment.

$$N \frac{dO_c}{dt} \tag{4.11}$$

Having explained the constituent parts and structure of the formula, in the following sections we demonstrate how the formula can be applied to data we gathered within a longitudinal research project. After presenting a brief description of the organization, we show how an interpretive assessment of the data pertaining to each variable can deliver an assessment of the state of social uncertainty (the "social uncertainty index") which is non-obvious and actually counter-intuitive, but which gives us insight into the behavior of the members of the organization. Using our formula, management might address the issues which lead to this state and create circumstances which promote activities that benefit the organization rather than only the individual.

4.5 Social Uncertainty in Unit 2

The case study organization is described in detail in Chap. 3, so we shall limit ourselves to direct observations pertinent to our theory development. The personnel in Unit 2 are highly-educated with considerable field-experience and strong groundings in professional and academic disciplines such as infrastructure, institutional or policy development work, large scale project management, etc. The consultants demonstrate an ability to work without supervision or immediate support for long periods. Although we visited Unit 2 five times, we saw most individuals only once, as they were frequently on assignment, and we constantly met people whom we had not met before. The staff, although friendly, had little inclination to stop and chat with us. They remained ensconced in offices or held conversations with each other about their work and assignments. The Director of Unit 2 was seldom visible and had a reputation for being removed from the day to day running of the Unit, and it was said his visions and goals for the Unit were somewhat aloof and unrealistic. There was a matrix management structure, organized around projects. Quality assurance and project reporting processes were tight. Each project had a wide variety of skills available to it, although some staff spoke of the divide between the hard and soft sciences (engineering and institution building, for example). There was a large number of contractors, and surveys showed that they had little desire to have a "sense of belonging" to the firm or to sustain its brand. One of the strongest impressions from interviews was of the "sense of self" demonstrated by staff: they were self-assured, articulate, open and insightful and evidence from the TST showed a very high individuality component. It emerged that, especially for contractors, the only really significant function of the firm was to supply interesting, well paid, ongoing work. In contrast to the high levels of personal competence and absorptive capacity (ability to accommodate new knowledge), there is little evidence of organizational learning. Experiences are not systematically shared or fed back into work processes. We noted low levels of group absorptive capacity in some areas, e.g., managerial attention to information from outlying regions seemed low, leading to important market information being lost.

Our data analysis led us to identify the four themes at a high level of abstraction. We summarize each of the themes below using statements made by the participants in interviews and workshops.

4.5.1 Theme 1: Concurrence

The level of group dispersal is high, with around 90% of the consultants being overseas on assignment at any given time. Several participants declared: "Out of sight is out of mind". One stated:

> But for people working abroad is where the chain breaks. You are sitting on your own there is no debriefing, no opportunity to share knowledge with colleagues.

There are no standards for e-mail responsiveness and no protocols for issue escalation when remote personnel have problems.

Collocation is also low. Although a monthly meeting had been introduced for each Department, only those in HO attended and minutes were placed on the Unit 2 intranet (the DIP). There was no technology support such as webcam or webcast to allow remote participation. Further, remote personnel did not participate in initiatives such as an electronic discussion forum, even though this was established with them in mind and consensual decision finding is the norm in TPC. One HO-based consultant observed:

> Any particular differences in the groups? ... A class that stood out were long-term external contractors. I think that management thought that the forum would be exactly for them, but according to admin staff – no way, they are lone rangers, out there, it's not for them.

More than half of Unit 2's staff were contractors who were permanently overseas and described as competent but not "belonging" in the same sense as permanent staff. "Permanent staff are much easier to work with" said one participant.

4.5.2 Theme 2: Coherence

Personnel in Unit 2 have a strong sense of personal identity: in the TST, they described themselves in terms of their position and role, but not in terms of their belonging to the firm or the unit:

> Individualism is a failure of management here. Things work in spite of the management, because of the self directed and hard working individuals. (Manager, HO)

> I am a project manager first, then a member of the organization.

This individualism and professionalism was associated with a strong commitment to high quality and project success but did not translate into a sense of corporate identity:

> Different sections have different ideas of what the unit is about (Consultant, OS)

Where there was identity drawn from a group, these were subgroups based on certain professional disciplines:

> Homogeneous? There is a good relationship – there is very little intrigue, but the subcultures are strong and usually along discipline lines. Science, management subcultures for example. And there is the technical subculture. There is however mutual respect. (7)

So, coherence was created by identities which were highly individual and aligned by a commitment to success in work or professions, not through a shared sense of being a member of an organization.

Ontology describes the lived reality of the Unit's members. This was shared to a high degree in some areas, particularly the reality of the professions, work standards and values, and work processes. The defining common factor here was the work process; there was no shared ontology of personal life:

> We might not even say hallo to each other as we meet Monday morning. We just say Hi and get on with our work. (Consultant, HO)

The shared ontology was devoted overwhelmingly to work practice.

4.5.3 Theme 3: Cognition

The ability of individuals to process information is obvious: they are highly educated and experienced, and information is quickly sorted and contextualized. But the organization has low processing power, hindered by poor absorptive capacity and poor inter-group communication: a restrictive project code mentality hindered time being spent on non-project specific activities. So, while individuals have high learning and cognition capability, the organization as a whole did not learn from the acquired knowledge of its members:

> Personal learning is fine but organizational learning is not. (Manager, HO)

It appeared that requisite variety was low, as the organization did not process signals particularly well from the outside environment:

> Our organization is suffering because it is not making use of field intelligence. It is sent in by field staff, but Head Office does not respond. Only when it is public does the organization respond, and then it is too late. (Consultant, OS)

4.5.4 Theme 4: Conformance

Control was exercised in indirect and direct ways within Unit 2. Direct control was clear and unambiguous and present in explicit lines of management, reporting procedures, regular phone calls and e-mails, audits and incentives. Strong peer control was exercised by colleagues, who shared a commitment to good quality work: if you do not do a good job, there will be someone who will tell you so in no uncertain terms. We also saw indirect, internalized controls in the form of strong professional commitment, personal motivation, team loyalty, fear of failure, self-interest and, to a smaller extent, organizational culture. In effect, we saw a complex and effective web of control which induced consistent and conformant behavior which as aligned by default (rather than desire) with the commercial objectives of the organization.

Trust, as a means of integrating staff, appears to have been strong at the personal level. The observed and espoused behavior of the personnel towards each other was collegial and generous. Indeed,

There is a culture, a discipline of relying on each other, trust, dependability. Not just knowledge, but a way of working together. This culture is very important, not only to grease the communication, but to keep people working here (Consultant, HO)

The attitude of staff toward Unit 2 was more varied: while they respected the management values and reputation of TPC and Unit 2, they did not give of themselves easily: some resented that they attended (voluntary) monthly lunchtime general interest seminars on their own time and did not feel there was any particular need to have a "sense of belonging" to Unit 2.

Table 4.1 summarizes the estimated values of the variables which are suggested by the qualitative results. While the scores are simplifications, we feel they reflect the data gathered in the interviews and workshops.

Table 4.1. An interpretive assessment of the case study data

Conceptual Category	Variable	Score
Concurrence	Dispersal	High
	Collocation	Low
Coherence	Individual Identity	High
	Shared ontology	Medium
Cognition	Information	High
	Knowledge	Medium
	Requisite Variety	Low
Conformance	Power structures	High
	Trust	Medium
Total		Medium-High Social Uncertainty

How do these observations compare with the results the formula might generate? We appear here to have a large organizational unit which functions effectively at some levels, but not at others. The self-confidence and individual performance of staff is in stark contrast to the general lack of *esprit de corps*. While individual uncertainty is low, it seems to us that social uncertainty is quite high. Our basic tenet is that, under these circumstances, the organization will implicitly or explicitly engage in activities aimed at reducing or avoiding social uncertainty.

The members of this particular organization appear to orient themselves away from the larger collectivity and towards smaller groupings. There is no common, coherent social view in the organization and, as a consequence, consent has been withdrawn and performance is delivered within parameters which suit the individual rather than the group as a whole. In-

dividualistic attitudes and survival strategies developed in the face of uncertainty mitigate against the construction of shared, organizational intellectual capital. Thus, it appears that in the absence of suitable or desirable
in-group prototypes at the organizational level the members of the organization form smaller social certainty clusters around available, positively
evaluated prototypes, e.g., individuals with particular technical competence, project management expertise, or personal charisma. Consequently,
knowledge sharing and creation is successful in these groups, but fails at
the organizational level.

4.6 Conclusion

This is a conceptual paper, derived from literature review and personal
management experience and partly grounded in the longitudinal study of
an organization which is in the process of virtualization. The concept of
social uncertainty seems useful, and the notion that reducing social uncertainty – particularly under conditions such as geographical dispersal and
disciplinary or cultural diversity – is intuitively appealing. However, this
should not be taken to imply that social uncertainty should be eliminated.
Depending upon their environment, tasks and objectives, organizations require some level of unpredictability and uncertainty in order to generate
dynamism and innovation. Particularly in a world which is characterized
by discontinuity and change, the concept of social uncertainty may open
up a new area of thought for managers. The formula we have developed is
a first step in trying to gather and combine the contributing variables and
allow an assessment of whether the level of uncertainty is empowering or
dysfunctional. With the formula in hand, a manager can focus upon the individual components and ask him- or herself whether it is at an optimal
level for a particular organization. It is compact and transparent, allowing
simple heuristics or complex hypotheses to be derived to assist managers
to analyze and respond to anomalies or problems. From the research perspective, the formula can be extended and enriched as new insights and relationships are revealed.

We used the detailed Unit 2 case study to illustrate the face validity of
the approach and to demonstrate the particularity of social uncertainty. Social uncertainty may be high even where individuals feel certain in themselves. Under conditions of high social uncertainty, the shared meanings
which bind a group to its purpose are weakly held. The consequence of
this (or perhaps the thing which makes it possible for the group to continue
to exist and even prosper) is that certainty will be constructed around an

individualistic formwork – which has consequences for all those organizational initiatives which seek to build social capital. Future research will include a comprehensive review of the empirical literature pertaining to each variable, the derivation of individual hypotheses from the formula, and the development of a measurement scale for each of the variables which, taken together, will deliver a social uncertainty index.

References

1. Ashby WR (1956) An introduction to cybernetics. Chapman & Hall, 1956
2. Barabasi a-L (2003) Linked: how everything is connected to everything else and what it means for business, science, and everyday life. Plume, London
3. Beck U (1992) Risk society: towards a new modernity. Sage, London
4. Berreby D (2005) Us and them: understanding your tribal mind. Little, Brown & Company, New York
5. Boisot M (1998) Knowledge assets: securing competitive advantage in the information economy. Oxford University Press, Oxford
6. Clampitt PG, Williams ML (undated) Managing organizational uncertainty: conceptualization and measurement. Retrieved 7 June 2007 from http://www.imetacomm.com/otherpubs/research/manorguncertain.pdf
7. Devlin K (2001) Infosense: turning information into knowledge. Freeman, New York
8. Galbraith J (1973) Designing complex organizations. Addison-Wesley, Reading, MA
9. Giddens A (1991) Modernity and self-identity. Polity Press, Cambridge
10. Giddens A (1999) Runaway world: how globalisation is reshaping our lives. Profile, London
11. Goffman E (1990) The presentation of self in everyday life. Anchor, New York
12. Hatch MJ, Schultz M (2004) Organizational identity. Oxford University Press, Oxford
13. Hedberg B, Dahlgren G, Hansson J, Olve N-G (2000) Virtual organizations and beyond: discovering imaginary systems. John Wiley & Sons, Chichester
14. Hogg MA, Terry DJ (2001) Social identity processes in organizational contexts. Psychology Press, Philadelphia
15. Klein HK, Myers MD (1999) A set of principles for conducting and evaluating interpretive field studies in information systems. MIS Quarterly 23:67–94
16. Kramer RM, Cook KS (eds) (2004) Trust and distrust in organizations: dilemmas and approaches. Russell Sage Foundation, Washington
17. Kuhn M, McPartland T (1954) An empirical investigation of self-attitudes. American Sociological Review 1954, 1968–1976
18. Leary MR, Tangney JP (eds) (2003) Handbook of self and identity. The Guilford Press, London

19. Lewin K (1997) Field theory in social science. American Psychological Association, Washington
20. Luhmann N (1979) Trust and power. John Wiley & Sons, New York
21. Merry U (1995) Coping with uncertainty: insights from the new sciences of chaos, self-organization and complexity. Greenwood Press, New York
22. Naisbitt J (1984) Megatrends: ten new directions transforming our lives. Warner Books, New York
23. Negroponte N (1995) Being digital. Vintage, New York
24. Peters, T (1993, 29 March) [Interview]. Forbes ASAP
25. Scott WR (1998) Organizations: rational, natural and open systems. Prentice Hall, Upper Saddle River, NJ
26. Scott WR, Christensen S (1995) The institutional construction of organizations: international and longitudinal studies. Sage, Thousand Oaks, CA
27. Sedikides C, Brewer MB (2002) Individual self, relational self, collective self. Psychology Press, Philadelphia
28. Sennett R (1998) The corrosion of character: the personal consequences of work in the new capitalism. Norton, New York
29. Stacey RD (2002) Strategic management and organisational dynamics: the challenge of complexity. Prentice Hall, Upper Saddle River, NJ
30. Toffler A (1980) The third wave. William Morrow, New York
31. Wassermann S, Faust K (1994) Social network analysis: methods and applications. Cambridge University Press, Boston
32. Weick KE (1979) The social psychology of organizing. Addison-Wesley, Reading, MA
33. Whetten A, Godfrey, PC (1998) Identity in organizations: building theory through conversations. Sage, Thousand Oaks, CA
34. Zand DE (1972) Trust and managerial problem solving. Administrative Science Quarterly 17:229–239

5 When Communities of Practice Fail: Community Ties and Organizational Commitment

Gaela Bernini and Jane Klobas

5.1 Communities of Practice

Communities of practice (CoPs) are groups of people with significant interpersonal ties built through the process of collective learning about a common practice [27]. Research about CoPs has concentrated on their role in knowledge management, with results that demonstrate their value for knowledge creation, knowledge sharing and as repositories of knowledge [7; 14; 16; 25; 29].

The CoP is a social device which connects people around a specific practice within a domain of human endeavor. The domain is the field or discipline which draws members together. The practice is the particular application or work activity that is the focus of knowledge creation, transfer and storage within the CoP [7]. CoPs are associated more with problem solving and sharing of tacit knowledge than with procedures and rules. Recognizing that theories, process designs, manuals and other formal devices for explaining and organizing practice are unable to deal with the complexity of much modern work, CoPs aim to solve problems and draw out tacit knowledge. Often, they use collaboration and narrative to deal with aspects of practice that may range from the mundane but unplanned for to dealing with incoherencies and irrationalities in the formal system [19].

Successful communication within a CoP relies on trust, mutual respect and reciprocity as individual members express doubt, and ask for and provide advice to one another. The interaction between participants assumes a social contract in which mutual expectations of others' behavior during exchanges are satisfied. This tacit agreement implies individual willingness to shift from being a *worker* to being a *member* [13]. In fact, membership, the feeling that one invests part of oneself and therefore has the right to belong [2], is an important notion in relation to CoPs. There are people who belong to a CoP and people who do not. This distinction generates boundaries which provide members with the emotional security necessary to let them expose themselves and allow intimacy to develop [10].

5.1.1 CoPs in the Organization

While most of the literature has glorified CoPs as effective means of managing and generating knowledge, some observations by Wenger and his colleagues suggest that there are some organizational risks. Wenger, McDermott and Snyder [28] have identified cases where CoPs are unrecognized by the organization and there is therefore no reflexivity between the organization and the community, and cases where CoPs are legitimated to the extent that become a target of management strategy. In both sets of cases, it can be difficult for management to steer CoPs. There may be: an excess of personal commitment to the CoP, leading to arrogance and elitism; imperialism, particularly where the community domain is considered more relevant to members than other organizational fields; tight bonds (cliques) within a group which acts as a restrictive gatekeeper; and lack of documentation, or development of dialects specific to the community, or both, which make diffusion of knowledge within the organization difficult. Given the cohesive and exclusionary forces that may emanate from within CoPs, CoPs may weaken organizations as community members establish distance from non-members.

In this chapter, we examine the relationship between intra-organizational CoPs (i.e., CoPs that exist within the boundaries of a single organization) and the organization within which they reside. We consider CoPs as organizational resources which, along with other resources, need to be reconciled and aligned to permit the organization to pursue its goals. In particular, we concentrate on the relationship between CoPs and organizational cohesion. The negative effects of poor organizational cohesion are believed to be profound: "lack of shared identity creates dissonance and makes collective action ... impossible – groups disintegrate, organizations become less than the sum of their parts" [6] (p113). We ask if CoPs, with their strong internal ties, threaten organizational cohesion.

As an indicator of organizational cohesion, we focus on organizational commitment (OC), the willingness of individual members of the organization to contribute to organizational purposes and success [15; 18] absenteeism and turnover [18]. We expect the strength of ties within a CoP to be inversely related to OC, i.e., the stronger the ties to a CoP the weaker CoP members' commitment to the organization is expected to be.

5.2 Research Approach

We studied the relationship between ties to CoP and OC through social network analysis (SNA) of data collected by questionnaire survey. SNA enables a social structure to be represented as a group of interconnections among units of analysis. It has been used to analyze and represent networks of relationships in fields as diverse as anthropology, organizational studies and analysis of the Internet. Social network data consist of binary social relations that record the presence, absence or strength of relations among pairs of persons or nodes. These relationships are represented in graphs known as sociograms. A set of metrics provide additional information about the network as a whole and relationships within and among elements of the network. Together these tools enable SNA to be used to uncover the existence of communities [23; 26].

Working in Unit 2, we used SNA to uncover CoPs among members of the organization based on the strength of the connections or ties between pairs. According to Granovetter's theory of weak ties [12], the strength of ties indicates the opportunity for communication and diffusion of influence and information [22]. We therefore developed two sets of questions to measure ties. Our first question provided information about communication. Following common practice, we used a questionnaire survey to ask members of the organization the names (or organizational initials) of up to 10 people in the organization with whom they communicated frequently about work practices. Our second question provided data about the diffusion of knowledge, and suggested a level of trust about another organizational members' knowledge of a subject or practice [12; 20]. In this question, we asked each participant to name of up to 10 people they asked for professional advice.

SNA usually begins with a matrix of binary relationships. In our study, we began with two matrixes, one for the communication networks and one for professional advice networks. Both the rows and columns of a social network matrix contain the names of all potential members of the network (in our case, all people who responded to a question or who were named in another person's response). The value 1 appears in a cell when the person named in row i cites the person named in the corresponding column j.

Different techniques can be used to convert these binary relationships into sociograms, identify clusters of related nodes, and calculate metrics that describe relationships and clusters. In our study, we used oriented graphs which recorded the direction of each relationship [23].

5.2.1 Identifying Communities

SNA can be used to distinguish clusters of related nodes, but depending on the technique used these clusters may or may not be communities. A method to detect communities was suggested by Girvan and Newman [11]. They proposed an algorithm based on the "betweenness centrality" of each node in a social network. Betweenness centrality [23] measures the extent to which a particular node lies between or connects the other nodes in a graph. For a node k, betweenness centrality is calculated as the proportion of instances in which the shortest route between two nodes i and j passes through node k [4]. Using Girvan and Newman's algorithm, betweenness centrality is calculated for all nodes in the network. The node with the highest betweenness centrality represents the boundary of a community. This node is removed and betweenness centrality is recalculated for all nodes affected by the removal. This procedure continues until no nodes remain. The number of communities (clusters) selected from the procedure is based on the change in betweenness centrality between iterations. Only clusters defined by individuals with relatively high betweenness centrality are considered communities. Consequently, the algorithm identifies the individuals who form the boundaries (those with the highest betweenness centrality) and then uncovers the linked groups of individuals forming each community defined by the boundaries. This approach, in cases where the community structure of a network was known beforehand, has been found to be accurate and sensitive [11; 21].

Once the communities have been distinguished empirically, they need to be labeled or identified. Our questionnaire asked for information about several possible explanations for community structure and membership: participants' geographical location, tenure, role in Unit 2 (manager, administrative staff, HO-based consultant, external consultant), and Market Area. Each cluster was overlaid with these variables in order to identify the extent to which CoPs reflected these attributes of their members.

5.2.2 Measurement

To compare strength of ties with OC, we first needed to measure the variables. In both cases, a number of alternatives were available.

Strength of Ties

SNA provides a number of indexes which may act as indicators of strength of ties. One of the most commonly used measures is density: the ratio of the number of connections among members of a cluster to the total number of possible connections among members of the same group [26]. This measure is, however, dependent on the size of the group and therefore does not readily permit comparison of groups. A more appropriate index for our study was proposed by Radicchi et al [21]. The index, I_k, is based on the total number of connections or linkages to nodes within a cluster V (the indegrees, K^{in}) and the total number of linkages from nodes in cluster V to nodes outside it (outdegrees, K^{out}), as shown in Eq. (5.1).

$$i_k = \frac{K^{in}(V)}{K^{in}(V) + K^{out}(V)} \qquad (5.1)$$

Organizational Commitment

OC consists of identification with the organization, along with the desire to continue to work for it and to put in extra effort for it [18]. In this study, we used an OC Questionnaire (OCQ) developed by Mowday and colleagues [18]. This index has been found to have good psychometric properties and has been used successfully in a wide array of studies, from personnel management [3] to psychology [9] and business studies [17].

The original OCQ has 15 items, measured on a 5 point Likert scale. For practical reasons, shorter forms are often used in organizational research and we adopted a 9 item form that had been used successfully in other unpublished studies with which we were familiar. We also modified two questions after Unit 2 management asked us to replace American expressions that would not be readily understood by people for whom English was a second language.

The modified OCQ was distributed at the same time as the social network questionnaire. Once the data were received, inter-correlations among the items were calculated. Two items had low correlation with the others, and discussion with organizational managers suggested that these items were not appropriate for measurement of commitment to their organization. OCQ was therefore calculated, for our study, as the mean score on the 11 items listed in Table 5.1.

Because Unit 2 was organized as a matrix, commitment was measured in three layers:

- The Parent Company
- Unit 2
- the Market Area in which the respondent worked

Table 5.1. Modified OCQ used in this study

1. I feel deeply dedicated to …
2. I would accept almost any type of job assignment in order to keep working for …
3. I find that my values are very similar to those of …
4. I talk about … to my friends as great people to work with
5. … really inspires the best for my job performance
6. I really care about the future of …
7. I am willing to put in a great deal of effort beyond that normally expected in order to help …

Cronbach's alpha was above .82 for all of these layers, indicating that the 7 point scale was reliable. OCQ was calculated as the mean score over the seven items.

5.2.3 Data Analysis

For SNA, we used the freeware software UCINET [5]. UCINET 6 converts lists of relationships (in our case between one person and up to 10 others) to a case-by-case matrix. Attributes, such as geographical location, organizational role and Market Area, can be associated with each case (node). Drawing on the matrix, UCINET calculates the requested social network data. UCINET is distributed with Netdraw 2 which graphs the social network. Among the options provided by Netdraw 2 is application of Girvan-Newman's algorithm to identify boundaries and communities.

Multiple regression was used to examine whether OC was affected by strength of ties as measured by community density in the presence of other attributes such as location and time with the organization (tenure).

5.2.4 Participants

The results are based on data collected in the 51 questionnaires received (from around 55% of contactable members of Unit 2) at the beginning of our study. Nearly 60% (30) of the questionnaires were received from staff within HO while the rest of the respondents were based outside HO. Responses were received from staff working in all market areas, as shown in Table 5.2.

Table 5.2. Market areas in which respondents work

	Frequency	Percent
Social and Institutional Development	19	37.3
Rural Development and Natural Resource Mgmt	15	29.4
Water Sector Development	10	19.6
Francophone West Africa	8	15.7
Urban Development	7	13.7
A combination	17	33.3
Total respondents	51[a]	

[a] Total frequency exceeds 51 because multiple responses were possible.

5.3 Results

In this section, we identify communities based on the two sources of information, frequency of communication and requests for advice. We then compare the strength of ties in these communities with OC.

5.3.1 Communities Based on Frequency of Communication

We identified four communities based on frequency of communication. These communities all reflected the market areas within which the respondents worked. They were:

1. S&ID: People working in the social and institutional development Market Area
2. Water: People working mainly the water sector
3. Franc: People mainly from the Francophone West Africa Market Area
4. Rural: People mainly in the rural sector

These communities are shown in Fig. 5.1. Boundaries are drawn around each of the communities and the community density (measured by index I_k) appears next to the community name. It is interesting to note that both the largest community, S&ID, and the Water community, which is somewhat smaller, have similar density. Members of each of these communities communicate more frequently with one another.

The symbols used to represent each node in Fig. 5.1 reflect a combination of the role each person plays in Unit 2 and their geographical location:

- Square: management (all in HO)
- Triangle: administrative staff (all in HO)

- Diamond: consultant based in HO
- Circle: consultant based in the field outside HO
- Circle in a box: staff of an African office
- Plus node: undetermined

The graph shows that there is no particular pattern by location or role in membership of communities based on communication. This is consistent with the nature of Unit 2 as a highly dispersed organization.

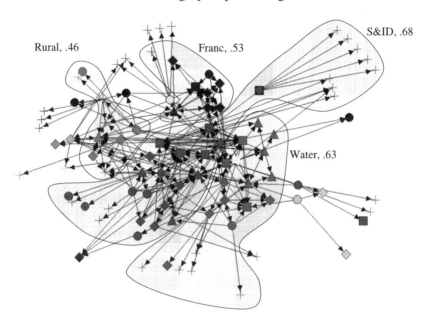

Fig. 5.1. Communities based on communication

5.3.2 Communities Based on Professional Advice

A different picture emerges when communities are mapped on the basis of requests for professional advice (Fig. 5.2). (The symbols used to represent the nodes in this figure can be interpreted the same way as in Fig. 5.1.) There communities can be identified:

1. SS: A large community formed mainly by social scientists and managers
2. Franc: The Francophone community
3. Admin: A community composed predominantly of administrative staff

Only the Francophone community is consistent across both frequency of communication and requests for advice.

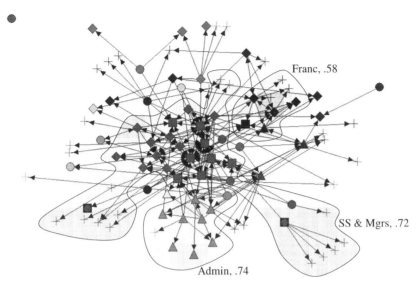

Fig. 5.2. Communities based on professional advice

5.3.3 Organizational Commitment

OC is summarized in Table 5.3. Commitment to the different layers of the organization varied, and the differences between people in different roles and locations were also marked. Managers and consultants based outside HO ("external consultants" in the table) reported the highest levels of OC overall. Consultants based in HO had the lowest OC, while the administrative staff were midway between them and the managers. When looking at commitment to the different layers of the organization, commitment to the parent company is lowest for all staff categories while Market Area commitment is highest.

Table 5.3. Organizational commitment by layer, role and location

	Management	HO admin	HO consultant	External consultant	Mean
Parent company	3.6	3.1	2.9	3.7	3.3
Unit 2	4	3.8	3	3.7	3.5
Market area	4.1	3.7	3.2	3.8	3.6

5.3.4 Relationship Between Community Ties and Organizational Commitment

The relationship between community ties and OC could only be calculated for those participants who were included in communities identified from the SNA. Table 5.4 reports the correlations between strength of ties measured by index I_k and OC measured by the modified OCQ.

Table 5.4. Correlations between strength of ties and OC

Community based on	Parent	Unit 2	Market area
Frequency of communication (n = 35)	-.39*	-0.23	-0.46**
Professional advice (n = 28)	-.75**	-0.62**	-0.49**

$*p < .05 **p < .01$

The correlations are all negative. They are statistically significant in all cases except commitment to Unit 2 based on frequency of communication. At all levels, the negative correlation between strength of community ties and OC were for those communities based on professional advice.

Regression analysis took into account the potential effects of location and tenure on OC along with strength of ties. Tenure was measured as the number of months worked for the organization. Table 5.5 contains the regression coefficients for commitment to each layer of the organization. Table 5.5a reports the coefficients for communities based on frequency of communication while Table 5.5b contains the coefficients for communities based on requests for professional advice.

Only in the case of commitment to Market Area, when communities were defined by frequency of communication, was OC affected by one of the control variables. People in HO had lower commitment to their Market Area than those working outside HO for whom their Market Area colleagues are their primary points of contact into the organization.

Table 5.5a. Regression coefficients for different layers of OC, communities based on frequency of communication

Layer	Parent	Unit 2	Market area
Strength of ties	-.4*	-.28	-.34*
HO	-.22	-.14	-.41*
Tenure	.02	.04	.2
R^2	.25*	.13	.46**

$*p < .05 ** p < .01$

Table 5.5b. Regression coefficients for different layers of OC, communities based on requests for professional advice

Layer	Parent	Unit 2	Market area
Strength of ties	-.76**	-.62**	-.36
HO	-.06	-.12	-.28
Tenure	-.12	-.07	.15
R^2	.57**	.38**	.34*

$* p < .05 ** p < .01$

5.4 Discussion

Before considering the substantive results of this study, we need to consider three potential limitations of the method that we used. Firstly, while we used a method that has successfully uncovered communities in the past, and our experience working within the organization suggests that the communities uncovered in this analysis reflect the communities within Unit 2, we need to ask if we have really uncovered communities of *practice*. Only one community, the Francophone community, passed both our tests, forming a community based on both frequency of communication and requests for practical advice. On reflection, we should expect this community to be strong and enduring because it is the only group within the organization that uses a language other than English (or the language used in HO) and some members of the Francophone community do not speak these other languages. On further reflection, we might ask if communities based on frequency of communication are necessarily CoPs. CoPs form on the basis of exchange of knowledge about practice. This does not necessarily require frequent communication, but communication when it matters, i.e. when advice is sought and provided. Thus, the professional advice communities may more accurately reflect the CoPs in Unit 2 than the frequency of communication communities.

A second possible limitation is the method used to measure strength of ties within the communities. Is community density the most appropriate measure for strength of ties in a CoP, and if so, is Radicchi's index I_k the most appropriate index? We experimented with other indexes of density and found that I_k gave the most readily interpretable and consistent results for these data, but that does not mean it is the best possible index. It may be possible to develop an index of strength of ties specific to CoPs. For example, if CoPs were defined only by the exchange of professional advice, an index that incorporates frequency of communication may provide a basis for comparison between the communities.

Thirdly, we were only able to identify communities based on the responses of those members of Unit 2 who responded to the questionnaire. Around 50% of the members of the organization did not respond. With their additional information, it may have been possible to identify other communities, and indeed the boundaries of the communities that we did identify may have shifted. While it is possible that those members of the organization who did not have strong community ties chose not to respond to the questionnaire, we nonetheless recommend some caution in interpreting the community structure that we uncovered as representing the entire community structure for the organization.

With those limitations in mind, it is first useful to comment on the relationship between the observed community structures and the formal organizational structure. In both cases, the observed communities were readily interpreted with reference to the formal organizational structure. The communities based on frequency of communication clearly reflect the structure of work in the organization: project-based, where projects are sought, found and managed by market areas. It is not surprising that these communities reflected the every day working necessity to communicate about projects in market areas. The communities based on professional advice were more diverse: one community (Francophone) reflected the language of its members, while the other two communities divided the organization in terms of role. There was a community of administrative staff, who exchange knowledge in relation to their role as HO-based support for the project-based processes of the organization; we had observed the strong nature of this community in our visits to Unit 2 when administrative would call on one another and refer to each other with mutual trust, respect and affection. The other community joined managers and consultants working in all locations. This community, although including members of the Social and Institutional Development Market Area, extended beyond it to include managers in all locations. Its existence suggests strong links between S&ID and those who set the direction of the organization, and indeed, several of the managers have social science backgrounds. But, why were professional advice communities not identified in the other market areas? One possible explanation is based on the size of the teams that work on the Unit's projects: many projects involve one person working as an expert in the field or in another organization. In this case, these experts are acknowledged as the leading experts in their field in the organization, and in some cases they are one of a kind. Their professional advice communities may therefore be communities that are formed among professional colleagues outside of organizational boundaries. Alternatively, or additionally, they may be isolated from the professional advice structure of the organization.

The consistency between community structure and formal organizational structure suggests that the organization may lack a parallel informal structure. While the consistency between community structure and formal organization can facilitate management, lack of an apparent informal communication structure may also have drawbacks. In particular, it may restrict the transfer of knowledge across market areas and may be associated with such strong conformity to the formal organization that creativity, flexibility and criticism are suppressed.

Concentrating on the main purpose of this study, the evidence supports the hypothesis that organizational commitment is negatively influenced by the strength of ties developed within communities. Why might this be so? Perhaps the community-based exchanges offer more reward or satisfaction than exchanges with a more distant body, "the organization". A related explanation might be provided by the nature of learning in CoPs.

We start with the assumptions, common to writers about CoPs, that individual learning is inseparable from collective learning and that learning grows through social interactions which generate the ground for a CoP [1; 7; 29]. Members voluntarily and mutually engage in a CoP because they are motivated to apply and exchange knowledge related to practice, i.e. to learn and to exchange knowledge with others as they learn. Learning about a practice within a CoP is more than intellectual exercise. It is a collective experience that affects not only "doing" but also "being". It is thus associated with the development of a person's identity as a member of the professional community represented by the CoP [8](p138). But, identity to one group is developed at the detriment of other group identities [24]. Group identity is formed and maintained through the use of rules of exclusion: in-group solidarity; out-group exclusion. To reinforce common features, it is necessary to deny what is different. As a result, it is possible that community ties and OC are in competition because professionals feel part of their community rather than the organization ("other groups"). Thus, although productive for knowledge and learning, CoPs may also be associated with organizational costs.

5.5 Future Research

This chapter describes a first attempt to examine the relationships between strength of CoP and OC. The study was conducted in a single organization headquartered in Northern Europe. Further research across multiple organizations based in different countries would be necessary to confirm our preliminary observations. It would also be useful to examine the relationship between strength of CoP and other organizational characteristics. While we have speculated on why the relationship between strength of CoP and OC should be negative, it would be useful to further explore these and other potential explanations so that we can better understand how to harness the benefits of CoPs without weakening other key aspects of the organizations in which they exist.

References

1. Andriessen JHE (2005) Archetypes of knowledge communities. In: Proceedings of the Second Communities and Technologies Conference, pp 191–215
2. Aronson E, Mills J (1959) The effect of severity of initiation on linking for a group. Journal of Social Psychology 59:177–181
3. Benkhoff B (1977) Disentangling organizational commitment. Personnel Review 26:114–130
4. Borgatti SP (2005) Centrality and network flow. Social Networks 27:55–71
5. Borgatti SP, Everett MG, Freeman L (1999) UCINET 5 for Windows: Software for social network analysis. Analytic Technologies, Natick, MA
6. Brown AD, Starkey K (2000) Organizational identity and learning: a psychodynamic perspective. The Academy of Management Review 25:102–120
7. Brown JS, Duguid P (2001) Knowledge and organization: a social-practice perspective. Organization Science 12:198–213
8. Brown JS, Duguid P (2002) The social life of information. Harvard Business School Press, Boston
9. Crossman A, Abou-Zaki B (2003) Job satisfaction and employee performance of Lebanese banking staff. Journal of Managerial Psychology 18:368–376
10. Ehrlich JJ, Graven DB (1971) Reciprocal self-disclosure in a dyad. Journal of Social Psychology 7:389–400
11. Girvan M, Newman ME (2002) Community structure in social and biological networks. Proceedings of the National Academy of Sciences 99:7821–7826
12. Granovetter M (1973) The strength of weak ties. American Journal of Sociology 78:1360–1380
13. Handy C (1995) Trust and the virtual organization. Harvard Business Review 73(3):40–50.
14. Hildreth P, Kimble C (2004) Knowledge networks: innovations through communities of practice. Idea Group, Hershey, PA
15. Kinnear L, Sutherland M (2000) Determinants of organisational commitment amongst knowledge workers. African Journal Business Management 31:106–123
16. Lave J, Wenger E (1991) Situated learning: legitimate peripheral participation. Cambridge University Press, Cambridge
17. Mitchell TR, Holtom BC, Lee TW, Sablynski CJ (2001) Why people stay: using job embeddedness to predict voluntary turnover. Academy Of Management Journal 44:1102–1121

18. Mowday R, Porter L, Steers R (1982) Employee-organizational linkages: the psychology of commitment, absenteeism, and turnover. Academic Press, New York
19. Orr J (1996) Talking about machines: an ethnography of a modern job. Cornell University Press, Ithaca, NY
20. Perry-Smith J, Shalley C (2003) The social side of creativity: a static and dynamic social network perspective. Academy of Management Review 28:89–106
21. Radicchi F, Castellano C, Cecconi F, Loreto V, Parisi D (2004) Defining and identifying communities in networks. Proceedings of the National Academy of Sciences of the United States of America 101:2658–2663
22. Scholten V, Bhagavatula S, van de Bunt G, Elfring T (2004) A measurement model of tie strength for business networks: the case of a Dutch high-tech and an Indian low-tech organization. Paper presented at XXIV International Social Network Conference, May 12–16 2004, Portoroz, Slovenia
23. Scott J (1992) Social network analyis. Sage, Newbury Park, CA
24. Sedikides C, Brewer M (2001) The individual self, the relational self, the collective self. Psychology Press, Philadelphia
25. Ward A (2000, Mar–Apr) Getting strategic value from constellations of communities. Strategy and Leadership Magazine, pp 1–9
26. Wassermann S, Faust C (1994) Social network analysis. Cambridge University Press, Boston
27. Wenger E (1998) Communities of practice: learning, meaning and identity. Cambridge University Press, Cambridge
28. Wenger E, McDermott R, Snyder W (2002) Cultivating communities of practice. Harvard Business School Press, Boston
29. Wenger E, Snyder WM (2000, Jan–Feb) Communities of practice: the organizational frontier. Harvard Business Review 78:139–145

6 An Exploratory Survey of the Structure and Components of Organizational Memory

Paul Jackson

6.1 Introduction

This chapter uses the concepts of organizational memory (OM) and organizational learning to analyze social, practical and technical issues facing corporate memory utilization in the distributed organizational setting of Unit 2. It advances our understanding of how to conceptualize, map and therefore manage and use OM by using inductive analysis of qualitative data to develop a conceptual entity-relationship model. This model refines and specifies our understanding of the concept of OM and its constituent elements, providing a theoretically based and empirically validated description which can be used as a platform for designing solutions to facilitate knowledge sharing in distributed organizations.

In economic sectors where success is predicated upon knowledge, responsiveness and the generation of innovation, making the best of what an organization knows, has become a key driver. What an organization knows and can apply to problem solving, decision making, routine tasks or innovation has been described as its memory; it is the availability and application of the appropriate memory when it is needed that lifts firm performance. This memory is present in a variety of forms and repositories within organizations. The general problem that this chapter addresses is that of increasing and making available these stocks of knowledge and experience, irrespective of the organizational unit or geographical location of the repository. We do this by developing a model of the general structure of OM which may support the development of technological tools for knowledge location and retrieval.

Because this is an exploratory study, several unanticipated insights are gained as well as some refinement and further development of existing theory. We confirm and usefully expand the relational model of Nevo and

Wand [17] to explicate our empirical data and advance the theoretical model of OM as well as continue their efforts to develop the foundations for the design of a practicable information system to manage OM metadata.

6.2 Background

In this research, we take the position that reality is socially constructed and that knowledge resides in the systems of thought and language that let us manage our way through day to day dealings with others and with the physical environment. A Tibetan lama knows things and so does a businessman on Wall Street, both dispose over explanatory concepts and interlocking axioms of perception, cause and effect [5]. This knowledge resides in "memory traces" in individuals, it is what people know but we come to apprehend it in social structures and recreate it in social processes [8]: there is no private language [32]. We can declare what we know, transcribe it, put it in databases, but we will always know more than we can say or write down [18].

Organizations are social groups which absorb and develop systems of knowledge to the extent that this knowledge serves their purposes and they can be interpreted and analyzed as information processing systems within which collective interpretations exist and emerge [7; 28]. Organizations, so perceived, have a particular memory, which is the knowledge of how to do things, how to approach problems and issues, how to treat each other. The instrumental view of OM is that it is that knowledge which can be brought to bear on present activities [25]. This knowledge can result in higher or lower levels of organizational effectiveness [23] so some memories may inhibit higher performance (the "not invented here syndrome", "core rigidities" [15] or defensive reasoning routines [3]). The sense-making view of OM says that it is that knowledge which gives structure and meaning to events and allows shared interpretation to emerge within organizations [14; 29].

There are processes such as acquiring, retaining and retrieving knowledge which fill and use this memory, ensure it is stored over time, and access it when it is needed. This is organizational learning. Argyris and Schon [4] stated that organizational learning is not complete until individual memory is embedded in the organization (making it OM). The organizational learning processes which interact with OM differ slightly between the authors who have researched this area, but they are generally similar in their approach and include processes such as acquisition, retention, and search and retrieval [12; 23; 24]. The performance of business activities may have organizational learning either as a by-product, when people learn and become accessible as experts, or it can be supported by explicit management techniques such as reflection in action, post-project review or six sigma process improvement. These knowledge processes can be facilitated through personnel being given capabilities (technology, training, time, space) and motivation (recognition, self-fulfillment, rewards) to contribute knowledge to the organization as a whole [20].

Along with economies of scale, the learning curve is widely accepted as a key factor in efficiency gain, not just from cumulative production experience, but "from the application of expertise culled from sources other than experience in producing the affected product" [21]. OM can improve productivity by improving routine work, developing better control over production, logistics and service delivery, and identifying the best skills for a job [2; 24].

Nevo and Wand [17] develop an initial entity-relationship schema which is capable of reflecting the metadata required for effective access to knowledge stored in OM using transactive memory systems [26; 27]. The three entities in this model are the retainer of the knowledge, the concepts which embody the ontology of the organization, and their combination into particular predicates, or propositions, which represent facts relevant to the organization. Nevo and Wand also describe four classes of meta-knowledge about these entities: conceptual (the meanings), descriptive (the general attributes), cognitive (the meta-memory of capabilities) and persuasive (the nature of the retainer). Their schema can accommodate both the instrumental and the sense-making view of OM in that practical, cultural and explanatory knowledge can be articulated in the predicate entity, while the conceptual instance entity contains the underlying ontology of objects which populate the organizational reality of invoices, orders and schedules, punctuality or quality. It is the schema that we seek to empirically extend in the course of this research. Furthermore, we pursue the approach of Anand, Manz & Glick [1] by viewing the metadata schema of OM as providing a map to any form of information, hard or soft, and seeing the processes by which metadata is maintained as consisting of a complex set of routine and ad hoc, formal and informal, technological and social interactions. Effective information management requires attention to all facets of metadata maintenance.

6.3 Researching Organizational Memory

To empirically explore the structure and form of OM and the role of the contributing processes requires access to rich data, delivered from within its natural setting. Therefore in-depth organizational case study is ideal. OM and organizational learning provide constructs for open-ended interview questions and allow the extraction of wide ranging data. As the patterns and structure of OM are not known a priori, factors which constrain or facilitate the performance of OM help in identifying OM's salient descriptive or structural features. We propose a research technique based upon the program proposed by Walsh and Ungson [25]:

1. Gain an understanding of what constitutes the memory of an organization by mapping it in some way. Gather empirical data about the organizational structure, purpose and work processes and use document analysis and in-depth interviews across a range of roles to identify knowledge types. Analyze the data inductively, grouping the data into clusters, proceeding along the lines of enterprise information modeling to develop a cognitive map or model of the organization's knowledge and knowledge domains. This map may have multiple layers. Examine the map to identify what structural features OM has: does it resemble work process or organizational structure and what repositories are used; are there any surprises in how it looks? What are the main abstract features about this memory – where is it stored, what kind of knowledge is it?

2. Conduct interviews or workshops about how people find and use the memory components. Ask people what they need to do to use or store the memory and identify factors which might influence the usefulness, availability and performance of each item of memory in terms of the organizational learning processes which store, retrieve and interpret the memories when they are required. Transfer these factors to the map by associating the memory components with the issues which impact upon learning or access. Then analyze the issues to see if there are any patterns in those which inhibit or facilitate memory access: these patterns may become useful metadata about OM. For example, difficulties accessing remote memory suggest distance is an important piece of metadata about OM.

3. Integrate the metadata into a diagrammatic schema which describes the OM. Review the metadata to identify any new or interesting discoveries about OM. Consider how you might design a solution to use and update this metadata to provide a current and practical set of

functions to facilitate access to OM in whatever form or location it is stored.

6.4 The Investigation

The intention of this research is to deepen our understanding of the nature of OM. The primary motivation is ontological and seeks to uncover and explore the characteristics of the underlying structure of OM. This objective requires rich, minimally filtered data from real life contexts where the phenomenon exists in the wild, in its raw form. We applied a qualitative and interpretive research and began with an examination of the structure, objectives and characteristics of TPC and Unit 2. The sources of the data were annual and management reports, the corporate intranet and Internet portals, and interviews with the Management Team. The engineering and institution building projects employed a high proportion of social scientists and natural scientists, most of whom are distributed throughout the world at any one time. Work is one of a kind, where consultant reports and engineering or institution building projects are specific to the needs of the client. This work, whilst thematically consistent, creates unstructured, unique problems which require novel approaches and solutions.

Data were collected in semi-structured interviews, workshops, documents and meeting protocols. A total of 42 interviews was conducted with 23 different staff members at six-monthly intervals over the 18 month study period. The participants represented the major roles in Unit 2: managers, administrative staff, consultants and project managers. Staff from HO and overseas and from different market areas were interviewed.

The first set of interviews was used to gain an understanding of the nature of the work and elicit the content and structure of the OM. This was done by asking what role the participant played and what information or knowledge they needed to achieve their objectives. This was followed by questions pertaining to the storage location of that knowledge. A second set of questions addressed issues of distribution, access and use of that knowledge and how the organization learns from its experiences. From this data, a map of OM was developed and annotated with the issues regarding using that memory for organizational purposes and learning. This map and the issues were demonstrated to the organization in a presentation and interim report. The subsequent three sets of interviews over the next 18 months confirmed the structure of the memory and asked follow up questions pertaining to any changes or improvements in use or storage of the memory types.

All interviews were transcribed and then scanned for principles according to which the OM clustered. These clusters were formed inductively, not from the extant organizational groupings or roles, and given a name which reflected the nature of the knowledge in the cluster. The classifications emerged from the data in a hermeneutic process of abstraction and generalization [13]: statements and constructs were grouped with other like-statements and categories were formed. A second pass over the data identified further elements which belonged to a particular cluster. This map of OM, not surprisingly, did correspond roughly, but not exactly, to the terminology of the Unit's business processes and responsibilities.

Comments and observations regarding issues and problems with elements of the memory were then linked to the memory items or the learning processes emanating from the memory. These comments were also interpreted for common threads and consistent responses. Signs of breakdown in particular were interesting as they identified memory access methods which would otherwise not be noticed if they were ready at hand and therefore not salient or obvious [9; 31].

6.5 Results

Fig. 6.1 is the high level map of the Unit's OM, which was derived from the mind map and is expressed in UML class notation (available from www.uml.org). Each class of knowledge can also, more generally, be described as a domain of expertise. In the following sections we analyze each of these to understand the contents of these domains and the processes of acquiring, storing and retrieving the memory from within the organization.

6.5.1 Customer Knowledge

Customer knowledge covers relationships and previous contacts with customers, knowledge of their requirements and policies, previous history of the customer and of any cultural and political specifics of the customer environment, upcoming sales opportunities and how to become aware of these. This knowledge is acquired largely through close customer relationships and is largely kept in the heads of Market Area managers at HO and, because of their close customer proximity, the heads of outside staff.

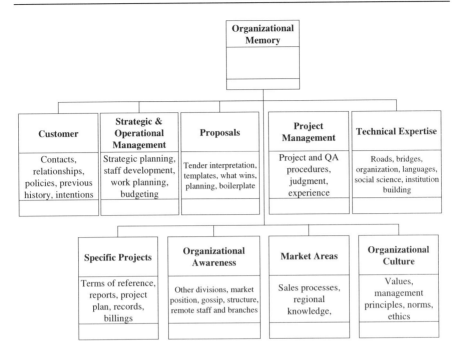

Fig. 6.1. Knowledge map, highest level

In the past there seems to have been little interest in using remote knowledge at head office ("out of sight, out of mind"), a situation which has been recognized by management.

There is a lot of business opportunity which is embedded in communication structures: this is not being properly exploited … (Manager, HO)

Customer knowledge is acquired through engagement with the customer in projects or sales activities and includes customers' idiosyncrasies, preferences, plans and so on. Because the knowledge is in people's heads, to find out anything interesting about customers, the name, role and location of local consultant or project manager or HO Market Area manager are required, as well as the length of their relationship with the customer (which reflects the level of their knowledge). The way of dealing with customers is defined through management guidelines (or propositions) which explicitly exclude any form of corruption, but it is also part of the organizational culture. These rules of engagement are clear to all within the organization but are specifically the responsibility of the Market Area managers. Telephone or conversation is the usual method used to gain access to information:

Face to face is best, then comes phone, and then e-mail. (HO Manager)

6.5.2 Strategic and Operational Management Knowledge

Management knowledge includes strategy, staff planning and development, creating staff work plans, project logistics and the general art of management. Methods of handling a wide ranging set of issues, problems, escalations and queries are stored in the heads of managers and they serve the gatekeeper function of locating knowledge for others when required:

> The Market Area managers are the main way of learning – they have time and the overview and learn from each project and provide information in future when needed. (Administrator, HO)

Nonetheless, management procedures and guidelines for budgeting, personnel management, strategizing and planning have been codified into office procedure manuals and staff management guidelines and principles of value have been codified into an organizational management handbook. However, although it is a global organization, many of these handbooks are in the firm's non-English national language, which precludes their use in international branch offices. The method for deciding IT investments is interesting. It is highly procedural and codified; each senior manager has a certain number of points (100) to allocate to a set of potential projects, the overall proportion of points that each project receives then determines the allocation of funds and resources. The fact that it is a manager who is involved (and that funds are made available according to the points) legitimates the decision. But the memory input into that managerial decision is diffuse and based upon experience, belief and gut feeling.

6.5.3 Proposal Knowledge

Proposal knowledge supports the activity of responding to requests for tenders and includes knowledge of project proposal preparation (templates, previous proposals, what wins), knowledge of skills and people, knowledge specific to market areas, project management (to prepare estimates and plans) and technical knowledge (to define solutions and review feasibility).

> The proposal secretariat was developed specifically to improve efficiency and reuse of information. (Administrator, HO)

Information management of proposals, employee CV's and so on is efficient and highly explicit. Technology is used to store templates, text standards and previous bids but there seems also to be effective management of tacit knowledge: there is consistency in who prepares proposals and experienced consultants are involved in discussion and review.

Knowledge of what constitutes a winning proposal, a successful project, where good templates are stored, what approaches have worked in the past and so on is a very good use of tacit knowledge in groups. Proposals are also reviewed in a formal process by a third party within the Unit who is known to be expert in the specific domain or with the customer. So while the final output of the proposal process is a codified document, the creation of the "high impact" parts of the document is largely dependent upon "lessons learned" which reside in the heads of experienced managers, administrators and specialists:

> those who are good, we use to write proposals and give advice. (Manager, HO)

At the same time, there is high use of codified templates to reduce the transaction costs in creating standard, general purpose parts of the proposal such as the approach to quality management, project references or organizational background.

> Proposal preparation is now really quick because of the effort put into preparing standards and templates (Administrator, HO)

6.5.4 Project Management Knowledge

The knowledge relating to project and quality management is sophisticated and much is explicit in procedures and technology, including project management software. Project procedures and control systems for best practice budget management, milestone control, reporting and escalation are of high quality, very specific and rigorous and published in manuals and on the intranet. They are considered to be a competitive advantage of the firm and are regularly reviewed and enhanced by a community of practice of experienced project managers.

> We have some excellent systems ... when I see how other companies perform in this respect, they are miles behind... It is by virtue of the good project management procedures that I can sit in another part of the world and run a project just like that! (Project Manager, OS)

Good project management is highly regarded and the procedures are widely used, very portable and so are used by HO and remote staff alike. At commencement and during projects, a major project control activity is "sparring", which is the location and utilization of experienced staff (who are usually located and assigned through a manager's mental maps of expertise) who review and quality assure in-flight projects and spar with project leaders and managers. This is a very effective form of access to memory stored in the heads of experienced people:

But the best knowledge sharing we do is still sparring – doing quality assurance with an experienced colleague. It is a formal requirement, so it almost always happens. (Manager, HO)

However, several Market Area managers stated that the more experienced a project manager is, the less the project procedures are followed, and the less the managers bother to monitor a project or concern themselves with a lack of reports.

6.5.5 Technical Knowledge Required to Perform Consulting

Technical knowledge exists for each of the specialist consulting areas and covers expertise such as road engineering, construction, social science, hydrology and water, and languages and dialects. This knowledge comes from many years of education and experience and is applied in diverse situations, which limits the degree to which codification is useful:

It depends upon the work – we are process consultants and we do studies but the context is changing every day and you cannot use the experience of someone else. We are not like bridge builders. You could get a framework for reports, but not much more than that. There are always new stakeholders, new ministries. (Manager, HO)

It is not practicable (or perhaps even desirable) to codify this knowledge and so it is located in the heads of the respective consultants, who increase their knowledge overwhelmingly on the job (it is in fact an explicit management guideline to learn on the job) in projects and interactions with colleagues:

Within projects, especially multidisciplinary, there is a lot of learning. It happens on the job from association with other staff and external consultants, and is tremendous. (Manager, HO)

When needed by another, the knowledge is found through a network of personal contacts or by asking a manager "who knows something about …?" and accessed via conversations or e-mail, or when it is applied in quality reviews or for advice. The memory of technical experts can also be located through an online CV system, which contains up-to-date information of what each consultant has done and where they are expert. This system can be searched via keyword:

The CV system is the life blood of the organization, as these are what are sold. (Consultant, HO)

It is in the interest of consultants to keep this system up to date, as their next consulting assignment may be dependent upon how powerful and current their resume is. The CV system is an example of codified metadata being itself a part of OM, instantiated in technology, but pointing to memory in individuals, thereby transforming the individuals' memory from personal to organizational. External consultants are increasingly being hired for one-off jobs: there is a database of independent contractors who are used as a kind of external memory, again made organizational through metadata:

> Jobs are also increasingly smaller, so there is a decrease in the usefulness of standard approaches. Heuristics, rules of thumbs are important. One way we have approached this is to hire in specialists for this. It is hoped they will pass this on to the people they work with. (Manager, HO)

6.5.6 Project Specific Knowledge

There is much explicit knowledge specific to individual projects stored in formal documentation and e-mail records which represent high levels of control and monitoring over project progress and budget. This is stored electronically during and after projects and is always accessible from a shared network drive and, more recently, the intranet. A small number of projects use project portals, available via the Internet, to facilitate intra-project communication and store all project documentation. But working project documents and information inputs (such as publicly available reports, periodicals or assessments) are not managed within this framework. The detail of what is going on in projects is kept in the heads of the project manager and the participants (and of course the clients up to a point, who are also quizzed by Market Area Managers as part of the project control process). The project specific memory which is stored in documents is generally project management knowledge (schedule, budgets, reports, quality control), whereas the knowledge acquired to execute the project (content knowledge for specialists to analyze) is kept informally or in people's heads (except for the actual project deliverables or consulting reports, which are documented and kept electronically). Generally, there is no post-project review to turn specific project knowledge into OM, although several participants said this should be done.

6.5.7 Organizational Awareness

Organizational awareness is knowledge about the organization as a whole, other organizational units and other classes of staff within the organization. This category of knowledge was not anticipated by us at all, but evolved from the data because of continued referral by participants to its absence. It refers both to practical knowledge about the organization, its market position, structure and any gossip, as well as awareness of the existence and needs of classes of staff such as outside workers or non-native language speakers:

> Outside experiences are not used enough ... but this is the problem with all professional services companies where everything in the company is between people's ears (Manager, HO)

The lack of awareness ranges from lack of contact details of external staff, lack of protocols when visiting remote locations where there is an office, not responding to e-mails in a timely way, even to not sending Christmas cards:

> There is low mindfulness of the needs and knowledge of outside staff. The level of mindfulness is the same as six months ago... Knowledge sharing is poor: this means that they don't know what other people know. This is what bad at knowledge sharing means... People could be drowning yeah – easy. We don't intend this: but it happens (Administrator, HO)

Awareness appears to be a kind of sensing metadata, which potentially supports not only the retrieval of memory from known sources but also the transfer of knowledge to relevant targets, where one is aware they have a need (or interest) to know. The absence of awareness leads to staff feeling left out of the loop or ignored. It also results in a lack of knowledge of organizational direction or expertise which could be exploited for a current problem, although the development of awareness depends not only upon organizational measures but also upon personal interest and motivation to become aware:

> Curiosity is required to seek knowledge that could be applied (HO Manager)

6.5.8 Market Area Knowledge

The Unit is divided into areas responsible for certain market areas such as water management, urban development, and rural and natural resources management. Knowledge within these areas includes solutions to certain problems, knowledge of sales and marketing processes and techniques, relationships, client needs and policies which are relevant to a particular Market Area and type of service offering or solution:

> There is lot to know – how to deal with a Ugandan civil servant, what to wear, what traditions exist here? (Manager, OS)

While they draw upon certain types of more or less persistent specialization, market demands change continually. Customers demand more experienced people who have specific knowledge of an area. The projects in some market areas are becoming smaller and more complicated, so opportunities to spend time and resources on learning are diminishing. Within market areas, technical and social science knowledge must be combined into holistic system of knowledge to deliver comprehensive solutions. This is learned on the job, but is not explicitly managed. Each Market Area manager has a map in their head of skills and capabilities of the staff. They depend upon reports from projects and regular phone meetings to track progress.

6.5.9 Cultural Knowledge

Culture is a shared system of meanings which is learned, revised, maintained and defined in the context of people interacting [11; 19]. "Culture is the acquired knowledge that people use to interpret experience and to generate social behavior" [22]. The organizational culture in Unit 2 is represented very strongly in management guidelines and the espoused company values: this spirit has strong convictions of belonging, excellence, and respect for the individual and participatory decision making. There is a strong value orientation to "quality" in the firm, where people are identified with the standards of the results they have delivered. At the same time, modesty and humility are strong norms: people are passively discouraged from promoting themselves. Correspondingly, it seems people do not actively praise their colleagues if they have done a good job, although poor work is openly criticized. The responsibility for promulgating the culture lies with managers, who can be seen as the living repositories of these values. The company management guidelines state: "The Manager is fully responsible for communicating the values and norms that inform the company's work."

The company is seen from without and within as having high ethical standards. However, increasingly, as a condition of winning work, indigenous employees at remote locations are involved in projects. Because they have different national and organizational cultures to the organization, it is not clear they will deliver results with the same quality or scrupulousness. As one consultant noted

For a variety of cultural and historical reasons, our internalized national values do not work on local consultants in the third world. The project funding parties increasingly require us to use them but still expect quality and timing of outputs as those produced under our system of values.

Similar to using external consultants to gain technical competence, we see external cultural memory playing a role in executing work – in this case to the possible detriment of the organization. Expressed another way, this aspect of OM is not available to these employees. On the other hand, remote permanent employees complain:

The company spirit – the longer you stay abroad, the more it decreases.

6.6 Discussion

In analyzing the results, we use the dual perspectives of memory and learning. The concept of *memory* is used to analyze the structure of organizational knowledge and its descriptive characteristics. *Learning* describes the processes which maintain this memory and retrieve it when it is required. The use of both analytical perspectives gives us both a static and a dynamic insight into what we need to know about OM in order to manage it effectively.

6.6.1 Organizational Memory

Some general characteristics of OM emerge from the case study. OM can be divided into domains of expertise, which are important signposts to locate the knowledge for retrieval and for which there appear to be fairly clear responsibilities. A domain can have its memory kept in several repositories. A repository can also store knowledge of several domains. There are different types of repository, which have different capabilities of retention and use. There may be contradictory elements within memory, where some subgroups have a different understanding of the meaning of a word or the truth value of a knowledge proposition. The nature of the work done using the memory is a factor in determining the most appropriate repository. The way in which the memory is acquired is also a factor in determining the repository – where is it convenient to store it, is storage a natural part of the work process, is the acquisition embodied so that acquisition and storage are achieved in the same act? Several repositories may have to be used simultaneously to get a job of work done. Personnel in an organization use their personal knowledge about the memory to retrieve it when required, or they use other people's knowledge to track it down. Or they use maps which exist in technology or structures to locate it.

It becomes clearer that OM metadata is actually an active component of OM, which is used for accessing and storing OM, rather than being a theoretical superstructure. In this regard, it requires its own particular set of processes for keeping up to date and being useful. That is, the directories and signposts to memory are part of the memory itself and can transform instrumental knowledge into organizational knowledge. While clearly these maps are important for using OM (and this is appreciated by the personnel) in the case study organization there does not seem to be any form of explicit memory mapping, or information architecture, but there are many processes by which staff maintain their maps (conversations, meetings, using technology). The organizational awareness or mindfulness of the existence, capabilities and needs of the rest of the organization or remote staff seems to be a substantial vacuum in the Unit's OM. For example, the knowledge, intelligence and on the ground expertise of outside staff is not part of OM because of a lack of awareness and mindfulness. It is not used, for example in gathering market intelligence or preparing proposals. Some form of knowledge mapping is required for this as well as a mindfulness of its usefulness. Outside staff whose knowledge is not part of OM feel unappreciated and not included. While they function autonomously, they feel keenly that they are not adequately valued either as people or for their professional knowledge.

The use of sparring is an excellent method of triggering and sharing tacit knowledge of experienced people. The mode of use of this form of memory (quality assurance, review) is highly interactive and contextual, suggesting that tacit memory is the best repository. This is turned into OM through the use of maps of expertise, usually kept in the minds of managers and administrators.

We also see more clearly that a single body of knowledge can be distributed across different types of repository and that this allocation is fluid and organic. There are different costs associated with different repositories, different access modalities and advantages and indeed different organizations and individuals have varying preferences regarding where something should be stored. We see that there is bad memory too, leading to unproductive behaviors. This has led us to posit a further category of required metadata for OM, namely normative descriptors. For example, where should a memory be stored, how valuable should this knowledge be perceived to be by the organization?

Importantly, we see that whilst the concept of OM suggests a monolithic, coherent structure, in fact, the existence of conflicting, contradictory and non-intersecting memories imply that there is no single OM. This is perhaps a sin of commission, an over-objectivation of the concept. There are in fact different groups with different memories which are bound together by the common purpose of the organization. This is important, as the design of an information system which contains *the* organization memory may be a chimera, for there are multiple, contradictory interpretive systems which reflect the preferences of sub-systems (the engineering interpretation, the human resources perspective, the sales world view and so on) or individual inclinations.

6.6.2 Organizational Learning

In Unit 2, there is no process of institutionalized organizational learning, for example where project experience might be passed into some general pool as a codification of professional reflections or conveyed to others as stories. There is little deliberate building of OM, although some happens in the form of proposal templates, project reports and CV updates. There is certainly an enhancement of a knowledge map in the form of updated CV's and in the minds of managers, but the informal and conversational method of building these maps is probably confined to those with whom one comes into contact (and so excludes, for example, outside staff). Therefore, when memory is kept mostly in heads, and there is no institutionalized organizational learning, the OM is enhanced through the development and updating of personal relationships and maps of who knows what. As such, the nature of managing knowledge in the Unit is cartographic and behavioral [6]: so the appropriate form of support for this sort of organizational learning would seem to be to develop maps to facilitate connections between people rather than codify their expertise and experience.

6.6.3 The Emergent Structure of Organizational Memory

Our objective in this study was to deepen our understanding of the structure of OM through first mapping the constituent elements of a live workplace ontology and then analyzing the performance of learning processes which utilize that memory in order to identify salient features which could be part of OM metadata (i.e. entities, relationships or attributes). This section describes the resulting information model for OM and the empirically observed attributes. The model seems to support both an instrumental and an interpretive approach to OM.

The model, represented as an information schema in Fig. 6.2 builds on Nevo and Wand's entity-relationship model [17], which contained the three entities of retainers, concepts and knowledge predicates. Our analysis of the empirical case data and the creation of the schema is a design process, and therefore still a "black art" [16] and "pervaded by intuition, tacit knowledge, and gut reaction", [30]. Nevertheless, in Table 6.1 (p 106) we propose further entities and specify some attributes due to their importance within the case study.

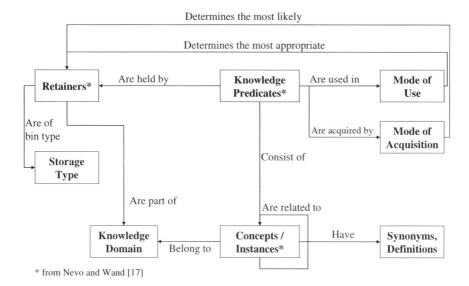

Determines the most likely

Determines the most appropriate

Are held by

Are of bin type

Are part of

Belong to

Consist of

Are related to

Are used in

Are acquired by

Have

Retainers*

Knowledge Predicates*

Mode of Use

Storage Type

Mode of Acquisition

Knowledge Domain

Concepts / Instances*

Synonyms, Definitions

* from Nevo and Wand [17]

Fig. 6.2. Schema for OM

After having clarified the key entities, we were able to identify their key attributes. These are shown in Table 6.2 (p 107). We have taken Nevo and Wand's [17] classification of metadata types, adding the new class of normative attributes, and indicated the attributes which emerged as significant.

The data suggest that there are indeed multiple interpretive systems and often diverging or conflicting definitions and understandings. The schema here can capture these distinctive interpretations using the domain entity (which provides the interpretive framework such as management or hydrology) and the Synonyms/Definitions entity, which represent divergent language or understandings. Many of the attributes are fairly obvious, but there are some interesting insights.

An additional metadata dimension emerged which we have called the normative" dimension. The attributes are generally descriptive in some way. But our data contained many comments like: "This should be stored here, this person should know this". Secondly, certain breakdowns or successes in access to OM (for example through distance or sparring) indicate that there is an appropriate place or medium to store something which is different to where it is actually stored. Confusion in communication between subgroups indicates that language is not used consistently and that divergences in memory need to be understood if they are to be improved. This normative knowledge is itself part of OM and OM metadata.

Table 6.1. Participating entities in the OM schema

Entities	Description
Nevo & Wand [17]	
Retainers	Where a specific memory can be stored, a retainer or "bin": this is the storage dimension of OM.
Concepts/Instances	The subjects and concepts of knowledge which reflect the socially constructed workplace ontology.
Knowledge predicates	The combinations of concepts into memories/propositions.
Emergent in this study	
Storage Type	The type of bin (technology, person's head, procedure etc) where a memory is stored. This is described as an entity rather than an attribute, as different bin types represent different levels of communicative potential, require further description and need to be salient.
Knowledge Domain	The area of expertise which characterizes the concepts. This is a major signpost within organizations when searching for a particular memory or possible repository. Concepts associate quite naturally into a domain.
Synonyms and Definitions	Other expressions for the concepts. There are often conflicting definitions or overlapping names for the same concept, which can confuse access to knowledge predicates. Organizational glossaries are a way of dealing with this and the mapping of multiple meanings helps identify areas of conflict or divergence in meanings between, for example organizational subgroups.
Mode of Use	The activity and context within which the knowledge predicates are applied. The mode of use defines the work process and context and introduces the dimensions of retrieval and use of memory, which are significant determinants of the most appropriate retainer for the memory. So, for example, quality review is best done using responsive, tacit memory.
Mode of Acquisition	The activity and context within which the knowledge predicates are acquired. The mode of acquisition introduces the memory acquisition dimension and is a significant determinant of how and where the memory will be subsequently stored. Learning on the job seems to lead to embodied knowledge and will be most naturally stored in people's heads.

Table 6.2. Key attributes of OM entities

Entities	Attributes Conceptual	Descriptive	Cognitive	Persuasive	Normative
Retainers		Name, location, capability, scope, accessibility, experience, role, duration at the firm, internal/external to the firm	Meta cognitive knowledge about skills	Source credibility, trustworthiness, likeability, historical connection	Certain retainers should have certain expertise
Storage Type		Bin type	Different bins allow different communication modes, diffusion, explanatory capabilities	Personal/ Oganizational preferences for retrieval	Some bins are more suitable than others for certain requirements
Concepts/ Instances	Ontology/ vocabulary		Meaning of concepts		
Knowledge predicates	Propositions of instrumental or cultural knowledge	Volatility of the knowledge, rate of decay	Tacit/explicit	Value, legitimacy and mindfulness of the knowledge	Some kinds of knowl and attributes imply certain bins (tacit, highly volatile)
Knowledge Domain		Subject matter, role/department which is expert, role in department to approach first	Domain of knowledge		
Synonyms/ Definitions	Other meanings or emphasis for the same object.		Other words for the concept		Preferred words
Mode of Use		Conversation, physical, quality review, product development and innovation, broadcast to many	Purpose of concept		Current retrieval mode, most suitable retrieval mode
Mode of Acquisition		Learning on the job, training	Purpose of concept		Current storage mode, most suitable storage mode

For the Retainers entity, we see the emergence of likeability and historical connection between people as a persuasive attribute: of course these are quite personal. But firms with a congenial culture and a matrix-project system with dynamic teams may find a systemic optimization of these attributes. There is also a normative element here, that specific repositories (i.e. roles or positions in particular, but also computer systems) should have certain levels of expertise or knowledge.

The knowledge predicate entity should be able to accommodate any form of memory, some of which may be tacit, or cultural, for example. Tacit knowledge can be described (but not captured). Cultural knowledge can expressed as propositions (or "postulates") from which certain forms of behavior logically follow [10]. The value, legitimacy and mindfulness of the knowledge need to be known, both to improve the management of the knowledge (for example to secure it from attrition or loss or conversely not over manage it) and to increase its visibility if it is not perceived as important. Just because something should be part of OM, does not mean that it is.

The entities for mode of acquisition and mode of use emerged as significant determinants of where memory resides and how it is most appropriately accessed. For example, learning is on the job and so knowledge subsequently resides in heads; proposal preparation requires a document to be created, so the memory of previous proposals is instantiated in templates, boilerplate and document chunks; quality control of a project requires the context to be understood and searching questions to be asked as a kind of sparring, so the OM to be applied is found in a qualified person. If the mode of use is distributed or remote, then certain repositories (i.e., technology based) will be useful, though perhaps not sufficient. This kind of metadata about OM needs to be stored if the management of OM is to be improved.

6.7 Conclusion

In this study, we have been able to use empirical data to extend the conceptual schema for OM metadata. An information system based upon this schema would provide a directory and functions supporting locating and retrieving OM when it is required. Using mapping techniques was an effective method for identifying specific items of memory but also issues in organizational learning, which in turn revealed useful metadata which are required when accessing the content of the OM. We saw that OM has attributes such as mindfulness, awareness of value and most appropriate repository, some of which have a normative component which gives members of the organization a sense of how better to plan or manage their OM.

This work has continued the research program of OM, following the approach proposed by Walsh and Ungson [25]. We have mapped the memory of an organization and identified key types of memory objects and the characteristics which constitute their useful metadata. We have continued the conceptual work of Nevo and Wand [17] with an exploratory empirical investigation of the contents of OM and the metadata in a case study organization. This metadata has been drawn as a conceptual information schema. The next logical step would be to develop a prototype information system based upon this schema design and conduct an action research project which would implement and observe the adoption of such a system.

Finally, technology is a major driver of virtual organizations and distributed work. The development of technology tools to manage and navigate through OM while considering the different modes of knowledge medium, storage and retrieval would greatly aid efficiency in distributed and networked organizations.

References

1. Anand V, Manz AA, Glick WH (1998) An organizational memory approach to information management. Academy of Management Review 23:796–809
2. Argote L (1999) Organizational learning: creating, retaining and transferring knowledge. Kluwer Academic Publishers, Massachusetts
3. Argyris C (1999) On organizational learning. Blackwell, Oxford
4. Argyris C, Schon DA (1978) Organizational learning: a theory of action perspective. Addison-Wesley, Reading, MA
5. Berger PL, Luckmann T (1967) The social construction of reality: a treatise in the sociology of knowledge. Penguin, London
6. Earl M (2001) Knowledge management strategies: towards a taxonomy. Journal of Management Information Systems 18:215–233
7. Galbraith J (1973) Designing complex organizations. Addison-Wesley, Reading, MA
8. Giddens A (1984) The constitution of society: outline of the theory of structuration. University of California Press, Berkeley
9. Heidegger M (2001) The being of entities encountered in the environment. In: Solomon RC (ed) Phenomonology and existentialism. Rowman & Littlefield Publishers Inc., Lanham, MD, pp 354–361
10. Hoebel EA (1972) The law of primitive man. Atheneum, New York
11. Hofstede G (1991) Cultures and organizations: software of the mind. McGraw-Hill, New York

12. Huber G (1991) Organizational learning: the contributing processes and the literatures. Organization Science 2:88–115
13. Klein HK, Myers MD (1999) A set of principles for conducting and evaluating interpretive field studies in information systems. MIS Quarterly 23:67–94
14. Krippendorf K (1975) Some principles of information storage and retrieval in society. General Systems 20:15–35
15. Leonard-Barton D (1995) Wellsprings of knowledge: building and maintaining the sources of innovation. Harvard Business School Press, Boston
16. Nardi BA (1993) A small matter of programming. MIT Press, Cambridge, MA
17. Nevo D, Wand Y (2005) Organizational memory information systems: a transactive memory approach. Decision Support Systems 39:549–562
18. Polanyi M (1973) Personal knowledge: towards a post-critical philosophy. Routledge & Kegan Paul, London
19. Schein E (1985) Organizational culture and leadership. Jossey-Bass, San Franciso
20. Shapero A (1985) Managing professional people. Free Press, New York
21. Sinclair G, Klepper S, Cohen W (2000) What's experience got to do with it? Sources of cost reduction in a large specialty chemicals producer. Management Science 46:28–45
22. Spradley JP, McCurdy, DW (1980) Anthropology: the cultural perspective. Wiley, New York
23. Stein EW (1995) Organizational memory: review of concepts and recommendations for management. International Journal of Information Management 15:17–32
24. Stein EW, Zwass V (1995) Actualizing organizational memory with information systems. Information Systems Research 6:85–117
25. Walsh JP, Ungson GR (1991) Organizational memory. Academy of Management Review 16:57–91
26. Wegner DM, Erber R, Raymond P (1991) Transactive memory in close relationships. Journal of Personality and Social Psychology 61:923–929
27. Wegner DM, Guiliano T, Hertel P (1985) Cognitive interdependence in close relationships. In: Ickes WJ (ed) Compatible and incompatible relationships. Springer Verlag, New York, pp 253–276
28. Weick K (2001) Making sense of the organization. Blackwell, Oxford
29. Weick KE (1979) The social psychology of organizing. Addison-Wesley, Reading, MA
30. Winograd T (1996) Introduction. In: Winograd T (ed) Bringing design to software. Addison-Wesley. Retrieved 7 June 2006 from http://hci.stanford.edu/bds/bds-intro.html
31. Winograd T, Flores F (1986) Understanding computers and cognition: a new foundation for design. Ablex, Norwood, NJ
32. Wittgenstein L (1958) Philosophical investigations. Basil Blackwell & Mott, Oxford

7 The Organization as a Transactive Memory System[1]

Paul Jackson and Jane Klobas

7.1 Introduction

Several forms of repository have been proposed for organizational memory, including people, culture, routines, technology and software, organizational structure and workplace ecology [5; 16], but what if we change the focus from repositories to processes? By observing couples and small groups, psychologists have found that the storage and retrieval of knowledge is transactional, i.e., that people develop systems for sharing responsibility for storage and retrieval of knowledge in such a way that no single individual needs to know everything that the group needs to know – it is sufficient to know who knows what and to be able to retrieve the information from that person. Transactive memory systems (TMS) essentially consist of sets of directories containing metadata which point to knowledge locations and the processes that maintain and utilize those directories. In this chapter, we introduce the notion of the organization as a TMS and consider how this perspective can assist with design of human and technology-supported systems to improve knowledge sharing in distributed and virtual organizations.

7.2 Background

Transactive memory is a system for encoding, storing, and retrieving information in groups: it is a set of individual memory systems in combina-

---

[1] Portions of this chapter are published in Jackson PD, Klobas JE (2007) Transactive memory systems in organizations. Decision Support Systems doi: 10.1016/j.dss.2007.05.001. Copyright Elsevier. Published with permission.

tion with the communications that takes place between individuals [17; 20]. Wegner distinguished the knowledge of members of a group from the directories which they have about the knowledge of others in the group. The directories indicate the existence, location and form of retrieval required to access the knowledge of others. The effective knowledge of an individual in a group consists of internal knowledge (held in the mind of the individual) and external knowledge (which the individual can effectively access using the directory). Originally, TMS was used to describe the ways in which members of dyads (such as married couples) who are close to one another share knowledge and allocate responsibilities for knowing. Three processes supported couples' communication: directory maintenance, information storage and retrieval of information [17].

Directory maintenance is the ongoing upgrading of mental maps held by people in a group about the knowledge of other members of the group. Directories can be maintained in several ways, the default being through the assumed roles (e.g., job titles or family position) and characteristics (e.g., gender or age) of others, which indicate their likely domain of expertise or interest. Directory maintenance can also be influenced by perceptions of the relative expertise of others gained through familiarity, conversation and self-disclosure of interests and knowledge; perceptions of the relative degree of access of others to information (through accident or design, duration of exposure and so on); or a person's public declaration that they will take responsibility for a certain area of knowledge [18].

Information allocation and storage is the assignment of knowledge retention to a member of the group. Access by other group members requires directories of who has been allocated responsibility. Allocation involves transactive encoding of information and deciding where and how in a group information is to be directed or stored. This may involve a progressive differentiation or specialization of group members.

Retrieval is the process of determining the location and accessing the knowledge of a group using the directory. Retrieval may require the use of multiple, linked individual directories before the required information is actually found and accessed. It is based upon the recognition of superior expertise and will usually be associated with judgments regarding the speed, accuracy and convenience of retrieval and the reliability of the source [18].

7.2.1 TMS and Group Performance

The research shows that well developed TMS can improve group functioning. There is a positive relationship between strength of TMS and team performance [10]. Group performance is believed to reflect the ability of a group with a well functioning TMS to store and recall more knowledge than any individual [7], to use the knowledge of others better [12; 15], to match problems with the person most likely to resolve them [13], to coordinate activities more effectively because of better anticipation of capabilities of others and appropriate allocation of roles and tasks [21], to make better decisions through the recognition and evaluation of the expertise contributed by group members [15] and to reduce cognitive overload where others act as external memory stores and allow greater specialization [8; 17]. TMS developed through group training can improve group performance more than individual training in team building [12].

7.2.2 TMS in Distributed Groups

The information systems (IS) literature suggests that TMS will be constrained for groups that are distributed or virtual. Constraints on transactive memory are believed to be a substantial inhibitor of the effectiveness of virtual teams to integrate their knowledge resources [1]. One explanation of the knowledge management problems encountered by virtual teams is that those that are more virtual develop lower levels of transactive memory than those that are more virtual [6]. Shared task training [11; 12], shared mental models [11], spending time together [4] and intimacy [11; 19] are all factors which improve TMS function but which are likely to be degraded by physical separation.

7.2.3 Organizational TMS and the Potential for IS

Extending the notion of TMS beyond groups and pairs, several authors have speculated on how organizations might function as TMS. Anand, Manz and Glick formulated a model which shows how organizations can be perceived as collections of TMS [3]. They proposed that certain forms of IS, such as intranets, search engines, standardized concepts and vocabularies, could be used to enhance the functioning of TMS. Nevo and Wand examined how an organization might function as a TMS. They proposed that an organization may be viewed as "a workgroup of groups that work together" [4:552]. It seems to us, though, that the key characteristic underpinning the notion of organizational (rather than group or personal) TMS is that the directories and processes involved in the TMS would be used to access knowledge anywhere in the organization – without the need always to access that knowledge through subgroups.

We suggest that organizational TMS can be observed where knowledge of what others in the organization know is accessible and current, and where retrieval of that knowledge from individuals can be observed in a number of ways. Retrieval may occur through direct contact between the knowledge seeker and the person who has the knowledge (i.e. we propose that people have TMS directories that extend beyond their workgroup to individual experts in the organization) and through individuals who act as intermediate directories of who knows what in the organization as a whole. If we extend the ideas of Anand, Manz and Glick and Nevo and Wand, retrieval might also occur through chains of group TMS where an individual contacts a member of a group who activates the group TMS to retrieve the sought knowledge. This seems a special case of retrieval through intermediate directories.

Moreland suggests that organizational TMS may have different characteristics to the TMS of pairs and groups [11]. Larger groups are less cohesive and willing to share, for example. He speculates that TMS might be constructed along technological and interpersonal dimensions, where the former is oriented towards the use of computers to create and maintain an organizational TMS and the latter is based upon those things that bring people together, such as a matrix structure and personal relationships in which knowledge about each other is shared. Nevo and Wand argue that the size of meta-memory (the TMS directories) required to access organizational knowledge and uncertainty regarding knowledge responsibilities inhibits the development of organizational TMS [14]. They propose a conceptual model as a basis for design of an information system to support an organizational TMS. Griffith and colleagues argue that lower transactive memory development in virtually distributed groups "will be mitigated to the extent that technologies or organizational systems are used to support transactive memory development" [6:278].Thus, it would appear that both interpersonal and technological approaches might be used to improve the functioning of organizational TMS.

7.3 Uncovering and Evaluating TMS

It is possible to uncover the structure of a TMS in a group or organization using interviews or questionnaires that ask people about their sources of information and their processes of allocating responsibility for certain information to others. A set of questions that might be used to uncover TMS are listed in Appendix 8. These questions can be asked in interviews which may be conducted with individuals or groups, in person or by e-mail. Answers to the questions can be classified by TMS process. They can used to identify the specialist knowledge of a given group in the organization, the location of key information, the processes used to find the information, and problems associated with finding it. A map can be drawn of knowledge locations (people, IS, physical files, etc.) and the processes used to allocate, store and retrieve the knowledge from these locations. A list of problems can be developed and compared to the location and process map to identify areas for improvement.

It is also possible to measure the quality of TMS in an organization. Two approaches are possible. The first is to conduct a two step study in which statements about each of the TMS processes in the organization are drawn from interviews using questions such as those outlined in Appendix 8. A second approach would be to use questions that have already been developed in other studies to measure TMS quality. Appendix 8 contains questions that can be used to evaluate the quality of each of the three TMS processes: directory maintenance, storage and allocation, and retrieval, as well as the quality of the directory itself. The derivation of these questions is described in the next section. The questions are designed for members of the organization to answer in their own time as a questionnaire distributed by mail or electronically across the corporate Internet.

We used the techniques described in the previous section in a mixed method study of the TMS in Unit 2. We first conducted a qualitative study in which we used the questions in Appendix 1 to elicit statements that described the organization's TMS. We used those statements to create items that were used in a survey of the quality of the organization's TMS. Survey responses were analyzed quantitatively.

7.3.1 Uncovering the TMS: Interview Study

We conducted 16 interviews in two rounds over six months. In each round, interviews were conducted with both HO and outside (OS) staff. Interviews were conducted in HO with staff who were either permanently in HO or visiting from the field. Telephone interviews were held with staff outside HO. We spoke with at least two staff from each of the defined staff roles in the organization: managers, administrative staff, HO-based consultants and consultants in the field.

All interviews were transcribed shortly after completion. All remarks that could be classified using Wegner's dimensions of TMS (directory maintenance, knowledge allocation and storage, and retrieval of knowledge [17]) were identified and classified by the dimension they represented. Interpretation of these remarks enabled us to describe the functioning of the organization's TMS and the effects of distribution on its functioning.

7.3.2 Evaluating the TMS: Survey Method

The survey was used to gauge the quality of the TMS and to identify if staff based outside HO experienced lower quality TMS as suggested by the literature. Twenty-five items that could potentially be included in the survey were drawn from the interview responses as well as from the theory of TMS [14; 17]. While most items were associated with one of the three TMS processes, some items (e.g., "I have a map in my head of who knows what in the Department") simply described the existence of a directory. The items therefore addressed four aspects of TMS quality: the directory itself, directory maintenance, knowledge allocation and storage, and knowledge retrieval.

The initial set of items was subjected to a "card sort" validity test. Twenty postgraduate management students in two different countries were asked to classify each of the items into one of the four categories of TMS quality. Eleven items were correctly classified by more than 50% of the participants, and three items were correctly classified by more than 30%. One of the items initially thought to measure directory quality was classified as retrieval by 62.5% of the respondents; this item was re-classified.

The 15 items identified in the card sort were included in the organizational survey. Forty-one responses were received from a potential sample of 94 members of the organization, a response rate of 43.6%. Thirty of the respondents (73.2%) were based in HO while the remaining 11 (26.8%) were based outside.

Exploratory factor analysis was used to identify a subset of items that could be considered to form a reliable TMS quality scale. The sample size was small for this type of analysis. Recent research has shown, however, that strong factor models can be reproduced with only 2 cases per item [7]. We used the measure of sampling adequacy (MSA) to identify those items that were likely to contribute to a strong factor solution and removed the other items from the analysis. The final scale consisted of the seven items listed in Appendix 8. Cronbach's alpha for this scale was .84.

7.4 The Nature of the Organizational TMS

All elements of the TMS emerged during the interviews.

7.4.1 Directory Maintenance

Staff actively update their personal knowledge of what others in the Unit know, in meetings, at lunch and in corridor conversations. The roles of manager and administrator function as a locus of directories: their central role facilitates the ongoing maintenance of their personal directories and their role as intermediate directories is prominent in statements made by other staff about the way they supplement their own directories. Both managers and administrators are based in HO and there were few reports of staff having difficulty to access them. We also observed individual directories built up over time, and not related to the formal organizational structure. Staff recognized the importance of directory systems and lamented the loss of a lunch time forum in HO at which not only was knowledge shared, but directory systems were updated.

In directory maintenance, members of a TMS are assigned or accept the responsibility for domains of knowledge and become known as sources for knowledge (via retrieval) and repositories (via transactive encoding). Respondents commented on the development of specialization and responsibilities for knowledge:

> You get to be known to be a specialist whether you want it or not, yes you are responsible for certain reasons (Consultant, HO)

Managers continually update their directories through interactions with their subordinates and management colleagues. They act as gatekeepers [2; 9]. There are processes in place where project debriefs are performed with managers, reports are sent to managers, and managers physically travel to overseas projects to conduct reviews and audits. In this way they refresh their understanding of the location of capabilities and knowledge in the organization, both locally and remotely. References to managers' directory maintenance role include:

> It's pot luck to find the right person, but usually it's the manager who is asked... There are a lot of maps in my head (Manager, HO)

Administrative assistants and coordinators are also a major locus of directories. Although permanently based at HO, their role as a communications hub means that they develop extensive maps of the staff experience and skills and become known as gatekeepers.

> I'm always here and reachable: that's why all people come to me. And I know who to ask (Administrator, HO)

However, accessing the right person for knowledge in the Unit is not always a function of the role formally defined by the organizational structure. Individual directories are built up over time "through trial and error", says one OS consultant.

Poor knowledge sharing inhibits the development of directories. In particular, the absence of a forum for sharing what each person knows was regretted by many of the staff:

> It's about keeping maps in heads… it needs a small presentation to the group to let them know what you know (Consultant, OS)

Recently, a Unit knowledge portal was implemented to encourage communication that reached international staff as well as staff in HO. Staff have been reluctant to contribute to the written forums for reasons which are attributed to a national culture of modesty and anti-self promotion, a cultural trait in which standing out in a crowd through high performance or self-promotion is seen as unseemly, pushy or disloyal:

> People don't like having names mentioned on the Website, as this gives the impression of somehow publicizing them and raising them above others (Manager, HO)

Another information system designed to support directory maintenance is the CV database. CV's and professional resumes are an important codified set of maps to locate expertise, as well as a key asset for marketing and acquiring work. They are updated in a formal process at the completion of each project and are available using keyword search from within the corporate CV management system.

> The skills and expertise are in people's heads and the CV system is a crucial map in locating this for subsequent projects. (Manager, HO)

The CV system was seen to have some limitations:

> Using externals [outside staff] based upon their CV is risky and can go wrong: anyone can put anything in a CV (Administrator, HO)

Because of the strategic value of the CV management system, and the fact that project teams are put together by HO-based staff, the system is available only inside the corporate firewall.

Despite the existence of the portal and CV management system, even some HO staff felt that they did not know enough about the expertise of remote staff, both permanent and on contract:

> I don't think people here realize how much good professional regional knowledge is sitting in this organization … they don't draw enough on it. (Consultant, HO)

Distance does not seem to be the only factor here. There are also limitations in the directories of collocated staff:

You are amazed by some people ... their (lack of) knowledge about what other colleagues sitting down the corridor – they don't know. (Manager, HO)

Personal directories in the Unit build up through involvement in successive projects and through mobility within the framework of the matrix organization. This has the effect of building strong networks across a wide range of staff who develop extensive and detailed directories of other people, their skills, their compatibilities and their strengths and weaknesses.

This [matrix] structure of moving from one project to another helps you build a network – so you know if so and so is good at doing budgets and you are lousy at it ... next time you put a team together you have an idea of skills and knowledge. (Consultant, OS)

But these directories degrade as people move onto new projects with different project teams over time. This degradation is observed by both HO-based and international staff, but international staff appear to suffer more because they are not able to speak informally with colleagues over the lunch table:

The "knowing who" is very important ... but after a long time abroad, my old group has been moved, so I know few in the current setup (Consultant, OS)

For people working abroad is where the chain breaks. You are sitting on your own, there is no debriefing, no opportunity to share knowledge with colleagues. (Consultant, OS)

One term used to characterize the absence of directories about remote staff is lack of "mindfulness" which is an awareness of the existence and characteristics of other parts of the organization. This mindfulness of HO staff for outside teams and workers is under-developed and the members of these outside teams suffer from a feeling that they are not cared for or considered.

Absence of mindfulness ... indeed this is a major absence ... the overall level of information has improved but it is that of those who are in the building ... not the systematic gathering of information from those who are out in the field (Consultant, OS)

There is low mindfulness of the needs and knowledge of outside staff (Administrator, HO)

This mindfulness can be seen as a partial absence of TMS directories regarding remote staff, which deal with who needs to know what and who knows what. There appears to be a lack of directories pointing to the capabilities of staff based outside HO and this leads to ongoing under-utilization (retrieval) of their knowledge as well as poor updating of their knowledge of HO.

These observations suggest that organizational TMS directory maintenance may have the following general characteristics:

- Specializations develop and become known to others in the organization, thereby developing differentiated directories of knowledge locations.
- The publication of knowledge specializations need not happen automatically and such specializations may remain hidden.
- Directories to knowledge can be stored in a number of places, including the heads of managers and administrative staff who have directory maintenance roles defined by organizational structure.
- Staff with long company experience have more extensive directories than newer staff.
- Certain organizational forms such as the matrix and project-based organizations are enablers of directory maintenance.
- Maintenance of personal directories requires a forum for knowledge sharing and finding out who knows what.
- Personal and cultural factors such as curiosity and modesty influence the active updating of personal directories.
- The kinds of information stored in the directories include the person's name and contact details, previous experience, knowledge and capabilities, reliability as a source of information, and personality traits.

The effects of geographical distribution on directory maintenance appear to be:

- Physical separation leads to fewer opportunities to maintain directories of "who knows what" in the organization.
- Physical separation hinders the update of personal directories about those who are remote.

7.4.2 Knowledge Allocation and Storage

In TMS, the storage of knowledge is shared among people who recognize that each person has their own domain of expertise (as identified in the directory). Allocation and movement of knowledge to the appropriate repositories is essential to TMS maintenance.

Each domain of expertise observed in the organization was generally associated with a formal organizational group or a formal role; for example, managers are responsible for strategic management and project managers for specific projects. Certain directions are encoded in organizational structure and procedures: the proposal secretariat gets requests for tender sent to it because it is their job to process them; Market Area managers receive information about changes to bidding procedures because they must act on this and so on. Identified knowledge domains included typical forms of instrumental knowledge of customer, sales, technical and project management, as well as that of the specific culture of the organization and the country.

Technical knowledge and knowledge related to specific projects appears to be gained and stored by the person assigned to complete the project or task to which the knowledge is relevant:

> Not much information comes to me through being given information by others. Most of the information that I receive comes from my own research. And learning on the job. And I get the job because I am the specialist. (Consultant, OS)

Sometimes the allocation is inadequate, for example remote staff do not transfer their customer knowledge to the proposal secretariat or Market Area managers at HO:

> Communications with outside staff has been so poor there is a big need for improvement... If we gave them better support, we would be able to take advantage of their business intelligence and closeness to what is happening. (Manager, HO)

These observations suggest the following characteristics of knowledge allocation and storage in an organizational TMS:

- The allocation of knowledge responsibilities mostly, but not entirely, reflect organizational structure and defined organizational roles.
- Knowledge storage may be done not only through transfer of knowledge from other people to the responsible person, but also as the result of work and research performed within a defined role.
- While responsibilities for acquiring and storing knowledge may be clear, the role of the TMS in transferring knowledge to the responsible repository does not seem strong or pronounced.

Distribution of staff appears to have the following impact on TMS allocation and storage:

- The specializations of remote staff are more likely to remain hidden from head office and therefore the allocation process may be less effective.
- Remote staff are out of sight (and therefore out of mind), and less likely to receive information, even when their information needs are formally known.
- Remote staff are less likely to know who needs what at head office and therefore to pass knowledge on to them.

7.4.3 Retrieval

Much information in the organization was stored electronically or in reports which can be accessed via computer networks or hard copies. But knowledge retrieval is overwhelmingly performed on a personal basis, by simply asking someone who might know, by asking a manager or an administrative assistant, or by pursuing one's own personal directory:

> People just walk down the corridor when they need to know something or get pointed to the right documents. It is casual and informal. (Consultant, OS)

Physical access to HO resources is difficult from outside locations. This is due to poor technology links, the arduousness of the relationship in not being able to walk down the corridor and the greater efficiency in simply asking someone for directions to a knowledge source. The access appears to be through a particular relationship (such as to a manager or administrative assistant) or a defined role, such as a particular group who are responsible for certain types of project.

> The "know who" is very important: knowing who to approach, or who to ask or who to approach for certain skills and questions. There is a map in my head of all the requirements. CV search would be very useful, but it is not useable from Africa (Consultant, OS)

Retrieval by staff often involves access to a manager's personal directory as an intermediate access point:

> The motivation to share (in particular as a manager) is very high, as this is what creates success in projects... people come to me and I know where to go for it. Having said that, a lot is done informally, where local people come in ... the remote people cannot do this and I do not have the time to build relationships with remote people to make myself available and discover their needs. So time and space are restricting the remote staff from accessing my knowledge as a gatekeeper and source of advice and wisdom (Manager, HO)

This also demonstrates that remote workers have greater difficulty accessing information via a manager's directories. The same happens when the manager is traveling, for example, they themselves become virtual:

> Knowledge is all kept in heads... It is a problem when [we managers are] traveling... traveling can disrupt availability. Writing it down and putting it on the net is not a solution, because if you "have isolated small flowers in a big jungle, people will never find them". (Manager, HO)

One international specialist gives an insight into the difficulty of retrieving knowledge from overseas. The following statement shows how the dynamics of interaction and knowledge retrieval become more difficult over distance and how different strategies apply:

With regards to finding information, this is through a map in my head, my personal network, where I know where to go. This is far easier when I am in head office. It is more difficult to access the network when I am overseas: the bandwidth is too low and you need to be far more specific in what you need. You can't discuss something and build up to your question; you have to formulate it quite precisely from the beginning. You tend to communicate when you have a problem. The point at which you decide to use communications is far higher. However, you normally get a good reply from head office. Personal contacts are very important (Consultant, OS)

Retrieval of knowledge from known sources depends upon motivation. This motivation seems to be influenced by several factors, including a desire to be original and not reuse material, a curiosity to see what others have done, and perceived time and availability of other staff:

Many people ... are academics. They like to reinvent the wheel... what are your best practices ... what are my best practices (Consultant, OS)

Accessing performance knowledge of what is happening outside HO is also problematic:

Accessing and finding knowledge is not a problem. However, in remote cases it is far more difficult to gain a true picture, especially when things are going wrong and there are conflicting reports. (Manager, HO)

When the TMS does not function, and personnel do not have access to each other's specialist knowledge, it is a source of frustration as one annoyed specialist states:

I have a lot to contribute ... and I would have benefited from gaining the perspective of my colleagues – for example about water supply. In developing countries water quantity is the issue, in industrial countries it's about quality. The exchange could have been very fertile (Consultant, OS)

These observations suggest that organizational TMS retrieval may have the following general characteristics:

• Retrieval of information depends upon some personal characteristics, such as the desire to reuse the work of others.
• A culture of personal contact influences organizational preferences for retrieving knowledge
• In this organization, codification of knowledge seems inferior for building directories than conversing with a knowledge holder and using a human directory is perceived as more reliable than a technical one such as an electronic CV
• Retrieval may have to go through intermediary directories.
Regarding the impact of distribution upon TMS retrieval:

- Physical separation makes it more difficult to use the knowledge of others.
- Physical separation requires different strategies for formulation of inquiries.
- Managers may act as information gatekeepers, but when they are remote there are access difficulties.

7.5 Quantitative Evaluation of the TMS

These observations on the TMS, and deterioration of the TMS of staff working outside HO, were supported by the survey. Table 7.1 maps the questionnaire items to the dimensions of TMS and matches each item to one of the interview remarks that reflect the dimension (in most cases, there was more than one relevant interview remark).

Scores on items measured in the reverse direction were reversed to calculate a mean score for each group across the TMS scale as a whole. The average TMS quality score of HO staff on the five point scale (where 1 is very poor and 5 is very good) was 3.5, indicating that there was a functioning TMS, but that it could be improved. On the other hand, the average score for staff working outside HO was 2.1, indicating that they had an inadequate TMS. The difference between the two groups was statistically significant ($t = 6.58$, $df = 38$, $p < .001$).

Our instrument measures TMS quality using a single score to represent quality across all four TMS dimensions taken together. The results reported here show that our short scale provides a reliable and valid measure of the overall quality of an organizational TMS. It would, nonetheless, be useful to have an instrument that would permit separate diagnosis of each of the four dimensions. Such an instrument would need to have a minimum of three items per dimension to measure the dimension reliably. Future research could use a more complete set of remarks taken from interviews to develop a multidimensional TMS quality instrument using a larger sample than that available in the research reported here.

7.6 Implications for IS to Support TMS

As [3] and [14] have argued, IS are a natural solution to the difficulties of maintaining, storing and accessing organizational TMS, particularly in distributed contexts. In this section, we transform our observations about the organizational TMS into a set of requirements for an information system.

Table 7.1. TMS questionnaire items

Questionnaire item	Sample interview text	TMS dimension	HO mean score	Outside mean score
I have a map in my head of who knows what in the Department	There are a lot of maps in my head.	Directory	3.8	1.9
My map of "who knows what" in the Department includes people outside Head Office as well those within Head Office	There is low mindfulness of the needs and knowledge of outside staff.	Directory	3.3	1.9
I keep my knowledge of what others in the Department know up to date	After a long time abroad, my old group has been moved, so I know few in the current setup.	Directory maintenance	3.1	1.9
It is difficult for me to keep up to date with who knows what in the Department*	Working abroad is where the chain breaks. You are sitting on your own; there is no debriefing, no opportunity to share knowledge with colleagues.	Directory maintenance	3.0	4.2
My colleagues in the Department contribute little to the knowledge I need to complete my tasks*	Not much information comes to me through being given information by others.	Allocation	2.1	3.0
My personal map of "who knows what" is an effective way of finding knowledge in the Department when I need it	The "know who" is very important: knowing who to approach, or who to ask or who to approach for certain skills and questions. There is a map in my head of all the requirements.	Retrieval	3.7	2.7
The structure of the Department makes it difficult for me to get knowledge and information from the people who have it*	Knowledge is all kept in heads... It is a problem when [we managers are] traveling	Retrieval	2.4	3.0

*Reverse scored item

We do this by first representing an organizational TMS as a process model (Fig. 7.1) from which requirements can be drawn.

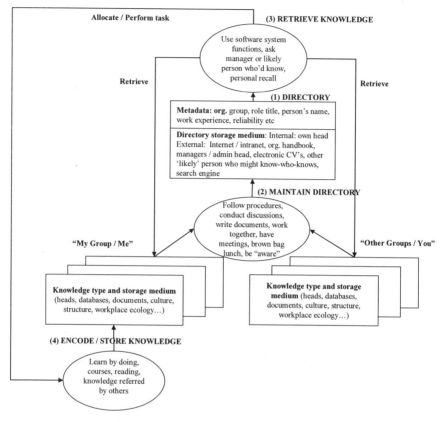

Fig. 7.1. Model of the operation of an organizational TMS

The model shows a TMS directory and the three TMS processes which maintain and use it, along with repositories of organizational knowledge. The directory, marked (1) in the figure, consists of metadata about people, including name, organizational role and formal group membership, work experience, areas of expertise and other information such as availability and reliability as a source of knowledge. The directory can be stored on a variety of media to support a variety of modes of access and maintenance. Some of the metadata for some people in a TMS will be stored in a person's head, but other metadata can be stored externally, in a CV or expertise database, a document management or knowledge management system, on the organization's intranet or in handbooks, or in the heads of intermediaries such as managers, administrators and other colleagues who act as gatekeepers or links in a chain to the ultimate source of the knowledge. The accessible knowledge in the TMS, represented in the boxes marked "My group/Me" and "Other groups/You" is the sum of the knowledge of each individual and the connected members of the organization. This knowledge may be held in many media, including people's heads (as tacit knowledge), and organizational databases and documents (as explicit knowledge).

The TMS processes, numbered (2) to (4) in Fig. 7.1, are annotated with the multiple types of activity which effectively constitute the performance of the process. Directory maintenance is a result of a combination of formal and informal processes. Formal processes might include the updating of metadata and other information in organizational IS and participating in normal work activities including projects and meetings. Informal processes include discussions held alongside formal meetings or serendipitous meetings in the corridor or coffee room. The directory allows knowledge to be retrieved – process (3) in the figure – from one's own work group(s) and from others in the organization. Much of the information retrieval from one's own group might be in the form of conversations although this retrieval might be supported by IS that record knowledge in the form of documents. Retrieval of knowledge from others in the organization relies on similar processes, but might also involve asking others to indicate who is likely to have the requested knowledge. Knowledge is allocated and stored – process (4) – on the basis of several activities ranging from formal allocation of responsibility and transfer of knowledge among people in the organization to individual learning.

The model shows that an organizational TMS is based on a range of formal and informal social processes interacting with a directory through functions which take personal, technical and structural forms. This view provides a framework to guide development of a holistic TMS for a particular organization. It allows a view of what an information system might provide and what is best done (or indeed must be done) through interpersonal means. Thus, while an information system can support an organizational TMS and satisfy several requirements, the different modalities of directory maintenance and usage imply that a rich and effective organizational TMS will include multiple forms of directory and require differentiated management techniques. This leads to an improved understanding of the enablers to be put in place to support desired social practices. While the following remarks refer to information system requirements, we caution therefore that any information system-based TMS be complemented by opportunities and programs for interpersonal contact, conversations and face-to-face meetings.

Based on the detailed observations from the case study, we propose that an information system to support TMS would have the following characteristics and limitations. Each of the processes can be assisted by certain IS functionality but we also point out where procedural or social measures may be required to ensure that the information system is updated and used or complemented through other activities.

1. A readily accessible directory or set of directories.

- The directories might consist of a storage area where labels and certain key metadata reside as a signpost to locating information. In abstract terms, the metadata can be classified into Nevo and Wand's categories of conceptual, cognitive and descriptive and cluster around the tripartite constructs of retainer/location, domain subject and perceived expertise [14].
- The entries in such a directory might include person's name and contact details, work experience (CV), CV author, an experience rating, formal group memberships and role title. The entries regarding experience should use standard terms which reflect the ontology of specific knowledge domains.
- We also expect that a useful form of directory entry point would be the specific codified outcomes of projects (such as project closure reports, consulting reports or information products). These are often in a domain language, and therefore (hopefully) anchored in a domain discipline, and can be linked specifically to the general role played by a person in creating that outcome. A search over a document management system could reveal not only specific documents but also the author or participant meta-knowledge. The matching human knowledge retainer can then be contacted in order to use their tacit knowledge for more flexible, contextualized analysis.

2. A method for maintaining the directories so that they reflect the available capacities and capabilities of the organization.

- A formal process of updating computer records is required, so for example electronic CV's should be updated from post project debriefs as a matter of routine procedure.
- It is more difficult to imagine how a TMS might support the maintenance of those personal directories that form the foundation of a TMS. For the personal directories of managers and administrative assistants, maintenance is performed in the execution of their duties; project reviews, performance reviews, conversations, meetings, hiring, fielding questions and so on. People's personal directories are built up in the course of work and through meeting people in and be-

yond their project team. They meet in the corridor, have discussions about work, attend group meetings, participate in projects which dissolve but leave personal directories intact. These directories point to skills which people can call upon later, without having to remember the actual details of the knowledge content. Participating in special interest groups and brown bag lunch sessions builds knowledge of who knows what. A function that allows any member of staff to add information about the perceived expertise of another may enable some of this directory information to be captured and shared with staff in all locations, regardless of whether they have participated in the activities.

3. A set of functions to use the directory to retrieve information:

- Where the directory store is electronic, computer access and search functions over the metadata from all corporate locations are required.
- Where directory information is in the heads of human beings, including managers, key administrative staff and company long-timers, an effective TMS would also provide access to those individuals. This may act via particular indicators linking roles and individuals to knowledge domains as the "gatekeeper". Finding a gatekeeper with a wide personal network might be done via a TMS directory or an electronic substitute such as a domain-specific forum product which is monitored by the gatekeeper.
- Work conditions should be created to give knowledge gatekeepers an incentive to function as intermediaries, knowledge retainers an incentive to share their information and knowledge seekers the confidence that their knowledge reuse efforts will be rewarded and responded to in a supportive manner.

4. A method of allocating responsibilities for storing knowledge and routing it to the person responsible.

- A TMS, or a KMS that adopted TMS principles, would include a method for alerting people to the addition of information in their field of knowledge to corporate databases, including the CV file.
- In the TMS that we observed, the allocation of knowledge stores is based primarily on the role that a person plays in the organization, so role and "interests" are important metadata for the allocation process.
- An information system based TMS may also include a mechanism that allows a person to declare expertise in a particular field of knowledge, although the use of such a mechanism may be bounded by cultural mores.

Finally one must consider the possible deficiencies of an information system based TMS when compared to the interpersonal networks of directories developed and used by people:

1. A directory built upon personal experience of others may be perceived by that person as more credible and rich than an anonymous information system based directory entry.
2. An information system based directory makes a claim for objectivity and universality, whereas it may be the case that TMS directories, of necessity, reflect highly individual preferences.
3. An information system based directory may never (be allowed to) include the really interesting information, such as personal habits, likeability, reliability or effectiveness.
4. Although the IS-based directory is the product of a TMS, it may be that the social processes of developing TMS in conversation, meetings and mutual projects are valuable in themselves and require support and nurture.
5. At the time of directory maintenance, it is likely that social signals are exchanged which transmit the preparedness of the knowledge retainer to share knowledge. These signals cannot be readily incorporated in an information system.

We surmise that while an information system based TMS may be useful, in particular as organizations become larger, more anonymous and more dispersed, it will probably achieve its greatest utility when it is embedded and implemented in the context of the interactive and communicative practices within the firm. These other practices also require ongoing management attention and support.

7.7 Conclusion

The analytical process described in this chapter can be used by organizations to uncover, describe and evaluate the quality of their TMS. The process model of TMS presented here provides an indication of the sequence of events in the operation of TMS and acts as a tool from which the requirements for sociotechnical systems to support and enhance organizational TMS might be derived. We have made the following observations:

- TMS suggests a form of knowledge management that focuses on using directories and metadata to find and use knowledge, rather than codifying the knowledge itself. Thus, systems that enhance TMS may be suitable where a "personalization" strategy is pursued or where knowledge is largely "embedded" in people.

- Organizational TMS directories appear to consist of multiple storage media (formal groups, roles, informal groups, people, computer-based systems) containing certain metadata about the knowledge holders and their expertise.
- It seems possible to identify gatekeepers, either by organizational role or by personal characteristics, who provide TMS directory information "services" to others. Organizational systems should acknowledge and support the TMS activities of people who play these roles.
- Personal directory storage media appear to be maintained and used largely through interpersonal contact, discussions which allow a contextualized abstraction of the knowledge by others for future reference. They are influenced by proximity, opportunity and personal characteristics. This approach appears to favor staff who are collocated or who come together in formal and informal meetings.
- TMS processes are influenced by physical distribution of staff. In the absence of systems that explicitly support development of TMS, people seem to be less likely to include distant colleagues in their directory systems even when these people might want to share knowledge with one another.
- It may be possible to develop IS that support TMS, but these systems would need to be supported by the actions of individuals and procedures to keep directories up to date. Computer-based TMS may provide wider access to the organizational TMS, but may be less credible and informative than personal directories.

While we have speculated on the characteristics of IS that might support organizational TMS, future research should examine in more detail how IS might be designed and implemented to support an organizational TMS, and in particular, the TMS of organizations whose staff are geographically distributed. Some form of action research in which a system based on the generic requirements that we have listed here is implemented and its effects tested might be appropriate in this regard. The relationship between the formal and informal elements of TMS can be studied further. It would be useful to know more about the relationship between the social and technical systems needed to support organizational TMS. What, for example, are the contingencies that permit technology-mediated systems to be effective and when might direct human contact be necessary for directory maintenance, retrieval and allocation? Addressing sociotechnical issues from a different point of view, future research could provide a deeper insight into the ecology into which the directory IS and their functions are to be embedded.

References

1. Alavi M, Tiwana A (2002) Knowledge integration in virtual teams: the potential role of KMS. Journal of the American Society for Information Science and Technology 53:1029–1037
2. Allen TJ (1977) Managing the flow of technology: technology transfer and the dissemination of technological information within the R&D organization. MIT Press, Cambridge, MA
3. Anand V, Manz CC, Glick WH (1998) An organizational memory approach to information management. Academy of Management Review 23:796–809
4. Argote L (1993) Group and organizational learning curves: individual, system and environmental components. British Journal of Social Psychology 32:31–51
5. Argote L (1999) Organizational learning: creating, retaining and transferring knowledge. Kluwer, London
6. Griffith TL, Sawyer JE, Neale M (2003) Virtualness and knowledge in teams: managing the love triangle of organizations, individuals and information technology. MIS Quarterly 27:265–87
7. Hair JF, Black WC, Babin BJ, Anderson RE, Tatham RL (2006) Multivariate data analysis. Prentice Hall, Upper Saddle River, NJ
8. Hollingshead AB, Brandon D (2003) Potential benefits of communication in transactive memory systems. Human Communication Research 29:607–615
9. Klobas JE, McGill TJ (1995) Identification of technological gatekeepers in the information technology profession. Journal of the American Society for Information Science 46:581–589
10. Lewis K (2003) Measuring transactive memory systems in the field: scale development and validation. Journal of Applied Psychology 88:581–589
11. Moreland RL (1999) Transactive memory: learning who knows what in work groups and organizations. In: Thompson JM, Meseick, DM (eds) Shared cognition in organizations. Lawrence Erlbaum Associates, Hillsdale, NJ, pp 3–31
12. Moreland RL, Argote L, Krishnan R (1998) Training people to work in groups. In: Tindale RS, Heath L, Edwards J, Posavac E, Bryant FB, Suarez-Balcazar Y, Henderson-King E, Myers J (eds) Theory and research in small groups. Plenum, New York, pp 36–60
13. Moreland RL, Levine JM (1992) Problem identification by groups. In: Worchel S, Wood W, Simpson JA (eds) Group process and productivity. Sage, Newbury Park, CA, pp 17–47
14. Nevo D, Wand Y (2005) Organizational memory information systems: a transactive memory approach. Decision Support Systems 39:549–562

15. Stasser G, Stewart D, Wittenbaum GM (1995) Expert roles and information exchange during discussion: the importance of knowing who knows what. Journal of Experimental Social Psychology 31:244–265
16. Walsh JP, Ungson GR (1991) Organizational memory. Academy of Management Review 16:57–91
17. Wegner DM (1987) Transactive memory: a contemporary analysis of the group mind. In: Mullen B, Goethals GR (eds) Theories of group behavior. Springer Verlag, New York, pp 185–208
18. Wegner DM (1995) A computer network model of human transactive memory. Social Cognition 13:319–339
19. Wegner DM, Erber R, Raymond P (1991) Transactive memory in close relationships. Journal of Personality and Social Psychology 61:923–929
20. Wegner DM, Guiliano T, Hertel P (1985) Cognitive interdependence in close relationships. In: Ickes WJ (ed) Compatible and incompatible relationships. Springer Verlag, New York, pp 253–276
21. Wittenbaum GM, Vaughan SL, Stasser G (1998) Coordination in task-performing groups. In: Tindale RS, Heath L, Edwards J, Posavac E, Bryant FB, Suarez-Balcazar Y, Henderson-King E, Myers J (eds) Theory and research in small groups. Plenum, New York, pp 177–204

8 Adoption of Technologies for Virtual Work

Stefano Renzi, Jane Klobas and Paul Jackson

8.1 Introduction

A prerequisite for the success of a virtual organization is use of the technology that enables people to communicate and collaborate with one another across time, distance and organizational boundaries. In this chapter, we examine factors that motivate and enable members of the organization to use the information and communications technology (ICT) that underpins the virtual organization. The research was guided by Ajzen's theory of planned behavior [1] which, when applied to technology use, enables us to distinguish between four different sets of influences: beliefs about outcomes of use, social influences on use, perceived control of use and external factors that facilitate or obstruct use (see Fig. 8.1.).

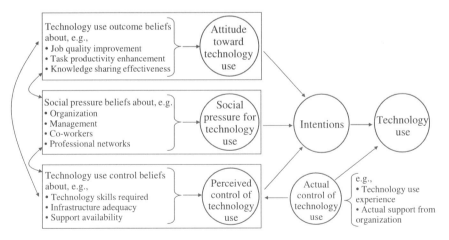

Fig. 8.1. The theory of planned behavior [1] applied to technology use

Attitudes to technology use may be, to a greater or lesser degree, positive, negative or neutral. Fig 8.1 shows that attitudes reflect beliefs about the outcomes of using technology. Beliefs which might be associated with attitudes to using ICT in the virtual organization include that use of the technology might improve job quality, enhance productivity or improve the effectiveness of knowledge sharing.

Social or normative pressures may arise when potential users perceive that their managers, coworkers, professional colleagues, or even parts of the organization want them to use the technology. They influence use to the extent that these external norms motivate the potential user to use the technology.

Perceived control of use can have a positive, negative, or neutral effect on use. Potential users' perceptions that they do not have the tools, skills or support necessary to use a technology may act as barriers to use, while positive perceptions of control may have the opposite effect. When perceived controls influence use they may do so because the more that people who perceive they have the tools, skills and support necessary to use technology, the more they use it. Perceived control may reflect the fourth influencing variable in the model, actual control, which encompasses both the users' actual ability (which may be based on past use of the same or similar systems) and actual provision by the organization of tools and support. The arrow between actual control and use indicates that, even in the presence of positive perceptions of control, lack of ability, tools or infrastructure will prevent use.

8.2 Technologies for the Virtual Organization in Unit 2

The ICT available to support virtual work in Unit 2 was very limited as our project began. The only ICT available for communication and collaboration were the telephone (terrestrial national and international carriers), Skype (for voice over IP, VOIP), e-mail, and Unit 2's intranet, the Development Information Portal (DIP). Administrative staff and consultants did not have corporate mobile phones (and were not provided with corporate mobile phones at any stage during the study).

When we first spoke with the Director of Unit 2, he pointed to three technologies that he believed would support his Global Network Organization (GNO) strategy: Skype, the DIP, and a discussion forum that was yet to be developed. While an early version of the DIP was available as we began our research, the DIP was modified in two significant ways during the study period: the underlying technology used to deliver the material in the DIP was changed, and the content and structure were upgraded. The goal was to deliver more up to date information in a more easily accessible way to more members of the organization. While the DIP remained a one-way communication tool, two-way communication was to be supported by the discussion forum. The Dialogue Forum (DF), a tool for two-way communication, was introduced in the second half of the study period.

8.3 Method

In order to study and explain adoption and use of the two technologies, we first gathered some baseline data about organizational members' access to the Internet, the use of information and communications technology (ICT) available to the staff at the beginning of the project and explanations given by the staff for use or non-use. We updated this information six months after the project began, after the organization had completed its review of systems accessibility and the bulk of the DIP upgrade. Twelve months after the study began, and three months after initiation of the DF, we reviewed the organization's own assessment of the DF and asked users more detailed questions about their use and reasons for use or non-use. Each of these stages of the study involved the collection of quantitative data in the organizational surveys described in Chap. 2 along with qualitative data gathered in small group seminars and interviews conducted with Unit 2 consultants, the administrators and managers responsible for ICT in Unit 2, and managers of the parent company TPC's IT Department. Six months later, we went back to see what, if any, changes had occurred in interviews with Unit 2 and TPC IT managers and administrators.

8.4 User Response

We begin this section with information about Internet access, an aspect of actual control: regardless of other factors that might motivate Unit 2 staff to use the GNO technologies, they would not be able to use them if they did not have suitable Internet access. Next, we describe use and user response to each of the three technologies, Skype for VOIP, the DIP and the DF. Finally, we consider lessons that can be learned about adoption of technology for the virtual organization.

8.4.1 Internet Access

Access to the Internet varied according to where the staff member was based and whether or not they were traveling. More than half the staff had no choice but to use a dialup connection either in their base location or when traveling outside HO (most managers and consultants spent more than half of their working days outside HO). About a quarter of them had no alternative but an Internet café or other public computer when in the field. In interviews, consultants pointed out that dialup network speed and reliability was a critical problem which limited their ability to download project documents and access online applications. Staff who used computers provided by the organization but did not visit HO often encountered access problems associated with security software or lack of password synchronization between their computer and the applications needed to use. There was little change in this situation during the study period.

8.4.2 Skype for VOIP

Despite formal adoption of Skype for VOIP in Unit 2, few staff were aware of its availability until they were asked about it in the baseline survey. Only 3 of the 51 respondents (6%) had used Skype. There was little support for Skype among staff working and traveling outside of HO. These staff already had trouble with e-mail access at a distance and were not confident that Skype would be usable. Staff who had tried to use Skype while traveling reported disappointing results. Despite positive attitudes to the ease, usefulness and economy of using Skype for communications, actual use was blocked by perceptions that it would be difficult to obtain access or sufficient quality while traveling. These perceptions reflected the reality that few staff had access to Internet connections that would permit use of VOIP while traveling or in the field.

8.4.3 The Development Information Portal (DIP)

The DIP was more widely used than Skype. Sixty-one percent of respondents reported using it (Table 8.1). The highest proportion of users was among HO administrative staff (80%) and the lowest among managers (50%) while around 60% of consultants reported using it.

Table 8.1. Number of DIP users by organizational role

	Users	Percent of total
Management	2	50
HO admin	8	80
HO consultant	9	56.2
External consultant	10	58.8
Other	2	50
Total	31	60.8

Different Perspectives on the DIP

Before reporting data survey data about the DIP, we present an overview of the DIP from the point of people in the different organizational roles.

Most managers viewed the DIP as a useful tool for disseminating information. They published a wide range of information to the DIP, but little technical information and few project reports. Some felt that this may perpetuate the idea that only special information should be published on the DIP. Occasionally, managers used the DIP to publish information for which they sought feedback and review – generally without success. Managers seldom used the DIP to access information; they felt the level of detail was insufficient for their needs and, in any case, they had ready and direct access to the sources they needed.

From their point of view, the DIP, while a useful innovation, was only an information repository: personal contact and the telephone were, and should remain, the most important means of communication. In their view, most staff would prefer to go to a manager or get pointed to another person to talk to in order to get information. They described Unit 2's work as very interpersonal, requiring closeness to clients, an ability to be flexible and responsive and to make the best of situations; reuse of organizational knowledge is generally not relevant. Further, in developing countries, the conceptual working environment is often quite simple.

Managers based in HO thought that the poor infrastructure in remote locations was a hindrance for outside staff, even though the DIP was designed to use relatively little bandwidth. This situation led some managers to comment that the rhetoric about the networked organization was too far ahead of the capability to deliver what is needed.

We interviewed three managers who worked outside of HO. Two of them had positive views of the DIP. They used it to read news about BU2, market alerts, and opportunities, goings on at HO and what is happening in neighboring countries. They used it to advertise for consultants and gain feedback on plans or gain assistance on proposals, and saw it as an opportunity to promote their region within the parent company. They saw the content as being largely HO focused and would have liked to see the DIP used more for collaboration and sharing rather than as a broadcast vehicle from HO. The other remote manager did not use the DIP at all, and saw no use for the DIP or the other GNO tools. The remote managers all saw HO as being overly security conscious, which restricted access to the DIP for non-permanent staff. They did not think HO promoted the DIP sufficiently and suggested it should include much more current information and be on every meeting agenda and should be provided with much more current information.

The HO-based consultants who used the DIP saw it as a useful system for sharing information and expected it to continue to grow over time. They could not identify any content that could be added or improved, but did suggest that better navigation or search would be useful. Consultants on short-term contracts did not have access to the DIP. Long-term contractors based outside HO did have access, but were not very interested.

Administrative staff (all based in HO) believed that the DIP was a good idea but would take time to evolve. They saw potential to improve the DIP by adding project reports, information about how to reach people, and information which would allow the distributed development of proposals. Putting administrative forms and procedures on the DIP had proved very useful. The staff who were responsible for managing the DIP would have liked to receive feedback about use, whether the information it contains in sufficient, and if not, what is missing.

Reasons for Using the DIP

Respondents who used the DIP were asked why they used it and under what conditions (they could mention up to three) they might use it more. Twenty-eight described their reasons. These are summarized in Table 8.2.

Table 8.2. Reasons for using the DIP

Reason	No. of respondents	%
Keep updated about Unit 2	16	57.1
Looking for (external) information or news relevant to Unit 2's work	16	57.1
Upload information	4	14.3
Get information about new projects	2	7.1
Total	28	100

We classified the 37 suggestions into the five main categories summarized in Table 8.3. The most prevalent categories were: if the DIP were more relevant or contained more up-to-date information (15, 40.5%) and if it provided more interaction with people (10 respondents, 27%). It seemed that there was a group of people who were ready to use the DIP more if only it provided more relevant content and access to people to interact with. Consistent with Internet access difficulties, there was also a call for better connections to the DIP from outside HO.

Table 8.3. Situations in which the DIP would be used more (baseline study)

Suggestion	No. of respondents	%
More relevant or up-to-date information	15	40.5
More interaction with other people	10	27
Faster connection from outside	4	10.8
More tools for virtual work	4	10.8
News and tools more targeted at the staff	4	10.8
Total	37	100

Reasons for Not Using the DIP

Respondents who did not use the DIP had space to describe up to three reasons. From 20 people we got 32 reasons which we classified into the five main categories (summarized in Table 8.4): access and communication problems (19, 59.4%), never heard of it (2, 6.3%), no access based on staff category (2, 6.3%), not interested in content or no time to access (5, 15.6%), can get the same information with different media (4, 12.5%).

Table 8.4. Reasons for not using the DIP

Reason	No. of respondents	%
Access and communication problems	19	59.4
Not interested in content or no time to access	5	15.6
Same info is available with different media	4	12.5
Never heard of it	2	6.3
No access based on staff category	2	6.3
Total	32	100

It is worth noting that lack of use was not associated with a perceived or actual lack of IT skills. All respondents described themselves as competent users of IT and this perception was borne out both by remarks made in interviews and the research teams' observations of and discussions with Unit 2 staff.

The number of respondents who claimed access and communication problems was also notable. Problems included lack of bandwidth: "I can't get access in the countries where I'm working", "very poor local ISP & telecommunication network", but also user support problems like "I have informed [the help desk] that we always get the answer: 'can not find the server' – [they have] worked on it, but never solved the problem" and "user info from [the organization] nil". These comments were supported to some extent by comments made in the interviews, although several external consultants saw the problem more as a lack of familiarity with the context of ICT use in the field than as a failure to respond: "IT people supporting [us] are not completely aware of work conditions in remote and isolated locations". Nonetheless, there were significant infrastructure problems which prevented or made cumbersome access to this basic tool designed to be easy to access.

Increasing and Explaining DIP Use

Six months after the baseline study, and following the organization's attempts to improve access to organizational systems including the DIP, we asked survey respondents which three applications were most important to them, and what would bring them to use these applications more. The DIP was the third most important application, ranked by 40% of respondents, after e-mail (ranked by all respondents) and the World Wide Web (ranked by 80%). The proportion of DIP users outside HO had dropped from the baseline survey. More than 80% of respondents noted that they would use all of these applications more if they had better Internet connections from outside HO. As at the baseline, about 40% said they would use the DIP more if it had more relevant information. Thus, despite the efforts made during the first six months of the study to improve access to and quality of the DIP, users and potential users still felt the need for more relevant information and better infrastructure for connection and use. They wanted to have an environment that allowed them to use computer systems from all locations in the same way as if they were at HO.

Overall, this review of the DIP suggests that use reflects the perceived relevance and currency of the material it contains (and, thus, one might think, its perceived usefulness) along with perceived and actual accessibility and support. These observations are consistent with other research that has used the TPB to study adoption of Internet-based electronic information resources [2].

8.4.4 The Dialogue Forum

The stated goal of the DF was to "provide a forum for online discussion and exchange of ideas, allowing all staff to participate regardless of whether they are based in HO or outside". It was introduced immediately following a Unit 2 strategic planning day in HO. The managers who directed the face-to-face strategy discussion established a discussion area in the DF to enable that discussion to be continued and to be joined by people outside HO.

During the two months after its introduction, about half the staff with access to the DF entered it. About half of those (a total of 29) made at least one contribution. Nine months after its introduction, a total of 95 contributions had been made to 42 threads by 31 contributors. Almost all contributors (27) were based in HO. Seventeen (17) threads attracted some dialogue (at least one reply). Most posting occurred during the three weeks following the face-to-face strategy discussion in HO. Apart from a spike of activity in the fourth week, when the facilitator personally solicited contributions from staff, activity steadily dropped off from the date of introduction to the point where facilitation ceased, two months after the DF was introduced. Only four threads were started after facilitation ceased. The DF had failed to engage its target users and had failed to meet its goal.

Four months after introduction of the DF, we interviewed 13 potential users and obtained 41 responses to questions about the DF from the Veronica study survey. The questions we asked were guided by the TPB.

Attitudes to Using the DF

To uncover attitudes to using the DF, we asked several questions in the final questionnaire (see Appendix 9). Responses are summarized in Fig. 8.2, in the form we reported them to the organization where we described them as "perceived value".

Overall, the perceived value of the DF was only modest. The mean value, taking into account all questions was 3.3 on a 5 point scale from 1 (strongly disagree) to 5 (strongly agree). There was some interest in using the DF, a moderate sense that a respondent could make a contribution to Unit 2 using it and a similarly moderate sense that it was relevant to the respondent. Slightly more respondents appreciated the interaction that the DF and thought they would enjoy using it than not. The DF was not seen as a means for keeping up to date with what is happening in Unit 2 or as important for work in Unit 2. Staff based outside HO had lower scores than HO-based staff on all items except appreciation of interaction and keeping up to date with what is happening.

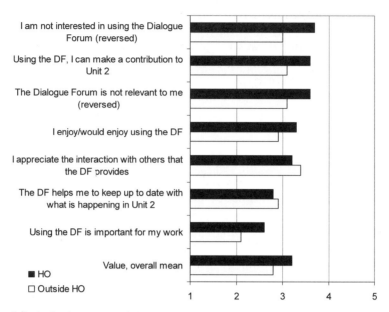

Fig. 8.2. Attitudes to use of the Dialogue Forum (perceived value)

Comments about the value of the DF ranged from statements about the relative advantage of other approaches to communication to comments about the nature of information sharing in the DF itself. The comments expressed a strong preference for one-to-one conversation, preferably face-to-face or by telephone. These preferences were coupled with expressions of fear associated with lack of confidence and trust in posting material to a public space where it can be judged by others. Strategy was considered to be a particularly risky topic to begin with because the risk of managers' negative judgment seemed high, and there was reluctance to participate in discussion on the DF of any controversial topic. One respondent said:

> If I was reading something that I was really against … I rather would go and knock on the door in person than actually write this, rather than putting another controversial message on the Dialogue Forum… these delicate things take time.

There was reluctance to use the DF as a place to ask questions when you know, personally, the person who can answer the question:

> If I have questions, I'll never put these questions onto the Dialogue Forum because I know the people.

Associated with this, there was some questioning of whether the DF could be a place for dialogue, or is rather another place where management can disseminate information and ideas:

I'm just not convinced that a Dialogue Forum is a way you get in depth understanding. It's an excellent way of conveying information but that's not dialogue. Dialogue goes in two directions and I'm not convinced that you get meaningful feedback that way unless you know people and unless you trust people.

There was also a perception that the discussions will not bring changes in working life:

This is more like something for voicing opinions but ... I don't have a sense of how we move from that electronic series of statements into some action or change or progression in our working life. What are we going to do about this? It's like, oh you read, written it, that's nice. Thank you for contributing. Finished, that's it.

DF Accessibility

In the questionnaire, we asked a number of questions about the accessibility of the DF including knowledge of its existence, technical access to it and access to the time and help needed to use it (see Appendix 9). Overall, accessibility was moderate and just a bit higher than perceived value (mean of 3.5).

Fig. 8.3 summarizes accessibility on each of the items we assessed. The most striking aspect of this figure is how much lower the scores on each item are for staff based outside HO. Even among the 40% of external staff who had technical access to the DF, there were problems with access on all the measured dimensions. They scored below the midpoint of the scale on all indicators: knowledge about the DF (mean = 2.4), knowledge about how to use the DF (2.9), access to help to use the DF (2.9), time to use the DF (2.7) and a sense that trying to use the DF from their location would be frustrating (2.3).

The comments confirmed that Internet access in developing countries is still a big problem. There was a call for more corporate support for the use of mobile phones, not just for access to the DF but also as a way to have Internet access through GPRS where it is available (and, as noted by consultants, it is becoming increasingly available):

I have my own mobile and I now have another one which I take with me and buy the local SIM cards. You don't get a mobile phone as part of your job. You can borrow one occasionally [in HO] but on two occasions I have tried that and they were all out. I think everybody should have a laptop and a mobile phone provided by the company.

Intended Future Use of the DF

We used cluster analysis to divide questionnaire respondents into two groups based on their intention to use the DF in the future. (The questions

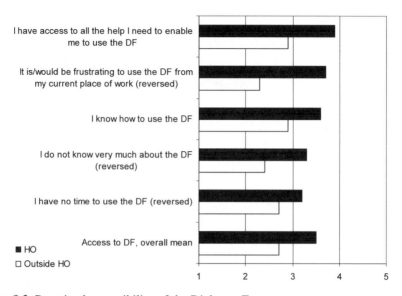

Fig. 8.3. Perceived accessibility of the Dialogue Forum

used to measure intention appear in Appendix 9.) Two distinct groups were identified from this analysis: a group who would never use the DF, or if they used it, would use it rarely; and a group that thought they would read the DF most weeks and would make an occasional contribution.

Table 8.5 shows that none of the staff based outside HO intended to use the DF with any intensity in the future. That is, the primary intended beneficiaries of the DF did not plan to use it even if they had access to it.

Table 8.5. Intended future use of the DF

Intended use of the DF	Respondents based in HO	Respondents based outside HO	Total
Never or rarely	11	17	28
Read most weeks, and contribute occasionally	0	13	13
Total	11	30	41

The relative influences of perceived value and accessibility on intended DF use are illustrated in Fig. 8.4 which shows that, while both low perceived value and lack of accessibility affected intentions to use the DF, lack of accessibility had a greater effect than perceived value. Even if the value of the DF could be demonstrated, its use would not significantly increase if accessibility (ranging from technical accessibility to the availability of time to use it) were not increased.

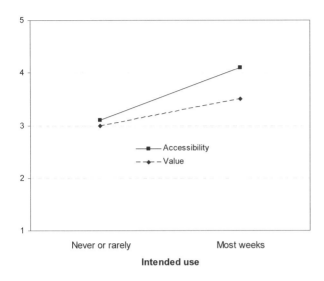

Fig. 8.4. Intended future use of the DF reflects perceived value and accessibility

Role-Based Perspectives on the DF

Our interviews with staff in different organizational roles shed some more light on reasons for the failure of the DF to meet expectations. Staff in all roles shared some points of view. All believed that the DF was well implemented, from the way in which it was rolled out to the way in which it was facilitated. There was a shared sense, from most but not all interviewees, that the DF had potential but that it had not yet found its appropriate use. There was some criticism that there were few contributions from managers to any of the forums (and none from the Director); this lack of participation detracted from the credibility of the DF and robbed it of momentum. The comment that face-to-face discussion and use of the telephone and e-mail were the most important means for communicating and developing culture in Unit 2 was reiterated across all groups, but there were some differences in the perceived need for technology such as the DF to augment these means.

Managers believed the strategy discussions were a genuine attempt to improve communication and participation. Some managers saw the DF as a drain on time and resources or a loss of control or both. Some said that they were not of the generation of chat rooms and that online discussion is simply not their métier; these managers were not convinced of the need for networked knowledge sharing or discussion technology or of the need for what they saw as high-tech sophistication while other managers believe that more modernization is important, partially because of increasing competition.

Managers outside HO said they only used the DF themselves because it was expected of them. They felt that the topics should have been more closely linked to work concerns and that people did not have time for things like strategy. Opinions diverged on the potential of the system, with some thinking it was pointless and others saying it was something whose time would come with better technology and a more useful application. In the terms of the TPB, use by this key group of users reflected the social pressure of their managers rather than their perception that participation was valuable.

HO consultants, although believing that a system like the DF might have potential, had trouble seeing its value. One consultant said it would feel silly to put something on the forum when you had just been talking about it down the corridor. Another said that people are simply not used to computer-mediated dialogues: apart from lack of exposure to them, this may be linked to factors such as nationality, disinterest, shyness or age. Staff who had worked in English and American environments described the use of such forums as far more everyday and usual.

Some HO consultants made some insightful speculations upon the reluctance to use new technologies. One was that there was a general lack of a personal sharing culture or sharing of information about oneself. Perhaps personal sharing is a foundation for volunteering and sharing on a public forum. Without a culture of personal sharing, one consultant speculated, the threshold for contributing to a public forum was higher and more difficult to overcome. There was also the high level of public exposure: perhaps smaller forums geared towards special topics would be more successful than a unit-wide forum geared towards a general theme?

Another suggestion was that people did not really understand why these tools and ways of working were important. Not only had they gotten along fine for many years working in a certain way, but they did not perceive any threats or opportunities in the marketplace or from clients which made wider knowledge sharing or reuse important. A continued fixation with job numbers and being able to bill as much of their time as possible mitigated against people simply spending a bit of time on a forum.

Very few long-term contractors with access contributed to the DF. Like the DIP, it did not seem important to them.

DF Conclusions

There was some interest in using the DF and a sense that it could be relevant, but its role was unclear. Are large, open dialogues likely to be valuable? Could the necessary conditions of trust be created to encourage participation? Would external staff – believed to be among the primary beneficiaries of the DF – use it? Do they have any need for it? There were significant barriers to use: lukewarm support from some managers, formal definition of valuable work in terms of billable projects rather than participation in activities such as the DF, and poor access to the Internet and the DF from outside HO.

8.5 Discussion and Conclusion

As expected, attitudes toward using the technology, social pressure for its use, perceived control of use and actual control all influenced whether Unit 2's managers and staff used the technology made available to them to work in the GNO. Regardless of perceptions of the potential of the technology, its use outside HO was limited by poor Internet access and the failure of support staff, despite good intentions all round, to resolve access problems. But access problems should not be permitted to mask other issues. While there was some appreciation for the DIP, there were calls for higher relevance. While there was a sense that the DF had potential, it was not highly valued. Even if the access and support issues could be addressed, use of these systems would be unlikely to increase without an increase in perceived relevance. Furthermore, although they felt they had the skills to use the technologies, the accessibility problems were translated into perceptions of poor control of use; these perceptions could well endure even after access issues are resolved. Finally, we see that institutions and principles of action vary between roles, and that the same behavior (i.e. non-adoption) may result from planned action based upon different premises.

References

1. Ajzen I (1991) The theory of planned behavior. Organizational Behavior and Human Decision Processes 50:179–211
2. Klobas JE (1995) Beyond information quality: fitness for purpose and electronic information resource use. Journal of Information Science 21:95–114

9 Monitoring, Control and the Performance of Virtual Work[1]

Paul Jackson, Jane Klobas and Hosein Gharavi

9.1 Introduction

When personnel are removed from the immediate sphere of their colleagues and managers and engage in virtual work, one of the most significant concerns of management becomes that of monitoring and controlling
performance. There is a sense amongst many managers that without observation and correction, the performance and commitment of distributed
staff will deteriorate. In this research we observed the constraints and rules
which keep virtual workers delivering high performance in Unit 2. We applied the dual lenses of direct and indirect control to our observations and
found that the range of constraints is actually more pronounced and pervasive than is initially obvious. Taken together, these controls suggest that
the grip over performance is not as tenuous as managers might fear and,
conversely, there is a range of managerial instruments available to monitor
and control performance.

In this chapter we focus on the monitoring and control of knowledge
worker performance in virtual work relationships. These workers can be
non-permanent and physically remote from central offices and management contact and are exemplified by telework, customer site frontline work
and remote project work [4; 13]. In these configurations, new systems for
the regulation and monitoring of employee performance are needed [1; 6;
11], as the effectiveness of systems of direct control and observation are
reduced. Haywood writes that when managers created prioritized lists for
her research on the challenges of distributed teams, "70% of the time the

---

[1] This chapter is based on Jackson PD, Gharavi H, Klobas JE (2006) Technologies
of the self: virtual work and the inner panopticon. Information Technology and
People 19:219-243. Copyright Emerald Publishers. Published with permission.

number one item had to do with control" [11:9]. From her survey of 514 managers at high-technology companies, 88% rated remote team members as somewhat or much more difficult to manage. Our motivation to pursue this theme developed as we noticed how hard the remote staff of Unit 2 worked, under difficult conditions and over long periods of time. We asked ourselves: why do they do it? We became intrigued by why these people subject themselves to these demands, conform to strict standards of quality and high performance and continue to generate company value, much of it in the apparent absence of managerial control or monitoring.

9.2 Background

We take an institutional approach to examining how virtual work operations can be managed and controlled [20]. Organizations can be seen as systems of normative, cognitive and regulative institutions which are created by and which form the members of an organization [21]. Institutionalization is the process of developing the durable social habits that give stability to the social order and therefore human interaction. These social habits are created when subjective processes become routines for overcoming day to day problems, externalized as perceptible behavioral patterns, and ultimately internalized by others and the self [3]. We seek to identify the institutions which exercise or imply control over staff engaged in virtual work. To guide our analysis, we use the distinction between direct control and responsible autonomy, which has been a common thread in the research literature about workplace control and performance monitoring [10; 26]. The main difference between these two ends of the control spectrum is that direct controls are external and involve observable artifacts and routines applied by a role other than the affected worker. Responsible autonomy is an internal control and exercised by the affected worker; for example, a desire to achieve good results, be recognized or gain a feel of belonging to a team. As information and communications technologies (ICT) are increasingly the major collaborative and communicative medium for virtual workers, we conclude by examining the role of technology in the exercise of external and internal control.

Control is the ability to manage a resource towards achieving a desired goal, in particular through maximizing the motivation and capability of staff to act towards specific commercial ends. It is any means of obtaining "the desired work behavior from others" [26:122]. Systems of control are the "mechanisms by which employers direct work tasks" and monitor conformance to a set of rules and the production of desired outputs. Procedures, quality management, hierarchy, rules, budget, task allocation and discipline are direct forms of external control, but indirect forms include job descriptions, performance appraisal, career development, compensation, training and flexible work arrangements. Traditional forms of management have emphasized command and control using procedures, measurement and standardization. While able to harness and direct work, these forms of organization are often adversarial and appear to be inadequate in increasingly unstable and complex environments.

Direct control over work can be divided into three forms: input, process and output controls [1]. In distributed organizations, input controls involve selecting and shaping all materials that are inputs to the work process, such that desired outcomes are more likely. Process controls are external controls which monitor or shape staff behaviors during their outside assignments. Output controls are external controls of the outcomes of remote projects. The literature suggests that knowledge workers are difficult to regulate and monitor using direct controls:

In the world of knowledge work, evaluating performance is … difficult. How can a manager determine whether enough of a knowledge worker's brain cells are being devoted to a task? [5].

In spite of this apparent difficulty, our analysis suggests that a number of direct controls are available to managers.

More recent management approaches seek to achieve self-generating commitment through motivation and attention to human resources: this is internal control. The more difficult command and control are (for example in the virtual business) the greater becomes the reliance upon self-motivation and "responsible autonomy" [26]. Depickere [6] argues that telework seems to have led to new forms of management, where managers seek to build a culture in which the worker independently performs tasks to the required level of quality and completeness. There has been a shift both from behavior control to empowerment and input control, and toward an increase in output control. In this situation, reinforcement of the discipline of work becomes an internalized process imposed consciously or subconsciously by the employee.

Drucker [8] maintained that knowledge work is a "volunteer" activity, not to be managed through command and control techniques: he is not the only author to note the importance of internal control of knowledge work. McKinlay states "The primary means of managerial control of knowledge work is the regulation of the employees' self rather than work flows or tasks" [14:245]. Professional groups and educational institutions evolved around disciplines and aim to maintain professional standards which enable them to fulfill comparable duties across different organizations [7].

Sets of knowledge workers, with their respective professional norms often have an orientation towards work which may override local, firm specific variations in control [17]. Members of organizations hold themselves accountable to the values generated and maintained by organizations and professions which provide intellectual muscle. This would seem to be even truer of virtual knowledge workers, who are in remote contexts and removed from the interaction with colleagues and the watchful eye of management. External controls can be superficial and are often impractical, and in most knowledge work, there is insufficient routine to provide the foundations for a regulatory framework. Internalized control becomes a far more effective means of ensuring the optimum application of effort in the service of the firm.

The role of workplace culture in affecting productivity and work relations has long been recognized [12; 18; 19] and culture change has generally been advocated as an avenue to increase work effectiveness [2; 22]. A positive corporate culture is also seen as a critical component in the effective transition to virtual working [6; 9; 25]. But when a worker is transplanted to a remote site, the means of perpetuation of culture are stripped away and a different, possibly competing, mindset may come to dominate social interaction. The virtual context demands adaptation to local mores and control requires perpetuation of the HO way. Furthermore, remoteness has a direct effect upon the maintenance of social institutions because of the reduction of face to face contact. Anonymity and the erosion of legitimacy increase with distance:

> because the anonymity of the typifications by means of which I apprehend fellowmen in face-to-face situations is continually "filled in" by the multiplicity of vivid symptoms referring to a concrete human being... The typifications of social interaction become progressively anonymous the further they are away from the face-to-face situation [3:46]

Technology has become a central feature in the development of managerial surveillance and control strategies and the effective use of technology enables and necessitates the deployment of the mechanisms of surveillance techniques for social management, planning and administration. The use of technology however is multi-facetted. Orlikowski analyzed how groupware technologies can operate as a means of surveillance while simultaneously fostering a sense of belonging to a group [16]. Although a poorer medium of interaction, technology can play a role in providing conversational forums and means of communication which maintain institutions over distance [15]. Sewell described the continuing use of technology to monitor staff, in spite of the rhetoric of trust and empowerment [23].

9.3 Research Approach

We set out to use the notions of external and internal control using an institutional approach to understand the nature of the systems of relations which cause virtual knowledge workers to continue to deliver high performance in accordance with the objectives of the firm. Firstly we analyze the data from the perspectives of external and internal control. Because ICT is a key enabler of distributed work, we conclude with a discussion of the role of ICT in monitoring performance and exercising control.

The data were collected in seminars and interviews over a period of three months at the end of 2004. Nine managers participated in a seminar primarily designed to uncover the Unit's virtualization strategy. Thirty staff attended a seminar in which the project was introduced. Three knowledge workers acted as a focus group designed to uncover issues associated with virtual organizing. Fourteen knowledge workers at all levels of the organization in several locations in Northern Europe and developing countries were interviewed about communication and knowledge transfer. In a second round of interviews, each was asked in a discursive form how the virtual organization can be sure that outside personnel perform to their best. All participants were volunteers in this research, remained fully anonymous and were free to withdraw at any stage. All participants have been given access to this article prior to publication.

Several methods were used to record participants' remarks. At least three members of the research team were present during each of the seminars. Key points were recorded on flip charts and white boards by one member of the research team. The management seminar and focus group were designed to encourage participants to comment on, correct, and add to these points. A member of the research team simultaneously took notes about participants' behavior and facial expressions in parallel with notes about the content. One member of the research team conducted the interviews, keeping notes as well a making a voice recording of each interview. After several of the interviews, the interviewer reported key observations along with his impressions of the meaning of these observations to other members of the research team, and the research team added information from their investigations of other research questions to question or support the initial impressions of the interviewer.

9.3.1 Data Analysis

Records of all the seminars and interviews were brought together and examined for remarks that addressed each of the questions that guided the analysis. Mind mapping software was used to assist with this process, and soon after analysis began, the structure of the meta-narrative regarding control and performance became apparent from pools of remarks addressing similar issues. We applied interpretive analysis to the remarks to generate insights into the network of concepts which describe and explain conformance behavior. The participants are represented in this section by a brief description of their role in the organization. Those described as OS are permanently based outside HO while all others are permanently based in HO are described as HO.

9.4 External Control of Virtual Knowledge Workers

Unit 2's managers spoke of the importance of input controls and when asked how they can get outside staff to achieve their goals and perform at a high level, they often referred to staff selection for overseas assignment. Reporting and monitoring were secondary.

Consultants were selected through resumes and qualifications, and where possible, face-to-face interview where one develops a gut feeling for the applicant's fitness for the job, and psychological testing of candidates.

The way control is exercised is at the input side: we match people to the jobs. We know the people well, can trust their ability and that they will do their best. Controls are at the input end. There is gut feeling, looking them in the eye. We also give bonuses for success. So the controls are before the project is even commenced, by getting experts and committed people... (Manager, HO)

If we recruit well, we can allow more trust, self-management and so on (Manager, HO)

But personnel are increasingly employed for tasks with no face to face interview, which is of great concern to managers. Input controls are complemented by process controls for explicit project monitoring. These controls include formal procedures for planning, reporting, budgeting and quality control. These are detailed, sophisticated and seen as superior to those of other firms. But consider the following statement from a manager:

We have people working for us now, long-term, who do not even provide one single report during an entire year ... we don't see any reporting from them ... at all ... this handover of power is part of the business ... hand over power ... we strengthen their capabilities. (Manager, HO)

Clearly procedural control has limited usefulness at a distance, particularly for experienced staff. A project specialist added:

In my view the company has a fairly decent QA process, I have always thought that performance relates to the output. If the QA process works, you would also know if the person produces decent reports. But that's only part of it. There are interactions working with external parties, customers that you cannot measure. Obviously as you have less face-to-face interaction you would be less aware of a person's ability to do this ... a person's qualities are so important ... how you would solve this I don't know ... (Consultant, HO)

Other stakeholders and client are located in close proximity to the outside worker. These are also a source of control: the HO managers will regularly contact various local stakeholders for feedback on staff performance and act upon any anomalies or underperformance. Further, in many cases there is a project team of some kind in place. These teams are collocated or distributed across the country in which the projects are based. According to the participants, local team cohesion is very high and there is a strong team spirit – and therefore strong collegial control:

I just came back from [the field]. There is an excellent team ... fully devoted to the job... It is incredible how they are sending mails... They have a meeting Monday morning ... coordinating ... and then off they go for the week ... They are a virtual team away from home. (Manager, HO)

We also have remote teams which work together and keep an eye on each other (Manager, HO)

An important means of control are annual management audits. Managers visit remote sites and gain a firsthand impression of the local state of play and of the commitment and competencies of staff.

The trips are a major form of monitoring ... I have responsibility for the staff in my area ... so I have to give them the chance to have a conversation with me. (Manager, HO)

Finally, output controls measure the timeliness and quality of results. There are formal completion procedures, signoffs and measures which indicate the success of a project and therefore a control upon the performance of the worker.

9.4.1 Discussion

Despite skepticism in the literature about the value of direct controls in virtual organizations, several direct controls were observed in this case. Input controls seem particularly important, suggesting that selection of the right kind of human "material" is crucial. The personal requirements mentioned in the case study suggest characteristics which are often cited in the literature about remote work: self-starters, flexible, independent and motivated and aligned to the organization (Haywood, 1998).

Statements of praise for the process controls (management procedures and reports) from outside and HO workers indicate that the management and reporting procedures have become internalized as serving the interests of the knowledge worker, not the management. Workers want these procedures, possibly because it means they can give early warning signals or actually help themselves to maintain control over their projects. But it seemed to us that the worker is driving the rate of work through their commitment to high performance and quality: the procedures only support this through providing transparency into some key management constructs such as time, cost and progress. But then there are the startling assertions from several sources that the reports don't actually mean that much! While they must be in place for administrative reasons, they are not decisive or regarded as that important. Other forms of control are considered far more effective.

Several monitoring and control methods also emerged: local teams, local clients, telephone calls and management audits. This net is not only relatively fine; it is also multi-sourced, meaning that data about low performance or deviation is more likely to be fed back to and triangulated by managers.

Forms of external control, such as sophisticated reporting and budgeting procedures, are implemented to maximize project success and reduce the incidence of breakdowns. According to the procedures, remote workers must report regularly, but are largely left to their own devices to run their work themselves. Nonetheless, the telephone, e-mails, visits from management, feedback from clients and the nearness of team and customer serve as process controls to absent managers. There is a combination of direct and indirect external controls in this mode of virtual organizing.

9.5 Internal Control of Virtual Knowledge Workers

In the case study, the discernible forms of internalized institution which control the actions of virtual knowledge workers appear to include professional pride, individual self-interest, management logic, creativity or self-expression in work, and a sense of belonging to the larger organization. Each of these is addressed individually below.

The virtual knowledge workers in the organization are highly educated and empowered professionals and invest a substantial amount of energy and dedication in their work:

She had deep ethics about why she is doing this job – and she is showing it ... and this makes the whole team very devoted to the job. When they advise clients, it shows that they are burning for the job ... it comes from the inside (Manager, HO)

This zealousness translates into hard work, as ruefully expressed by one outside worker:

One of the "problems" is that some of us work 18 hours a day, typically those who are on travel, in many time zones while others work from nine to four especially those working at head office. (Consultant, OS)

The research described in Chap. 4 describes how an overwhelming proportion of statements in the twenty statements test conducted during the study was individual, with very few related to the organization as a whole. Staff were strongly committed to individual institutions such as professionalism, high performance and personal friendliness, but not Unit 2 or TPC. Different managers offered different interpretations of this observation. The Director even exclaimed that his goal to increase organizational identity may be mistaken if staff were by nature individualistic. An outside project manager responded:

Individualism is a failure of management here. Things work in spite of the management, because of the self-directed and hard working individuals (Consultant, OS)

This individual self-interest has an obverse dimension in the fear of failure and the possible loss of their job:

Hopefully they're ambitious people who like to their job properly and get a good reputation to get another job ... you don't want to get blacklisted on the next proposal. Rumors travel fast in this business. In one proposal we presented a guy the local company didn't want him so he was taken off. That was their point of view ... he thought he was ok but the locals didn't like him. (Administrator, HO)

As mentioned, direct control over operational results is achieved through sophisticated project management planning and reporting processes. These are however also embedded in an organizational culture which has its origins in a project engineering mindset of order, clarity and predictability, and a managerial mindset of time, cost and risk control. This mindset is widely spread throughout the organization and at all levels:

We have some excellent systems ... the biggest strength of our company is that all of its staff are very good project managers ... then I see how other companies perform in this respect, they are miles behind... It is by virtue of the good project management procedures that I can sit in another part of the world and run a project just like that! (Consultant, OS)

Belonging to a large organization provides a certain sense of pride, confidence and belonging in remote workers. However, they yearn for greater inclusion in the processes which signify belonging to the culture. The organizational spirit is represented very strongly in published management guidelines and the espoused values: this spirit has strong values of belonging, excellence, respect for the individual and participation. These are genuinely admired by HO and virtual knowledge workers. Outside employees demand greater involvement in the cultural and nutrient life of the organization. They say:

> When we have new people ... someone who has not worked with us before ... it is difficult to absorb the company spirit. (Consultant, HO)

Interestingly, although the management audits mentioned previously are a form of direct control, they also generate internal controls in the form of relationships and loyalty. The trips are looked forward to by management and they speak very fondly of their experiences in the field, where tight bonds are formed as teams and visiting managers spend a lot of time together, working, visiting clients, socializing and gossiping. As one manager put it:

> Social capital is created which sustains the relationship until the next visit (Manager, HO)

The company is seen as having high ethical standards: "we are not corruptible" says one outside manager. However, both quality and integrity are social values. Increasingly, as a condition of winning work, indigenous employees at remote locations are involved in projects. Because they have different national and organizational cultures, it is not clear they will deliver results with the same quality or scrupulousness. As a participant noted:

> For a variety of cultural and historical reasons, internalized national values do not work on local consultants in the third world. The clients increasingly require us to use them but still expect quality and timing of outputs as those produced under our system of values. In short, we have a problem. (Manager, OS)

Conversely, it does not appear that the organization's remote workers adopt local ways of working:

> Do people go native? No ... I have heard of very few people going native, and not necessarily from our company, but only contract staff. I don't recall any company staff going native. (Consultant, OS)

Clearly there are some significant issues relating to the maintenance of the cultural and normative institutions relating to sense-giving and belonging and which therefore generate commitment and ownership. The available communication media provide poor interaction. Some staff recollected a time when annual conferences were held; all staff were brought together and discussed strategy, futures and experiences. They commented how energized and optimistic they were after these, and how the feeling was sustained for some time after.

9.5.1 Discussion

Unit 2 demonstrates the importance of internalized control in a professional organization. Professional values direct and constrain the behavior of the knowledge workers in the case study organization. The participants are self-aware and self-critical. There appears to be significant internalization of and adherence to the mores of the professions to which they belong. Knowledge workers are driven by internalized institutions of professionalism and high performance which transcends external surveillance and sanction. They don't wish to fail or be seen to fail. Further, we have seen in previous sections the risk of dilution of culture across distance in this case study: and yet performance continues to be high, as professional norms provide the focal point around which (self) control mechanisms cluster.

Individuals appear to exercise agency through commitment to social institutions and behavior which suit them or appear to them to be worthwhile. Where cynicism or distance was expressed by several participants about organizational culture and values, this was not once expressed about their profession or about "quality work". In Chap. 4, we surmised that although they viewed the firm and its principles in a positive light, staff saw it primarily as a provider of opportunities for them to enact and develop their skills, rather than as a place for belonging and nurture. The operational result however is that these individualistic institutions still deliver outcomes which serve the interests of the firm. A further demonstration of individual agency is the drive to be creative, which irritates management, who would prefer higher levels of knowledge reuse. The desire to be creative is possibly derived from a socially constructed institution of a good academic or professional, but stands in opposition to the form's actual need: this suggests that not all such controls are in the service of the firm.

Although direct controls such as procedures, reports and monitoring are present, staff have internalized the project management mindset to the point where it appears to be second nature to them and becomes a form of self control. In some respects, although most workers report formally, regularly and in detail to HO, there is an inversion of power relations with their management. Management acts as a central service to outside workers rather than a source of directives, subordinate to their subordinates to the degree that they are able to understand the detail of the work to the extent of the virtual knowledge worker.

The organizational culture in Unit 2 reflects its existence as a commercial consulting firm, in which project procedures, reporting and cost control by managers are accepted as legitimate institutions. While the espoused values and norms of the organization are participatory, tolerant and respectful of the individual, organizational culture is not just a feel good factor. As a giver of roles and identity, it provides a set of relationships and institutions for the enactment of personal roles and the affirmation of identities, in particular professional identities. This appears to be a significant vacuum for virtual workers (who are also frustrated at not being able to contribute their field knowledge to the firm). While there is an instrumental explanation (i.e. that the organization is missing important market intelligence and project learning by not adequately integrating outside staff), the meta-narrative of this discourse as revealed by the depth of feeling in interviews indicates that virtual workers feel denied the opportunity for professional development, the building of knowledge as a virtue in itself, and construction of their own identities within the firm.

There is a strong, durable value orientation to quality and performance in the firm, and people are identified with the results they deliver, but modesty is a dominant value: people are passively discouraged from promoting themselves and do not actively praise their colleagues if they have done a good job. Poor work is openly criticized. The uniformly high quality of staff which we observed in interviews, consistent high levels of performance, sophistication and education imply there are other forces which ensure that the organization is anything but mediocre. This is an apparent paradox worthy of further research.

The strong skills in project management techniques and procedures are bound up with the values of project management: to use certain methods to deliver according to the principles of timeliness, budget and customer satisfaction. We expect that these values would have been internalized with the instrumental skills as part of project management ontology and that personnel apply these institutions to shaping their own behavior.

How are institutions maintained over distance and in the absence of direct and regular contact in Unit 2? Previous observations have stated that virtual knowledge workers do not "go native": they maintain their commitment to hard work, quality and a job well done. Conversely, other statements suggest that the organizational culture and values do seem to attenuate over time and distance. These institutions are maintained in different conversations and it may be that the dialectic for maintaining culture (which is perhaps a synonym for HO) is interrupted more seriously by dislocation than that for professionalism.

To sum up, the underlying principles of the organization are commercial and the institutions are directed towards performance and profitability. Decision making, although participatory to a degree, is the domain of management. The personnel are acutely professional and directed towards high quality and high performance, and strong project management values, while being constrained by a national cultural norm of modesty and self-effacement. Virtual knowledge workers also clamor for a greater sense of belonging to the culture of the firm: their removal from the everyday social and interpersonal interactions at the workplace amplifies a need to be part of a social system which can be seen to simultaneously nurture and instill conformance in its members.

9.6 The Role of Technology in Controlling Virtual Knowledge Workers

Information technology use in Unit 2, particularly by staff based outside HO, is low level and non-critical and the role of technology in exercising control seems low. This is partially due to the fact that most projects are in developing countries where facilities are poorly developed, but perhaps most importantly the work processes themselves do not require much information or communications technology. These virtual knowledge workers function fairly autonomously in the field, with little need for information from HO to fulfill their project tasks. While there is some need from workers outside HO for the information available from the company's ERP system, better communications facilities are demanded by remote knowledge workers, primarily for maintenance of contact with the company and their colleagues. As one outside project manager said:

> The thing people want to know the most is the thing they need to know the least. (Consultant, OS)

The telephone is the technology of choice for regular contact. While responsiveness and media richness are given as reasons for this, there are two further reasons. The first concerns using e-mail instead of telephone as a form of defense against potential interpersonal conflict:

> I'm very much against e-mail communication … I'm pushing hard for people to use the phone … when things are getting a little difficult with the client, there is a tendency to write things in an e-mail … and that's exactly where you should NOT use an e-mail (Manager, HO)

The second reason is the increased scope for the development of personal relationships:

I called him with no reason ... that was so important ... somebody calling from home ... for no reason ... we will always have a good relationship. I had a feeling that he would appreciate it ... why not use the time to call XXX. Those little things can have such an effect (Manager, HO)

And another manager:

What does telephone add? One thing, it's faster. Second thing, it gives you a feeling of the mood amongst the people you are talking to... Showing that we care is one of the main objectives ... but you get more details in a telephone conversation. I remember concern expressed in a phone call better. (Manager, HO)

There have been some attempts to use information technology to promote sharing of professional experiences and stories and provide forums for professional exchange. A knowledge portal has been developed to distribute information about the markets, proposals, reports and staff. This is managed by the administrative staff and has changed lines of communication: all personnel are now expected to use it, both to publish meetings of minutes and items of interest, but also to "fetch" their own information when they need it. The system was explicitly implemented to support "out of office" communities, in contrast to the "brown bag" lunch session at which people present in HO present their projects and highlight interesting aspects. These sessions are very popular: indeed it is now "almost impossible to get a spot" (Manager, HO).

9.6.1 Discussion

The case study indicates that control can be achieved without the introduction of specific technology. The overall use of technology for communication and control in the case study organization is generally quite low: reports representing process controls are e-mailed to head office, as are ad hoc e-mails and requests. Overseas personnel are reachable via technology and must reckon with contact by their management at any time but there are no information systems whereby IT could be used to directly monitor the activities of staff. Gossip, what is going on, involvement, what are the staff movements and market successes are the kinds of needs articulated by virtual workers, to develop a sense of belonging. So technology for the transfer of instrumental knowledge is secondary to the requirement of its use as an instrument of perpetuating social institutions of belonging. This role of IT could be described as the transfer of "nutrient" knowledge [24] rather than monitoring or control.

Interestingly, in spite of the "informating" [27] capabilities of the technology, IT is demanded by virtual knowledge workers: there seems to be no consideration of its potential for surveillance. Instead, they seem to have transcended any reservations about observation and external control through the internalization of a management mindset and dedication to their profession.

The telephone is the preferred mode for communication and control. The consequences of this relatively rich media technology extend beyond the ability of channels of communication to transmit information. The observations suggest that voice dialogue nurtures the inclination to be more open, intimate and display care, encouraging the development of trust and closeness. But this may simultaneously spin a Web of obligations within the specific practice of media rich telephone communication.

9.7 Conclusion

Virtual work relations will continue to grow in response to the massive market forces which thirst for flexibility, frontline customer visibility and economy. We have sought to better understand how it is that virtual employees continue to conform to the expectations, requirements and standards of their employers. From an initially apparent small set of direct controls, our research led us to observe a complex, pervasive network of integrated and overlapping constraints. We see direct controls in the form of procedures, reporting, regular phone calls and e-mails, salary incentives, the presence of local teams, clients, stakeholders and regular management trips to audit projects and (more importantly) the people. We see indirect, internalized controls in the form of strong professional commitment, personal motivation, team loyalty, and fear of failure, self-interest and to a smaller extent organizational culture.

These controls are numerous. Secondly they are diverse. Thirdly they are fluid and complementary – where one form of control is strong, another may be withdrawn. Fourthly, the internalized forms of control appear to have primacy. The more decisive is the commitment which management perceives to be present, the less the significance of formalized direct controls. Fifth, remoteness does seem to exclude staff from participation in activities which enhance a sense of belonging and which maintain organizational institutions. It may be that some institutions are more stable and robust in the absence of face-to-face communication. Finally, the interactions of some controls with technologies amplify the control mechanisms in different ways: a telephone call will speak to the loyalty and obligation of the outside staff; an electronic discussion forum will appeal to their sense of professional identity.

References

1. Adami L (1999) Autonomy, control and the virtual worker. In: Jackson PJ (ed), Virtual working: social and organisational dynamics. Routledge, London, pp 131–150
2. Argyris C (1999) On organizational learning. Blackwell, Oxford
3. Berger PL, Luckmann T (1967) The social construction of reality: a treatise in the sociology of knowledge. Penguin, London
4. Crandall NF, Wallace MJ (1999) Work & rewards in the virtual workplace. AMACOM, New York
5. Davenport T (2005) Thinking for a living. Harvard Business School Press, Boston
6. Depickere A (1999) Managing virtual working: between commitment and control. In: Jackson PJ (ed), Virtual working: social and organisational dynamics. Routledge, London, pp 99–120
7. DiMaggio P, Powell W (1983) The iron cage revisited: institutional isomorphism and collective rationality in organizational fields. American Sociological Review 48:147–160
8. Drucker P (1999) Management challenges for the 21st century. Butterworth-Heinemann, Oxford
9. Fisher K, Fisher MD (1998) The distributed mind. AMACOM, New York
10. Friedman A (1977) Industry and labour: class struggle at work and monopoly capitalism. Macmillan, London
11. Haywood M (1998) Managing virtual teams: practical techniques for high-technology project managers. Artech House, Boston
12. Hofstede G (1991) Cultures and organizations: software of the mind. McGraw-Hill, New York
13. Jackson PJ (1999) Introduction. In: Jackson PJ (ed), Virtual working: social and organisational dynamics. Routledge, London, pp 1–16
14. McKinlay A (2005) Knowledge management. In: Ackroyd S, Batt R, Thompson P, Tolbert PS (eds). The Oxford handbook of work and organization. Oxford University Press, Oxford, pp 242–262
15. Orlikowski WJ (1992) The duality of technology: rethinking the concept of technology in organizations. Organization Science 3:398–427
16. Orlikowski WJ (1993) Learning from Notes: organisational issues in groupware implementation. The Information Society 9:237–250
17. Perrow C (1961) Organizational prestige: some functions and dysfunctions. American Journal of Sociology 66:335–341
18. Schein E (1985) Organizational culture and leadership. Jossey-Bass, San Francisco

19. Schein E (1996, Fall) Three cultures of management: the key to organizational learning. Sloan Management Review 38:9–20
20. Scott WR (1995) Institutions and organizations. Sage, Thousand Oaks, CA
21. Scott WR, Christensen S (1995) The institutional construction of organizations: international and longitudinal studies. Sage, Thousand Oaks, CA
22. Senge PM (1992) The fifth discipline. Random House, London
23. Sewell G (1998) The discipline of teams: the control of team-based industrial work through electronic surveillance. Administrative Science Quarterly 32:397–428
24. Shapero A (1985) Managing professional people: understanding creative performance. Free Press, New York
25. Suomi R, Pekkola J (1999) Management rationalities and virtual working In: Jackson PJ (ed) Virtual working: social and organisational dynamics. Routledge, London, pp 121–130
26. Thompson P (1989) The nature of work (2nd ed). Palgrave Macmillan, London
27. Zuboff S (1988) In the age of the smart machine. Basic, New York

Part 3
Understanding Virtualization

10 The Challenge of Becoming Virtual, Part 2

Jane Klobas

10.1 Introduction

On a sunny afternoon in June 2006, the research team looked out to the city that Peter Fischer had looked out on 18 months before. They had come to present the results of their research to Unit 2, but the mood did not match the weather. There was despondency in the air, staff stayed mostly in their offices rather than wandering out to discuss the results displayed on posters near the coffee room, and the researchers learnt that business had not picked up as hoped. No-one knew it at the time, but the Unit would largely disappear six months later in a major corporate reorganization.

10.2 Efforts to Build the Virtual Organization

Since her appointment as Department Manager that seemingly long-ago November 2004, Louise Kjaer had worked systematically – in an increasingly difficult business environment – on developing Unit 2's version of a virtual organization, the Global Network Organization (GNO). Peter Fischer had delegated full responsibility for the GNO to Kjaer while he concentrated on the wider business issues facing Unit 2 and TPC.

10.2.1 Access to Information and Communication Systems

One of Kjaer's first steps was to develop an up-to-date list of staff in all categories (including contractors) with current e-mail addresses. This list was matched against system access permissions: company applications inside the firewall, such as the TPC intranet, SAP and the "CV database" that recorded individuals' skills and experience, were available only to employees of the company, while the DIP, which resided outside the firewall, was available to selected long-term contractors as well as to TPC employees. The matching process uncovered a small number of people who had access to the DIP when they should not have and a group of long-term contractors who, in the opinion of Kjaer's team, should be given access to the DIP.

An e-mail message was sent to all people with permission to access the DIP, asking them to indicate if they were actually able to access it. The result was surprising. About one third of the messages identified problems: some messages were returned undeliverable, while no response was received to others. Around one quarter of the recipients was unable to access the DIP. Access problems were dealt with on an individual basis. This approach was successful in about half the cases, but infrastructure limitations meant that it was still not possible to provide DIP access to all staff and long-term contractors working outside HO.

A technical solution for staff working in TPC and Unit 2 offices in Africa was developed by the IT Services Department, but it could not be implemented: there was no budget for IT Services Department staff to go to the remote offices to implement the necessary modifications. After six months of work, Unit 2's IT staff felt they had achieved all that they could without specific funding for extending access. From the original list of 141 potential participants in the GNO, the exercise of checking authority and ability to access systems had identified 97 staff and long-term contractors who had the permission and technical capacity to participate. But, perhaps more tellingly, only 40% of authorized outside staff were able to access the DIP. Sixty percent remained unconnected because of problems with Internet access or authentication of their accounts from the locations where they logged in (e.g., Internet cafes in developing nations) or could not be contacted.

Recognizing that not all actions to improve communication and collaboration involved ICT, and in response to the requests of HO-based staff, Kjaer also reinstated Department meetings in HO. This move was very well received.

10.2.2 Improving the DIP

Considerable effort was also put in to improving the DIP. The administrative staff responsible for the maintaining the DIP under Kjaer's guidance upgraded DIP content and structure so that the information it contained covered a broader range of issues, was more up to date and easier to find through navigation.

Almost in parallel with this process, the IT Services Department introduced a new version of the Project Portal (PP2), implemented using Microsoft SharePoint. This necessitated several technical changes to the internal structure of the DIP which was re-structured as a set of inter-linked project portals. As Kjaer said, "it's much, much more complex; it's several portals in one". Unit 2's DIP administrators worked to ensure that these changes did not impact on users, but the new structure introduced complexity that slowed down access to some pages, including the DIP home page.

10.2.3 Implementing and Working with the Dialogue Forum

The Dialogue Forum (DF) was introduced in August. Technically, it was implemented through an open source add-on to SharePoint, MacawDiscussionBoard.

Unit 2's goal was to "provide a forum for online discussion and exchange of ideas, allowing all staff to participate regardless of whether they are based in HO or outside". It was introduced immediately following a Unit 2 strategic planning day in HO. The managers who directed the face-to-face strategy discussion established a discussion area in the DF to enable the discussion to be continued and joined by people outside HO. A project code was allocated for participation in the strategy discussion. Andrew Jones, a relatively new HO-based consultant who had experience with discussion forums from his previous work, was appointed DF facilitator for the two months that the strategy discussion was to be continued. Louise Kjaer identified five other topics to add to the DF, including technology for access to Unit 2 systems and a notice board for exchange of personal and social information ranging from holiday homes to rent to Christmas festivities.

At the end of each week during the two month period, Jones summarized discussion on all topics, not just strategy, and circulated his summary to all staff by e-mail. Nonetheless, participation dropped off steadily after the first week. In the fourth week, Jones walked the HO corridors and telephoned key staff outside HO, reminding people to contribute to the forum. Participation peaked during this week, but again dropped off steadily in the following weeks.

During the two months that Jones facilitated discussion in the DF, about half the staff with access to the DF accessed it. About half of those (a total of 29) made at least one contribution – but almost all contributors (27) were based in HO. The contributors from outside HO told the research team that they contributed only because they were "told to".

Seventeen (17) threads attracted some dialogue (at least one reply). Most posting occurred during the three weeks following the face-to-face strategy discussion in HO. Only four threads were started after facilitation ceased. The DF had failed to engage a critical group of target users (consultants based outside HO) and had failed to meet its goal.

10.3 Progress Toward Being Virtual

One year after their study began, the researchers asked staff to assess the level of virtualization using the indicators they had used at the beginning of the project. Ninety-four (94) members of staff were identified as eligible for participation in this review. Survey responses were received from 41 staff (45%). The distribution of respondents over location, employment categories, Market Area, nationality and language group was similar to that of the initial survey. This review also drew information from interviews, seminars and meetings with 29 members of Unit 2 management and staff and three TPC staff with ICT responsibility.

The survey used the indicators of virtuality and capability described in Appendixes 1 and 4. In addition, respondents were asked to give an overall rating of the level of virtuality in Unit 2. (The question appears at the end of Appendix 1.) Fifty percent evaluated it as Basic ("HO and international staff have similar levels of performance but difficulties are still faced as a result of being virtual"), 32% evaluated it as Ad hoc ("Effective only in HO and/or among senior staff"), and the remaining 18% evaluated it as Standardized ("Benefits of operating as a virtual organization outweigh the problems"). At first glance, this seems a moderately positive assessment, but when the figures were broken down, it became clear that most HO-based staff evaluated the level as Basic, while most consultants based outside HO evaluated it as Ad hoc, i.e., effective only in HO or among senior staff. If the virtual organization was not effective for people outside HO, it was not an effective virtual organization.

In interviews, HO consultants said that they felt not much had happened to develop a virtual organization. They did not think of outside colleagues much ("because I don't need to") and doubts were expressed about whether the GNO was needed to support the way Unit 2 works. Even for their own work, when they were on assignment in the field, they did not feel the need for HO let alone a distributed community of colleagues. One of the researchers summarized the views of HO consultants in this way:

Distributed communities of people develop where there is a common interest, and simple tools are used which work well (such as e-mail or phone), but this is not virtual. It is something that people decide to do based upon likes and dislikes and personal relationships.

10.3.1 The Virtuality Dashboard

The extent to which Unit 2 had reached its goals for virtualization in December 2005, after one year of activities directed toward becoming virtual, is shown on the virtuality dashboard in Fig. 10.1. The level in December 2004 is shown in grey. The dashboard includes a new dimension, trust, which was added after the first survey to capture a new organizational dimension which had been mentioned by managers and staff. The researchers' report on the rationale for the levels recorded in the dashboard appears in Appendix 3.

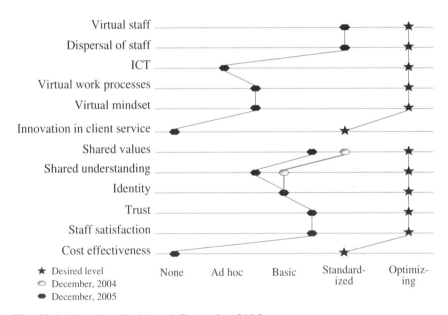

Fig. 10.1. Virtuality Dashboard, December 2005

After one year, the level of virtuality in Unit 2 had, if anything, decreased rather than increased. While the decrease was neither dramatic nor across the board, it was a clear indication that the virtualization strategy had not been a success. The two dimensions which were rated lower at the end of the year were shared values and shared understanding of the organization. In both cases, declines were seen among consultants based outside HO, yet one of the goals of virtualization was to increase the sense of belonging to the organization of remote staff in particular.

In their December 2005 report, the researchers challenged Unit 2 management to re-evaluate their goals:

> The goal of increasing the sense of belonging of remote and contract staff may be an illusion: are people really interested in feeling they belong or are they only interested in their next job? ... The major concern [of contractors] seems to be that they continue to be supplied with work which is secure, interesting and well paid: the job market on the DIP fulfils this function well, but the DF (on strategy) is of little interest to them.

10.3.2 Capabilities for Virtualization

Unit 2's capabilities for virtualization after one year are summarized in the capabilities dashboard in Fig. 10.2. The researchers' reasons for the reported levels of capability are given in detail in Appendix 6. Although there were some minor changes, all capabilities remained at or below the midpoint of the scale, and below the desired levels of High to Very High.

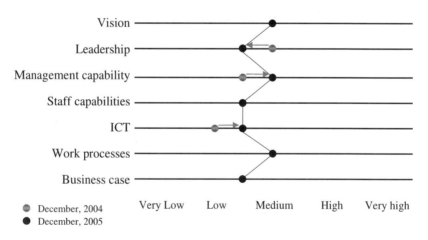

Fig. 10.2. Capabilities for Virtualization after one year

10.4 Subsequent Activities

After one year of working without an administrative staff member dedicated full-time to Unit 2's information systems and technology, Louise Kjaer obtained the Director's support to appoint an IT Expert. Funding was limited, but after a careful search, Kjaer appointed Charles Krogh, a recent graduate in anthropology who had completed field work in a large organization in preparation for his thesis on the adoption of information systems.

Krogh's appointment very quickly had several positive effects. Soon after his appointment, he conducted a study on the usability of the DIP, and work began to implement improvements. One project group held a successful videoconference with an overseas client after Krogh resolved problems – largely through human communication – that had hindered previous attempts.

There was some successful, unplanned innovation. The Francophone Market Area group began using Centra as a computer-mediated communication tool to support communication with their Market Area manager who is no longer based in HO. Although primarily used for audio-conferencing, Centra is also used to share documents. Other groups are not currently expected to adopt Centra to support their work, however.

On the other hand, problems have emerged in an area previously considered useful for, if not widely used within Unit 2. After the PP was migrated to SharePoint, people from outside TPC were unable to access project portals. This issue has not been resolved. It is not clear if the problem is the result of IT Services Department reluctance to allocate suitable levels of permission, or if it is a technical problem associated with the way the SharePoint application is configured to check permissions, or a combination of the two. Resolution of technical problems with access to the PP, like access to the DIP and DF, appears to be outside Unit 2's control, something which Kjaer and her staff find discouraging:

Investigating [access problems] ... is a very difficult process, it takes a whole lot of time and we don't have the resources so a few experiences [of failure to provide access] and you've just abandoned the idea.

As the researchers contemplated the future of Unit 2's virtualization efforts, Kjaer and Krogh set ICT goals for the year ahead: (1) continue the dialogue with Unit 2 staff to assess their ICT needs and define how ICT applications can be improved and (2) manage migration of the DIP and existing project portals to the parent company's new version of the project portal, PP2. But, there was another cloud on the horizon: budget constraints meant that Krogh's position was unlikely to be continued beyond his initial one year contract.

10.5 One More Survey

So, on that sunny day in June, the researchers were at a bit of a loss. Some progress was being made, but the Director's enthusiasm for virtualization had waned. Louise Kjaer was despondent at the meager return from the effort she had put in to improving the supporting technology, access to it and its use. She was also carrying the weight of knowing that she would soon have to tell Charles Krogh that, despite his effort and success, his contract would not be renewed. Several Market Area managers were openly hostile to the DF and the virtualization strategy. HO consultants were skeptical about the whole process having seen little change in their work apart from an apparent deterioration in the business market which carried with it the risk of less work. Consultants based outside HO had been largely untouched by it all, and if anything, had less of a sense of shared vision and understanding of the organization than one year earlier. What could be done?

Unit 2 managers and consultants had frequently referred to issues associated with knowledge sharing and communication in their interviews with the researchers. They had made several suggestions for improvement over the 12 months of the study. In June 2006, the researchers addressed these suggestions directly in a series of targeted interviews and a brief final survey. The final questionnaire contained two sections. The first asked Unit 2 staff to evaluate 18 different actions that had been suggested in earlier interviews. Many of the actions, such as "Hold more department meetings that address trends and developments in the market", had nothing to do with technology. The second section asked for opinions on the value of continuing or closing the DIP and the DF.

The attitudes of staff to the DIP were captured in responses to a simple survey question "How would you feel if the DIP was closed and no longer available?" Possible responses were: very pleased, pleased, indifferent, unhappy, and very unhappy. Most respondents (18, 72%) indicated that they would be unhappy or very unhappy if the DIP were closed, indicating a reasonable level of acceptance. Respondents from outside HO were a little less enthusiastic than those based inside HO, with half of them saying that they would be indifferent and half saying that they would be unhappy. Nonetheless, those for whom the DIP was intended were less interested in it than those in regular physical contact with one another.

Respondents were asked a similar question about possible closure of the DF and the responses were clear. All respondents from outside HO said that they were indifferent to its closure, as did more than half of the HO-based respondents.

The managers and consultants who responded to the survey strongly supported more visits to HO by staff based outside HO. Apart from agreement on this initiative, though, there were marked differences in the actions favored by each group. Consultants sought more Department meetings, while managers saw little need for them. On the other hand, managers favored continued use of an e-mailed newsletter and use of a project code to encourage participation in initiatives such as the DF, while the consultants were lukewarm about these ideas. Were managers clinging to a technology-driven vision of change that the staff did not share?

11 Reflections from the Frontline:
The Journey of a Knowledge Manager

Louise Kjaer

11.1 Introduction

After only six months in TPC I first met with the international group of re-searchers, the authors of this book. They were to become my companions throughout a cumbersome and yet exciting journey of organizational change; a change process that unfolded in Unit 2, one of ten units which form part of a large transnational consulting company, TPC. Setting off in December 2004, I was to become the knowledge manager of an innovation process which by means of new Information and communications tech-nologies (ICT) was designed to enhance communication and knowledge exchange and smooth interaction between colleagues working in our dis-persed "Global Network Organization" (a term used by the Unit's Direc-tor, shortened here to GNO).

During the following two year process the research group members have acted as "critical friends" rather than professional advisors. Based on their recurrent data collection, interviews and critical theory-based reflection they have been the sounding board against which I have been able to test new ideas, discuss setbacks, seek inspiration and begin to comprehend and overcome different kinds of complexities throughout the change process.

11.2 Infatuated by the Idea of Virtual Collaboration

The journey began back in 2004; an organizational change process had re-cently been introduced by the Director of Unit 2 in response to increased competition in an increasingly globalized market for consultancy services. The proposition was to meet the new challenges by enhancing measures of collaboration among staff members positioned in various locations across

the globe. Given that two-thirds of the workforce is working outside of HO
at any given time and therefore cannot benefit from face-to-face professional exchanges, the improvement of virtual communication was given
high priority.

Hence, it was decided by management to pioneer a unique system of
virtual collaboration, a system that would enhance communication and
professional exchanges among colleagues and administration at HO, local
offices in developing countries and traveling consultants moving from one
destination in the developing world to another. This while recognizing that
telephone conversations across time zones and one-to-one e-mails might
not be enough. In the attempt to compensate, for example, for the absence
of face-to-face meetings, the new strategy for virtual collaboration would
introduce an Internet-mediated technical dialogue facility, e-meetings, and
other knowledge exchange systems (see below).

The purpose of the strategy for enhanced virtual collaboration has been
many sided. With an increasingly dispersed workforce operating in ever
smaller units (if not as individual consultants) it is necessary to ensure
some degree of cohesion, i.e., that there is clarity about business processes
and that company values and code of conduct are disseminated and form
the basis of the way we work. High quality standards must be maintained
throughout the production cycle while ensuring at the same time that transaction costs are kept low. Furthermore, retention and continuous recruitment of the most qualified international consultants require a clearly articulated, communicated and enacted value system.

A separate target has been to optimize use of the knowledge, practical
experiences and multidisciplinary competences of all employees throughout the GNO. There is a need to constantly exploit frontier knowledge of
new demands in the international market as it is being obtained by traveling consultants. Contact with customers in all corners of the world provides excellent opportunities for innovation of our services.

Associated with the obvious advantages of a still more flexible, globally
distributed workforce are also a number of risks, however. Risks may relate to changes in the organizational culture, including a possible loss of a
sense of belonging or commitment to the organization, or to a reduction in
adherence to the company's values and quality standards. As it were, any
sense of corporate identity had been constituted within a number of separate organizational entities, be they subsidiary companies, local offices,
HO or specific business units at HO level, or through assignment on large
implementation projects with a smaller or larger number of colleagues and
a team leader on board. For individual consultants – increasingly operating
alone in a new virtual organization model – without closer affiliation to

any one of the above physical entities, identification with the company could become at risk.

11.3 The Notion of Virtualization

According to the Director's strategic intent, as stipulated in the 2005–2009 strategy plan, the Unit was already at the time regarded as being virtual:

A geographically dispersed organization close to the clients and their demands, characterized by a strong learning culture where knowledge is transformed into frontier quality services by all staff irrespectively of their location and sustained by our systems and procedures.

As knowledge manager I was yet to understand the difference between on the one hand the vision of a fully virtualized organization freed of spatial and mental boundaries and on the other hand, the underlying complexities associated with transforming a globally dispersed organization into a fully functional network organization sustained by means of ICT-mediated communication and virtual collaboration.

In retrospect, I was setting off without a bulletproof plan, but with a clear sense of direction. And I was excited at first. I was leaning on to the overall strategy of Unit 2 and the spelled out goals for increased virtual collaboration. The beauty of the approach was the creativity it allowed when thinking up new ideas and tasks and when seeking and inventing solutions to the challenges we were bound to encounter along the journey.

I was intrigued also by the privilege of being appointed to pilot test new corporate technology. Not only our Unit, but the much larger TPC was introducing new Microsoft SharePoint applications to support communication and collaboration and in this context we volunteered as test pilots of a new portal facility. In our unit we had created the Development Information Portal (to become known as the DIP) for the purpose of easy information exchange, knowledge sharing and virtual dialogue among colleagues posted inside and outside of HO. In doing so we positioned ourselves in the front line of development of corporate communication, with the right to invent solutions and influence decisions, but also exposing ourselves to the challenge of dealing with all the infant diseases of the new technology.

Another issue discussed was the potential of future marketing of our experiences. We discussed how our efforts of experimenting with virtual collaboration might in the future form part of a change management service product for similar organizations striving to learn to operate in the global marketplace.

11.4 Beginning to Grasp the Complexity

In line with the above idea of virtualization, I was inspired by INSEAD professor Yves Doz talking about potential advantages of "tearing down" the head office of one's organization and moving the different departments out into the world [1]. Only by allowing local (meta-national) inspiration to influence head office business thinking can the innovation game be won in the global economy, he claims. The future belongs to those corporations that know how to capture knowledge right when and where it is encountered, is the argument.

Doz goes on to challenge the perception of innovation simply as a means and possibility for saving money. Innovation has a price to it, and one cannot predict the result. But if you do not count on global knowledge sharing, you can be sure of losing out.

I was soon to understand that there were a great many things we had not predicted when embarking on our ambitious plans for "virtualization", let alone the financial cost of it!

Another fundamental mistake might be that we never made a distinction between organizational/managerial and communicative aspects of virtual collaboration on the one hand and on the other hand, the more sociological aspects of human behavior of those individuals inhabiting our organization and of their incentives for knowledge sharing.

11.5 All the Way Virtual – or a Two-Tier Strategy?

Out of eagerness to get on with the job we never spent time defining to which degree the organization was already functioning virtually (extensively using telephone and e-mail as means of communication) or exactly how virtual we would want to become, at what pace and at which cost?

The Director had his obvious reasons for advocating immediate advancement towards fulfillment of the agreed strategic goal of a fully operational GNO – tied together by means of virtual collaboration – and based on the above described motives for overcoming challenges in the global market. At an early stage in the change process he therefore suggested to suspend all analogue (face-to-face) meetings at HO in favor of only virtual communication, so as to enact the ambition of equal access to information for all members of the GNO.

Contrary to this position was a strong wish expressed by the consultants – particularly those based at and traveling out from HO – for more information from and interaction with the management group. When I took up my position as knowledge manager, the only analogue meetings conducted at HO were Friday morning gatherings where management passed on information about tenders won and lost and a few market specific subgroups conducting bi-weekly or monthly information gatherings about work in process. However, what consultants seemed to be missing was the opportunity to gather for the purpose of dialogue and peer group discussion about professional development and direction. The management group had henceforth not made this a priority because of time constraints and a strict focus on billable hours.

Against this background I took it upon myself to advocate a two-tier approach. A comprehensive annual meeting plan was introduced that would allow for both analogue and virtual interaction between colleagues. Managers agreed to conduct regular market specific/thematic, analogue meetings for relevant staff. In addition, the new Web-based Development Information Portal (DIP) would feature detailed minutes of these meetings along with specific supporting content items for out-posted or traveling colleagues to access and read while abroad.

Despite the Director's initial reluctance, the two-tier approach was agreed. The meeting structure has proven to be highly valued among colleagues as a vehicle for common reference and knowledge exchange.

11.5.1 Technological Hindrances

A lot of time was initially invested into making the DIP fully functional not only as a container of information but as a dialogue and knowledge exchange facility. The very first challenge encountered had to do with firewall constraints and access problems for consultants working outside of HO, i.e., the primary target group of our virtualization efforts.

I was soon to understand that our Unit was ahead of the game when it came to experimenting with connectivity between HO and traveling consultants. Whereas other units have their internal information displayed on the corporate intranet, we in our Unit have chosen to maintain a twin structure of sharing our Unit-specific information on a) a subsection of the firewall protected corporate intranet, and b) we have in addition copied everything onto an extranet version (project portal accessible via the WWW) for the benefit of traveling consultants and out posted staff.

Initially, the project portal software was not very useful in terms of allowing for interactivity or dialogue. Luckily the company was at the time planning to go ahead with investment in a new SharePoint project portal system and soon we could migrate all information onto a more advanced portal site, including both dialogue and virtual meeting facilities. In principle we could now foresee active involvement in IT-mediated discussions by consultants connecting from a Net café in Ouagadougou!

We were all the time aware that content on the DIP had to be "light weight". It soon appeared, however, that even if the new portal technology was making the above dialogue tools available, it became a larger than anticipated hindrance that Africa and Asia only offers connection on very thin lines. Still today it is not possible to download larger documents, slide presentations or even PDF files from many destinations in developing countries. All consultants working outside of high-tech continents complain that they are constantly thrown off their Internet connection so even e-mail correspondence can prove difficult. Hence, technological shortcomings in developing countries, where most of our consultants are operating, have become a major challenge for the realization of the vision of full virtual collaboration.

Alternative satellite connectivity had been explored by the corporate IT Services Department some years back, but found too costly. I was slowly realizing that only limited attention had ever been granted to supporting our target group of traveling consultants in low-tech countries, besides efficient help desk advice provided over long distance calls, or support to computer repair when pit-stopping at HO. Perhaps the scope had been unclear, the challenge too big and costs deemed too high and therefore not worth the trouble. But obviously no financial analysis had ever been made of the cost of *not* finding a solution to hindrances in communication with colleagues in developing countries and the missed possibilities for knowledge sharing.

One year down the road I therefore conducted a quick and simple baseline survey – only to discover affirmation that hardly any traveling, regionally hired or out-posted consultant would even attempt trying to access the DIP due to technological constraints! Hindrances to Internet connectivity was given as the main reason for lack of involvement. But there is more to the picture that meets the eye…

11.5.2 The Importance of Context

The following description may begin to explain why these technical constraints had not been anticipated or even taken care of. The Unit is functioning as one (smaller) organizational unit in a large organization structured as many units. The unique characteristics of this Unit is that we work in small teams or by means of individual consultants traveling in low-tech developing countries, or out of smaller local offices operating in some instances without even a high speed connection to the Internet. Although the other units are also operating internationally, they do so primarily via sub-sidiary companies or larger project offices (typically established for long-term, bigger scale construction projects) to which IT corridors have been set up to support high speed information exchange with HO.

In essence, although our Unit forms part of a bigger setup and enjoys the support and services of the central IT department, priority to our unique and relatively smaller challenges has not henceforth been granted. At times I have even discovered that corporate rules and standards have restricted our ability to develop individual IT solutions, e.g., when a client requested a database of our development consultants for their easy reference at coun-try office level, this wish could not be accommodated (and potential busi-ness opportunity may have been lost) because corporate IT could not dis-close a subsection of the overall corporate CV database.

11.5.3 Comprehending Resistance

As if technological hindrances were not enough, there seemed to be grow-ing skepticism against the very idea of virtualization among colleagues. A small editorial group had initially been formed by administrative assistants and members of the management group at HO level and was working with some degree of enthusiasm to make the DIP comply with the high stan-dards set for information exchange. But the remaining managers and a lot of consultants did not seem to fully embrace the overall vision.

In retrospect, one main reason for lack of commitment to the virtualiza-tion strategy may well be that top management had not from the start clearly articulated exactly how it would work to accomplish its vision. No tangible indicators had been established against which to measure progress (other than statistical measurement of users and contributions to the DIP). And it was assumed that involvement in virtual communication or knowl-edge exchange would take place on a completely voluntary basis.

11.5.4 Incentive Structures

So when the dialogue facility on the DIP was introduced, nobody felt in-clined to make use of it. That left both me and the external researchers wondering.

I, for my part, immediately appointed a dialogue facilitator/moderator who would encourage discussion by asking relevant questions and posting comments on to the DIP. But only a few comments were trickling in – and many of these were forwarded by e-mail to the moderator, e.g., from those consultants traveling, who did not have sufficient bandwith to gain direct access, rather than being submitted directly to the virtual forum.

Still the idea of virtual dialogue never really took off. Nor have very many individuals felt inclined to contribute with bits of information or better practice examples for the purpose of knowledge sharing among colleagues (although the structure is there and technical assistance is easily accessible by e-mail to an appointed DIP/Web manager).

But then it struck me: why would anybody want to get involved? What would be their incentive? Perhaps not in the longer term, but in the short term perspective it was hard to see why middle managers would spend much time engaging in knowledge sharing. Given the overall management structure their individual performance is measured solely by financial targets. Obviously their incentive is therefore to focus on current operations and to make money rather than to engage in thematic discussions and accumulation of best practices!

Much the same disincentives were prevalent when looking at the consultants' missing involvement. The billing structure prevalent in our organization simply does not support that time – other than personal time – is spent on active engagement in knowledge sharing. Many have referred to this phenomenon as "time code tyranny" and management has failed to address this problem. It has been debated, but never resolved, whether or not the overall budget could carry the cost of allocating time for consultants to engage in virtual interaction.

In the meantime, there have been very few voluntary contributions when it comes to, e.g., submission of subject specific knowledge to the designated DIP knowledge bank. This all suggests that there has been a mismatch between voluntary contributions and interest, available financial resources at unit level and top management's desire to enforce knowledge sharing for the purpose of enhancing future business opportunities.

The researchers, for their part, came back with new revelations about consultants' sense of belonging to our GNO based on questionnaire samples. It appeared that in our unit – populated by staff with different roles, positions and often expatriated or based far from HO – many do not necessarily feel a strong need to belong to an "all embracing community". Instead many of the consultants were ranking independence and scope for self-management high on their list of priorities, along with regular and timely salary payment.

11.5.5 Employee Capability

Another observation relates to the different virtual mindsets of employees. Although basic training has been provided to staff in the use of new ICT facilities, there has been a marked difference in its attraction to different individuals and to different age groups. Many of us aged 30 plus already belong to "the lost generation" when it comes to IT literacy. We do not throw ourselves with the same eagerness and confidence into testing and exploring the many new possibilities of the digital era!

And given that the staff composition in the Unit is dominated by individuals above 30 years of age, elements of resistance may also relate to such perceived IT illiteracy.

11.5.6 Willingness to Share Knowledge

Finally, it is worthwhile recalling that all consultants in my organization make up a highly skilled and internationally acknowledged group of knowledge workers who rightly see themselves as experts. Each individual consultant is educated, trained and experienced in delivering world class intellectual performance. Their guiding principles when providing advisory services are common business standards and company quality norms, blended with a large degree of individual freedom, "room for maneuver" and personal responsibility. In other words, it is part of the corporate spirit to trust in and profit from the human agency [2] of all individuals who make up our staff base.

The flip side of the coin may be that these same individuals may lose sight of the collective. Although belonging to the organization and paying respect to company rules and regulations, they may at the same time choose to behave rather according to the rules of the free market place. Even when contractually confined by the boundaries of the overall company, they may – more or less deliberately – be seen to behave as if they were marketing their own individual skills and profile instead of actively sharing their knowledge. Although knowledge sharing is described as a company objective, it is perhaps not explained clearly enough exactly how we would like to see this happening. Verner Petersen usefully elaborates on the span between duties and rights, which is relevant to the willingness of the individual consultant to share insight and knowledge [3]. In an extreme scenario individuals may even have felt inclined to withhold professional knowledge, rather than sharing it with others. This hypothesis is of course difficult to prove, but some examples suggest an element of truth in this assertion when talking about consultants hired on time-limited contracts.

11.5.7 Head Office, the Centre of Gravity

I have described above the technological hindrances for out-posted staff when attempting to connect to the Internet. Another possible reason for lack of involvement in virtual knowledge sharing may refer to the fact that the Unit is still organized and managed not as a networked organization but one that has HO as the centre of gravity and decisional power. The structure of communication is established as one where information floats from top to bottom – to the local project offices, subsidiary companies and individual out-posted consultants. Two-way streams of communication and dialogue have been confined to project-related exchanges, rather than discussions on matters of relevance to the organization as such. In other words, if there has been a lack of local incentives for participation in virtual knowledge sharing for the benefit of the organization (the collective) it may be because HO has never clearly articulated how highly the local voices would be valued.

11.6 Light at the End of the Tunnel

While embarking on a pioneer journey like this, one must be prepared for all kinds of experiences. We have constantly evaluated progress, made adjustments – and certainly we have learned a lot along the way. In spring 2006, well over a year after we began experimenting with new ways of virtual collaboration we took stock and made a few radical decisions.

11.6.1 Focus on the Project

It was clear that communication and dialogue have taken place all along (by e-mails and telephone) when it comes to project-related exchanges. We decided to look more exclusively at how to support and perhaps profit more directly from these "ideal networks" for knowledge sharing. We began looking into ways of technically supporting each of these project-related networks, e.g., by setting up project specific portal solutions (easily accessible on the WWW, but with firewall protected access) for the inclusion also of external partners or clients, and with systems for document exchange and common filing, work planning, announcements, dialogue facility, etc. Similarly, we began experimenting with ways of interlinking several already existing informal networks of consultants with a shared interest in specific thematic areas around which several of our projects evolve. One concrete example has been the creation of a professional network and common knowledge sharing platform for the subject of Capacity Building, Monitoring and Evaluation (many projects relate to this subject which holds a common interest for many consultants).

This professional network was built not only as a virtual platform, however. Conscious of the noted hesitancy towards ICT-borne knowledge sharing we decided to launch this particular knowledge sharing initiative as a dual undertaking. A small group of consultants was commissioned (with time/resources allocated) to establish and conduct a series of analogue training sessions – for consultants present at HO – in which participants' and facilitators' own professional experiences would be exchanged. Traveling staff were invited to take part in the learning sessions by making use of a new virtual meeting facility or to forward by e-mail contributions or questions in advance of the sessions. Secondly, the group was tasked with the responsibility to summarize the content of these training sessions and discussions for display at a designated project portal accessible for out-posted or traveling colleagues. This portal would feature also an annotated bibliography of relevant literature on the subject at hand, recent examples and experiences, up-coming related learning events, etc. By establishing this professional entry point – and while building on direct interest and work-related motivation – it was anticipated that more consultants would feel directly motivated to take part in knowledge sharing.

The idea of building a learning community of interested colleagues has been somewhat successful in that it has attracted wide interest in participation in the analogue meetings. The related project portal has also been frequently visited, however, only during the two month period when the training sessions were running. Thereafter the statistic for user logon declined dramatically, which suggests that virtual "attraction" requires simultaneous, real life encounters!

This assumption can be substantiated by another concrete example. In a few recent instances we have had the opportunity to test virtual collaboration in relation to preparation of project tenders. A lot of hectic activity normally takes place during the proposal writing processes. Many documents, contact details, updated time schedules and new versions of the same documents are exchanged, and telephone conversations are used to clarify specificities. In some of these cases we have seen users becoming familiar with the advantages of using project portals as a new means of information exchange and collaboration. They have also seen the potential for onward knowledge sharing should the tender process result in us winning the assignment and venturing into project implementation.

11.6.2 User-Driven Innovation

When deciding to hire a full-time assistant to help bring the vision about virtual collaboration alive, we chose to hire an anthropologist. This decision was based on the apparent fact that, in order to create interest and commitment among users we needed to gain a much better understanding of their needs. On top of the agenda we therefore put questions like "How do you work; which are your daily work processes?", "What kind of support do you need from HO?", and "What are you interested in?"

With the attempt to promote a different kind of "horizontal" communication we decided to launch an old-fashioned bi-monthly newsletter. Not as an alternative, but as a supplement to the DIP intranet site. This newsletter would be circulated by e-mail to every single inhabitant of our GNO, thereby ensuring that also those with Internet access problems (or those feeling reluctance towards logging on) would gain easy access to a lightweight and easy read! The journalistic style of this newsletter would focus on storytelling, with a relative small proportion of HO information, and the remaining space dedicated to personal accounts from consultants working across the globe. The ambition has of course been to spark an interest and build a sense of cohesion across time zones and individual assignments.

Based on assessment of user needs, working procedures and work life behavior of colleagues we have begun to identify other necessary initiatives and scope for improvement. One example worth mentioning is the development of a tailored training course for one segment of our staff, namely French-speaking consultants working in French-speaking Africa (although the corporate language of our organization is English). At an upcoming regional meeting in Western Africa a training session will – by means of French version video tutorials – offer simple guidance in the use of various tools for virtual collaboration and communication (project portal, Skype, etc.).

11.6.3 Overcoming Technological Hindrances

Along the way we have come to understand a great deal more about the multiplicity of technical hindrances and access problems people are faced with when traveling or being out-posted. Not only have we made a comprehensive baseline study of the different kinds of problems encountered by different categories of employees working from remote destinations, with some delay we are now in the process of costing what it will actually take to bring as many as possible of our many remote units (permanent regional offices, or project offices) up to speed with minimum technological standards, granting access to HO information and network exchanges to everyone.

Poor Internet connectivity, bandwidth that is too narrow and download times that are too long are some of the usual complaints. The ongoing scoping exercise will estimate the actual cost of bringing everyone up to speed, while acknowledging also the financial implications of lost business opportunities if not all critical players are connected. It is imperative to our business that information floats smoothly; this while recalling the stated vision for our GNO as

a geographically dispersed organization close to the clients and their demands, characterized by a strong learning culture where knowledge is transformed into frontier quality services by all staff irrespectively of their location ...

Earlier investigations and proposed coping strategies with low-tech developing countries had suggested that very expensive satellite connections were one, if not the only, solution to overcome problems of Internet connectivity from low-tech developing countries. Luckily times are changing. Wise men are now saying that the ICT revolution is shortly hitting Africa and that by 2010 high speed connections will be available in at least all capital cities at not too high a cost.

11.7 Preparing for the Future: Lessons for Knowledge Managers

We have learnt a lot from the mistakes we have made and also the many small victories we have celebrated. The latter inspire us to move on. Especially when it comes to sharing our experiences with other segments of the corporate group to which my Unit belongs. The future lies for the company as a whole in increased network collaboration among many actors across the globe. Colleagues are now looking at our "case story" for inspiration.

Other companies are faced with similar challenges. My primary advice in respect of new initiatives meant to foster virtual collaboration and/or knowledge sharing would be: The initiative needs to be relevant, necessary and directly related to line production.

It is imperative to critically assess a series of preconditions before launching any new ambitious initiative, and it is necessary to plan and communicate clearly about goals and objectives, to monitor, adjust and measure progress along the way.

Below are suggestions for any manager who is about to introduce ICT-enabled methods of virtual collaboration:

11.7.1 Scoping

Make sure that there is a shared understanding of the challenges related to virtual collaboration and/or knowledge sharing. Thoroughly assess the context and preconditions for introducing ICT-enabled knowledge management and collaboration methods

- Leadership and vision: Are goals clearly defined?
- Management capability: Can a long-term vision be matched with short term requirements of financial performance?
- Technology: Are all possible hindrances taken into account?
- Economics: How much will it cost to make it happen? Is it worth the cost?
- Employee capability: Are staff likely and willing to make the necessary time available, do they have the necessary skills? Are they motivated to learn? Do they have a virtual mindset?
- Incentive system: Can knowledge sharing initiatives be introduced as an improvement in daily work life?

11.7.2 Planning

Clearly outline the initiatives you choose to set in motion, including action plans. Mobilize the necessary non-cash resources and clarify roles and responsibilities, including management responsibilities

- Communicate broadly to the organization about overall objectives, expectations and terms of involvement.
- Communicate specifically with individual staff members and involved groups or networks.
- Lay out a roadmap (work plan, short term/longer term expected targets, end goal/future aspirations).

11.7.3 Implementing

- Conduct training.

- Establish a team of "ambassadors" or role models to show the way! (In addition to management's endorsement of the idea and practical adaptation.)

11.7.4 Measuring

- Monitor progress on a regular basis and inform people about it.
- Create a sense of ownership by asking for – and listening to – feedback from users.
- Make room for adjustments and changes.

11.7.5 Taking Stock

- Evaluate the impact of initiatives *vis-à-vis* the defined objective.
- Celebrate progress!
- Make sure to decide on whether to sustain or terminate initiatives or sub-initiatives or to eventually set in motion new initiatives

11.8 Conclusion

The journey traveled by all members of my Unit has proven the critical importance of shared and clearly communicated objectives. We might have been more successful had we more clearly from the start made a distinction between on the one hand a required strategic change management effort to accomplish a fully functional virtual organization and on the other hand the enhancement of knowledge sharing and business intelligence.

There is no doubt that it is critically important to understand the difference between management needs and user relevance. By user relevance I refer also to the need to understand user preconditions (difference in IT literacy, age groups, workload, distance, technical hindrances from low-tech countries): Sharing knowledge is not just about systems!

Equally important is it to create incentives for involvement ("What's in it for me?" need to know, instead of nice to know), and to acknowledge and seek to overcome disincentives.

The story told in this chapter is one about change management efforts enforced by new ICT. It is a story that contains anecdotal evidence of the risks associated with a gradual abolition of face-to-face communication. In essence, the vision of a virtual network organization related to both managerial change and cultural change. In retrospect, it has proven to be too ambitious a plan to launch new means of virtual collaboration, borne by (in some instances, alienating) technology, and with an expectation for unprecedented knowledge sharing.

Knowing what I know today I will in future efforts work to ensure that plans are much more thoroughly drafted, cost-estimated, endorsed and widely adhered to by all stakeholders involved. Equally important is that progress is measured regularly and impact assessed, and that there is an inbuilt willingness to either sustain or terminate initiatives originally agreed upon, based on evaluation of cost-efficiency.

Learning from our mistakes are some of the best lessons learned. This said in the true spirit of knowledge sharing.

References

1. Doz Y (2001) From global to metanational: how companies win in the knowledge economy. Harvard Business School Press, Boston
2. Giddens A (1984) The constitution of society: outline of the theory of structuration. University of California Press, Berkeley
3. Petersen VC (2003) Beyond rules in society and business. Edward Elgar, London

12 The Forensics of a Challenged Initiative

Paul Jackson, Jane Klobas, Gaela Bernini, Ivan Jensen, Stefano Renzi

12.1 Introduction

In this chapter, we analyze Unit 2's virtualization initiative, drawing on information gathered throughout the research study and from the perspective of all the points of view that our research team brought together. We begin with the overview of the initiative that we sent to Louise Kjaer at the end of the study. The rest of the chapter describes the method and results of a workshop in which the research team sought to explain the observations described in the overview.

12.2 An Overview of the Outcomes

There was little change in the virtuality of Unit 2 during the 18 months in which we observed the organization. If anything, there may have been a slight reduction in shared vision and shared understanding of the organization. In this section, we comment first on what progress has been made and then on some barriers that we perceive.

12.2.1 Progress

The organization has remained geographically dispersed without becoming significantly more or less so. There appears to have been an increase in the visibility of staff based outside HO, but this does not seem to have been translated into an increase in virtual mindset. Our conversations with HO-based staff suggest that, although they are now more aware that the organization is global, there is no apparent increase in interest to communicate more frequently with colleagues in different locations or to use new technologies to do so.

The DIP is a well regarded information dissemination tool, particularly valued by HO-based staff. The vision of the DIP as a tool to support sharing of culture and values, as well as knowledge, with staff and long-term contractors based outside HO has not, however, been achieved. There are patches of strong support for the DIP among outside consultants who are permanent employees of TPC, but there appears to be little interest from long-term contractors.

It appears that the sense of belonging to the organization of consultants and outside staff, and the shared values that may be associated with sense of belonging, are influenced by a complex blend of factors. Communication from HO about general organizational issues does not play as strong a role in maintaining sense of belonging as Peter Fischer thought when the notion of the GNO was first considered. We do not know what all the influencing factors might be, but we can speculate that these include interpersonal contact with project managers and – when they visit – members of the management group, along with an emotional commitment to the company brand. While theory suggests the last of these is influenced by general communication, there are many other influences on commitment to a brand and some understanding of branding may help to understand how to maintain the sense of belonging of people in the field.

In terms of capability for change, there is now a much deeper understanding of the issues associated with use of ICT to improve and change the organization. The appointment of a suitable IT Expert has increased capacity.

12.2.2 Barriers

Technical barriers to access were not solved during the 18 months we observed Unit 2. Even though the Unit's knowledge management team worked to understand the access needs of all staff and long-term consultants, we did not observe a serious attempt by the central IT Services Department to address either the issue of Internet access for staff in developing countries (apart from those in TPC offices) or issues associated with security-related barriers to access by people based outside HO. No matter what progress is made in HO, virtualization cannot be achieved until these access issues are resolved. Developments in communication systems coordinated by the central IT Services Department are driven by larger corporate concerns to which Unit 2's specific needs have been subordinated. Compromise has been required, and to some extent, obtained in order to approximate Unit 2's needs. Nonetheless, without specific commitment from the IT Services Department to understand and directly address Unit

2's needs, and funding to implement solutions that incur direct costs, the Unit may continue to find itself investing time and effort in suboptimal solutions.

While there has been a focus on technology, little attention has been paid to the process changes that need to accompany technological change if technology is to be adopted effectively. The competitive contract-based nature of resourcing also puts pressures on attempts at nutritional change such as improved organization-wide (rather than project-specific) communication. In addition to the financial restrictions this places on nutritional activities, this characteristic of the organization leads middle management, in particular, to take a largely short-term project-based approach to organizational activities. Middle management commitment to virtualization has been limited, but the support of this key group is necessary if the organization is to be able to put resources into nutritional change. Associated with this observation is that, although staff feel they understand the vision of the GNO, there has not been across-the-board commitment to the detail of how the vision might be achieved.

12.3 Method

Why was there so little change in the virtuality of Unit 2? In terms of the VAM, the business strategy demanded a high level of virtuality, but the level of virtuality remained low – as did the capabilities. There was a misalignment between what the business needed and what it had. The lack of capabilities appears to have been critical to the organization's failure to virtualize. Understanding the capabilities required for virtualization should give us an insight, then, into the factors critical for the success of virtualization. All researchers involved in the study therefore participated in a one day workshop six months after completion of the study.

Cognitive mapping [1; 5] was used to identify influences on the lack of change in virtuality at Unit 2. Each researcher wrote possible influences on the lack of virtualization on "post-its". The capabilities identified in Section 1 and summarized in Appendix 4 were written on a whiteboard in the form of a fishbone diagram. The researchers pasted their post-its to the board. The result was a set of clusters of post-its around each capability. Where a post-it did not fit anywhere or where several post-its seemed to form a new group, a new heading and cluster was generated. Each researcher explained their reasoning and any new perceived causes or consequences which emerged from the discussion were also written down and stuck onto the whiteboard.

12.4 The Critical Success Factors

We identified several new success factors, which we judged should be given high visibility in the preparation for virtualization. These are:

- **Staff motivation**. While the literature recognizes the importance of staff capability, Unit 2's experience also underlined the importance of staff motivation. Capability and expertise needs to be accompanied by the motivation to adopt new ways of working and to work under virtual conditions, where cooperation and interaction with colleagues takes different forms and where the direct supervision of work performance is secondary to indirect, internal incentives.

- **ICT governance**. The literature on ICT capabilities focuses on ICT infrastructure and implemented systems. Certainly, Unit 2 had problems with the implemented ICT, but many of these could be traced back to differences in the understanding of Unit 2 staff and the central IT Services Department of the needs of remote staff as well as difficulties in funding ICT initiatives that would primarily benefit Unit 2 rather than the organization as a whole. These issues are issues of ICT governance rather than implementation or operational management. ICT governance is

    the system by which the current and future use of ICT is directed and controlled. It involves evaluating and directing the plans for the use of ICT to support the organisation and monitoring this use to achieve plans. It includes the strategy and policies for using ICT within an organisation. [7]

  ICT governance involves ensuring alignment between business needs and implemented ICT, the responsiveness of the ICT unit to business unit needs and oversight of the realization of business benefits from ICT initiatives [8; 9]. Its role in organizations with a centralized IT services unit is underlined by Marwaha and Willmott [3]:

    Centralizing IT with other functions in a shared services unit reduces costs and improves productivity but can distance business units from technology capabilities they need. To promote speed and innovation, companies must govern IT as they govern their businesses: with different rules and metrics for different parts of the organization.

- **The communicative environment**. An authentic communicative environment is one in which issues and critique can be openly articulated and discussed. There is clarity about the attitudes and perceptions of group members so that, even where agreement is not reached, there is transparency regarding the motivations and actions of others. This is critical in virtualization, not only because it facilitates general communication, but because the very nature of the virtual organization, separated in space, time and structure, renders communication and issue resolution more difficult.

- **Planning**. Planning is the translation of vision into the activities which operationalize and instantiate the vision. This activity should involve identifying and assessing the capabilities required for effective virtualization, and developing actions to overcome deficiencies. This might include technology acquisition or enhancement, new work procedures or management policies [2; 4]. The need for planning and project management is strangely absent from the literature of virtual organizations.

With the addition of these capabilities, the list of capabilities for virtualization now covers: vision, leadership, management capability, staff capabilities, staff motivation, ICT, ICT governance, work processes, the communicative environment, business case and planning. In the following sections we discuss these and their effect on virtualization in Unit 2.

12.4.1 Vision

Vision is the articulation of a credible, realistic and attractive future for an organization. The vision for virtualization should describe and explain the virtual form of working that will occur in the organization, convey a feeling for the technologies that will be used and the working relations that will emerge, and articulate the reasons for the transformation.

The importance of vision was reinforced by our study of Unit 2 and we were able to identify some attributes of the vision which appear to be particularly important for the virtualization process. These are: the foundation of the vision, i.e., whether it is genuinely worthwhile; the efforts made to communicate and sustain or share the vision; and its clarity, i.e., its meaning and the ability to represent it in a form in which it can be clearly communicated and understood.

The Foundation of the Vision

At the beginning of the virtualization process, Unit 2's management team outlined three desired outcomes (see Chap. 2). At the end of the 18 month period, we asked questions about each of them. Taking each of them in turn:

- "To be more flexible and responsive to the market in terms of competence, countries and clients". Virtualization was expected to provide a basis for improved operations, sales and marketing, identification of opportunities and threats, and bid planning and preparation. Market information from the field would be more readily available to managers. Despite its importance, no explicit attention was paid to addressing this goal as part of virtualization in Unit 2. Changing economic conditions and government policies, allocation of budgets on a project-by-project basis and immediate client demands had a strong impact on Unit 2's success during the period and it is not clear how virtualization would have been able to address these immediate pressures.

- "To broaden a sense of belonging to the organization and increase the stock of shared values and goals". This goal was of particular importance to the Director at the beginning of the period. Over time, however, it emerged that a sense of belonging to the organization did not (at least at a conscious level) interest staff. As highly qualified individuals, their stated interest was in stimulating, well paid work. The project-based nature of Unit 2's work meant that permanent consultants continually kept their eyes on the potential for the next project, not only to have interesting work but also to meet the organization's performance requirements in terms of billable hours. External contractors emphasized the need for a pipeline of well paid, secure work, rather than any need or desire to contribute to or feel part of the organizational culture.

- "To attract and retain the best people wherever they are". As we spent time with Unit 2's managers and consultants, it emerged that, in their experience, the "best" people are attracted by a strong company brand (as external contractors told us, the TPC brand, rather than Unit 2) and the opportunities it offers. From a psychological point of view, a "cyber workplace" image did not seem important. While younger consultants with experience in American and British organizations commented on the operational benefits offered by use of ICT to support communication and collaboration, the virtualization (or non-virtualization) of Unit 2 played no role in attracting them to work for the organization. There was some evidence that effective communications technologies (but not necessarily a strategy of virtualization) helped retain people: when the Francophone Market Area manager moved permanently to France, he continued to work in his position, staying in touch with the members of his market group through some advanced teleconferencing.

Sharing the Vision

Although he was respected and liked by most staff, the Director's management style was not one in which he communicated directly and frequently with Unit 2's staff as a whole. Rather, he usually prepared thoughtful analyses of vision, strategy and goals which he shared in a Friday morning meeting and then made available to all across the DIP. Consistent with his communication style, he did not reinforce the vision by repeating its goals and benefits to the staff once he handed responsibility for implementation to a Department Manager in December 2004. In an early interview, Fischer had stated that his goal was to increase virtualization in order to improve the quality of working life for consultants and increase the sense of belonging; this would have the side effect of increasing loyalty and commitment. However, this vision was never decisively transmitted to staff, who thought the strategy was to improve operational effectiveness – and could not see how virtualization would do this. On reflection we realized that, while the Director described what the GNO might look like, he never fully or clearly explained to staff why the strategy was so important.

Clarity of Vision

The academic literature and industry press is replete with definitions and examples of "virtual organizations" and "global networks". The research team took this knowledge into the research project, but it is not clear that the organization and its members possessed the same understanding. The vision of working across time, space and organizational boundaries using email, discussion forums, VOIP, desktop videoconferencing and other CSCW tools may be clear to academic nomads and certain classes of business people, but in retrospect it is not clear that this was the vision of the Director. Perhaps a fundamental reason for the lack of progress towards virtualization was that, for the Director and management of Unit 2, "virtualization" really only meant the implementation of a knowledge portal (the DIP) and electronic dialogue forum, but otherwise, business as usual.

12.4.2 Leadership

Strong leadership is a common critical success factor for organizational change. We identified several specific aspects of leadership that were important in this case: the leader's commitment, the influence of external factors on leaders, leading by example and leadership team support. Leadership for a change such as virtualization is more than a characteristic of a specific individual, rather it needs to be displayed by all those who have some form of managerial or opinion building function.

The Leader's Commitment

The Director initiated Unit 2's steps toward virtualization with élan and enthusiasm, but once he handed responsibility to the Department Manager with responsibility for knowledge management, his interest seemed to wane. Several events occurred more or less simultaneously with initiation of virtualization activities. The Director encountered problems with acculturation of consulting staff who had joined the organization following two mergers. An organizational survey showed low satisfaction among all HO staff; this, we observed, affected the Director's motivation for the virtualization initiatives, making him hesitant about promoting them too strongly while he sought to improve satisfaction among new and continuing staff. At the same time, the general business environment became more difficult. There was a noticeable decline in the Director's commitment to and interest in the details of ongoing implementation of virtualization initiatives. The precise reasons for this withdrawal are difficult to ascertain: perhaps there was a genuine loss of commitment through the blows of the employee survey; perhaps the Director was distracted through his myriad other responsibilities; perhaps having handed responsibility for implementation to the knowledge manager, he felt he was able to direct his attention to other matters.

The Influence of External Factors on Leaders

As a senior member of a larger organization operating in a changing marketplace, the Director of Unit 2 was not in complete control of his own fate. Tight targets were in place for revenue and expenditure and it was difficult to find resources to staff a virtualization project by, for example, employing an information systems support person, or allocating time and resources to education, training and discussion. The market and the policies of the organization's largest client changed during the period, and this diverted attention and energy from the virtualization project.

Leading by Example

The Director was an enthusiast for technology. He introduced virtual meetings with managers of other Units, using VOIP conference calling and document exchange, simultaneously accessing, discussing and updating documents across large distances. In contrast, neither the Director nor most members of the Management Team used Unit 2's electronic Dialogue Forum at all. The inter-Unit management meeting process was not visible to the general staff. On the other hand, many participants in the study (managers, consultants and administrative staff, both from within and outside

HO) noted the lack of participation by the Director and other managers in the Dialogue Forum, describing it as a case of "do as I say, not as I do".

Leadership Team Support

All members of Unit 2's Management Team were interviewed at some time during our research. While it appeared that each had supported virtualization to a greater or lesser degree at the initial envisioning workshop described in Chap. 2, the espoused enthusiasm waned considerably over the 18 months of our study. After 12 months, several managers expressed their doubts that there was any need for virtualization and others professed to not understand what the Director was trying to achieve. In particular, the vision did not seem to be shared by the Market Area managers, the managers with whom the consultants had most day-to-day contact. Indeed, the vision appeared to stumble at this middle management level; for example, one manager instructed members of their team not to use a discussion forum, as they had planned, to discuss certain emerging specialist issues. The manager's argument was that the discussion could not be ascribed to any specific project code, although the consultants complained that the manager was simply afraid of losing control. Another manager stated that the work conducted by consultants was so personalized and the level of client expertise was so low, that any sophisticated tools or "virtual" approach was misplaced.

12.4.3 Management Capability

There are many issues in managing a distributed, virtual workforce which particularly concern middle and line managers: performance, performance management, expertise assessment, control and group cohesion. Often, managers need to acquire new capabilities if they are to understand and manage these increasingly complex issues.

In Unit 2, new management skills were needed to cope with and fully exploit the potential of virtual operations. These capabilities include competencies in written (e.g., email or discussion forum) as well as face-to-face or telephonic communicative environments; an understanding of the challenges involved in managing virtual work; a notion of how to develop appropriate management, communication and work processes; and an understanding of the available technical tools to support the virtual organization.

Although we reported on the need to develop specific management competencies for working in the virtual organization in each of our reports and presentations of the research results, no attempt was ever made by the organization to assess management capabilities. No inventory of new skills desired or required was developed. Staff commented that, while some managers had the skills to communicate effectively in writing, by e-mail or in the DF, others did not.

One capability for managing in the virtual environment is an understanding of technologies and a preparedness to use, assess and apply these. But there was low appreciation for the portfolio of technologies available to manage distributed work, accompanied by a low perceived need for these technologies. Indeed, telephone and e-mail were viewed as superior to known alternatives and adequate for the management of remote staff. There was also a somewhat deterministic approach to the implementation of the new collaboration technologies. Little thought was given, for example, to the human and motivational issues associated with discussion forums, the choice of arguments or the potential role of managers in leading by example.

Causes for the lack of attention to management capability can be speculated upon: perhaps the managers' self-concept revolved more around administration than leadership; perhaps the capability of "reflection in action" [6] was missing; perhaps there was insufficient commitment to becoming virtual to raise the question of management competencies to the level of consciousness needed if they were to be addressed; perhaps there was insufficient time to explore and understand new ideas and technologies and their implications for the ways managers worked.

12.4.4 Staff Capabilities

There was little attempt to develop staff capabilities for virtual working. The staff had high levels of competency and adequate levels of understanding of technology. They demonstrated self-reliance, independence and self-sufficiency and they were confident that they had the capabilities to work in a virtual organization. To this extent, the capabilities of staff to operate in this environment seemed high. New capabilities, such as those required to access and use a knowledge portal and Dialogue Forum were quickly and effortlessly acquired. It is not clear, though, that all staff were able to use the new tools effectively. No training on effective use of discussion forums was provided and we do not know if there may have been an increase in use if some of the fears of the potential participants were addressed through training on modes of expression and social interaction in online forums.

12.4.5 Staff Motivation

Motivation to participate is a key component in almost any process for transformation. We identified two specific aspects of staff motivation which require thought when moving to virtual knowledge work: the personality attributes of staff and motivation to share knowledge.

Personality Attributes

The personality attributes of independence and self-reliance were amply demonstrated by Unit 2 staff and indeed, the organization had specific recruitment guidelines which selected people with these qualities. But precisely these highly educated, individualistic staff may have greater difficulty in committing to a group culture or identifying with supra-individual goals. The literature about virtual work emphasizes strong organizational culture as an important condition for binding people and maintaining group cohesion, but we note a tension between this and the type of self-interested and self-motivated people required to sustain virtual work over time.

Motivation to Share

At an interpersonal level, high levels of knowledge sharing and collegiality were noted and staff were very willing to help others with their experiences and knowledge. However, this motivation to share did not extend to the wider organization when measures were put in place to feed knowledge back into the organization for its own benefit in discussions such as the strategy forum on the DF. We can speculate about whether a discussion forum for new staff, of the kind envisioned in our initial workshop with management would have attracted more discussion. Motivation is associated, too, with trust, and the lack of trust that many staff expressed in the way management might treat opinions expressed in the DF would have affected motivation to share in this environment. Recognition of contributions in terms of hours billable to a discussion project code did not seem to be a motivating factor for consultants, who it appears would participate in a discussion forum in any case, if they were motivated to do so by the argument and a trusting environment.

12.4.6 Information and Communications Technology

A critical issue that emerged from our study of Unit 2 was that, no matter how much attention is paid to other factors, the technology itself must be adequate and provide the appropriate functions at an acceptable level of access, usability and performance. When dealing with staff in remote locations and under the different forms of contractual relationship that might be found in a virtual organization, reassessment of conventional thinking may be required.

ICT Tool Functionality

The primary new tools made available to remote staff in Unit 2 were a knowledge portal (the DIP) and an electronic discussion forum (the DF). The applications were very simple and lacked functionalities such as effective search, e-mail notification and subscription that enable such tools to be integrated readily into day-to-day work. To deliberately access these tools on the chance that there may be a change, or a change worth knowing about, was cumbersome and slow. This substantially reduced the likelihood of adoption of the technology by consultants and managers.

ICT Performance

The infrastructure in many of the regions where the organization worked was slow and unreliable, reducing the capability of technology tools to make a difference. When planning infrastructure to support virtual work, the whole network of interacting components (both local and remote) must be considered, as it is often the case that a communications infrastructure is only as strong as its weakest link.

Management of Security and Access

One of the most frequently cited problems in our discussions with Unit 2 staff was lack of access to systems. While consultants based in developing countries cited problems with national and local infrastructure, consultants based in developed countries also had problems. The security systems that had been put in place to prevent unauthorized access to corporate systems also prevented authorized access from outside HO in many circumstances. No matter how good the new systems might have been, lack of access meant that they were not used by many of the people for whom they had been developed. Furthermore, the failure of the organization to resolve access problems added to the anger and frustration of consultants. It seems that new attitudes towards information security, and perhaps more creative solutions than those commonly put in place, may be required in the virtualizing organization.

12.4.7 ICT Governance

The IT Services Department in TPC provided, as it name suggests, information technology services, principally the management and day-to-day operations of installed systems and ICT infrastructure. TPC had no individual or unit concerned with a more holistic view of information systems (IS). In general terms, the IS function or unit in organizations is concerned with the alignment between the organization's strategy and operations and its IT. Among the activities of an IS unit are the identification of business opportunities to use technology, the strategic management of technology priorities, the development and control over standards, the analysis of business requirements and the effect of technology solutions upon work processes and staff. Given the need to align both business and technology, the IS function operates best in an environment that enables and controls these two aspects of the organization. IS governance, also known as ICT governance, has become an important mechanism in organizations that address this complex blend of business and technical issues. Specific aspects of ICT governance that emerged from our analysis of Unit 2's experience were the critical role of ICT governance in ensuring alignment between business and technology, the need for IS architecture and the value of an IS function in the organization.

The Critical Role of ICT Governance

The acquisition and implementation of ICT does not happen in a vacuum, but must be closely aligned with business strategy and operations. ICT acquisition in TPC was the result of negotiation between business units on the basis of recommendations made by the business managers. But there was no subsequent oversight of implementation, assessment of business effectiveness or benefits realization. The specific managerial skills required to exploit and oversee technology assessment and implementation were not present. Neither Unit 2 nor its parent had a structure or system of ICT governance in place to oversee the making of a business case in relation to organizational strategy or to ensure that any implemented systems met organizational needs and achieved their business goals. A system of ICT governance would have defined roles and responsibilities for needs analysis, acquisition, implementation and review of installed ICT, and encompassed processes for ensuring alignment between business needs and the installed systems. It is likely that such a process would have identified the differences between a virtualization or GNO strategy and the simple implementation of two new information systems, defined whether the organization was indeed pursuing a virtualization strategy, developed a clear statement of the need for and goals of the selected initiative, and monitored progress toward achievement of the defined goals.

IS Architecture

One aspect of ICT governance is attention to the design of organizational ICT in such a way that it meets business needs within budgetary and technical constraints. An integrated plan for ICT and its management is known as the IS architecture of an organization. TPC had no IS architecture. The acquisition of ICT and embedding of new technologies and systems within the existing communications and security infrastructure was the responsibility of the centralized IT Services Department. There was, however, no wider architectural plan, and no guidance on how the needs of an individual business unit might be dealt with when they differed from those of the rest of the business. This restricted the range of choices available to Unit 2. It slowed up implementation and deployment, limited the functionality of the implemented systems, and impacted critically on the ability of staff to access systems and the information they contained. Because the IT Services Department undertook a technology function, it did not supply, or see the need to supply, the embedding services required for needs assessment or implementation.

Information Systems Function

The absence of an IS function from Unit 2 and its parent company meant that there was no individual or group with the responsibility for implementing an IS architecture. In organizations which have an IS function, that function is typically responsible for supporting a business group in formulating its technology requirements, designing and acquiring IT solutions and implementing these into the business. In the absence of an IS function, solutions were adopted for which there did not seem to be a need, the solutions lacked functionality, and implementation was dealt with in only a rudimentary fashion.

12.4.8 Work Processes

Most work within Unit 2 was individual or small group consulting work or project management. The primary unit was the individual project, which was specific to client needs. Performance was delivered through personal knowledge; indeed, contracts were acquired through bidding based on individual competencies as presented in a curriculum vitae, not on the basis of company methodologies or accrued organizational knowledge. Therefore, generic work processes for service delivery did not exist. As a result, project work in the organization did not require work process definition and design; furthermore, the vision of virtualization never had the intention of changing or improving the process of project work. For this reason, virtualization may not have been perceived as relevant by staff involved in service delivery.

Nonetheless, generic processes did exist for the preparation and submission of proposals and for project management. No attempt was made to review or revise these generic processes, even though traveling and remote staff criticized management for ignoring their local knowledge of available projects and expertise when bidding for new contracts. Bidding processes remained centered on HO, but required managers to travel even more than before.

12.4.9 Communicative Environment

Our analysis of the lack of change in Unit 2 highlighted gaps in communication within the organization, at least in regard to virtualization. The Management Team did not communicate their views to senior management; staff did not communicate their views to their managers or the Director. Somehow the issue of the virtualization was "undiscussable" (or not important enough to merit discussion) – even though otherwise in the organization the level of openness, participation and consensus appeared high and the staff (being articulate, educated and confident) seemed to express their views directly and openly.

12.4.10 Business Case

A business case was never developed for virtualization and no catalogue of savings or benefits was documented. The achievement of a long-term material benefit was never compared to the short term material costs. Consequently, no indicators were developed for success and no targets were defined. This was particularly noticeable because the organization was otherwise very cost-conscious and costs were closely managed.

We cannot explain why no business case was developed. Perhaps virtualization was seen only in terms of the implementation of the two systems (the DIP and the DF), more as a general purpose internal infrastructure project than a multi-dimensioned, specific program, and therefore not in need of a business case. Perhaps the objectives articulated in the vision were considered to be business case enough. Perhaps there was a sense that the project should proceed "by stealth" given the other difficulties the organization was facing (although our discussions with the Director gave no indication of this). Regardless of the reasons for lack of a business case, its absence was notable. A business case is not only an aid to management decision making, it is also a method for sustaining management commitment; there does appear to have been a link between the loss of management commitment and the absence of the business case.

12.4.11 Planning

Strategic planning was well developed in TPC and Unit 2. The Director and the Department managers prepared thoughtful, far reaching and well articulated strategies and strategic plans for the unit. But, although the knowledge manager included virtualization activities in her own personal work plan, there was no formal plan for virtualization in Unit 2. Two related aspects of planning for virtualization were not addressed: project planning and IS planning.

Project Planning

No project plan was ever prepared for virtualization. No project code was assigned, no budget was developed, no milestones were established, no deadlines were set, no strategy was developed to communicate goals and achievements to staff. Activities were defined within the task sets of individual members of staff, but not within the context of a project. In her reflection on the virtualization process at Unit 2, the knowledge manager specifically noted the need for planning in future.

IS Planning

There was no analysis of the technology needs of the organization, not just in relation to virtualization, but also in relation to the specific technologies that were developed and implemented to improve virtual communications (the DIP and the DF). The usual processes of analyzing user requirements, designing solutions to work and management needs and issues, product selection, training and implementation were not carried out in the systematic way usually associated with IS projects.

12.5 Conclusion

This analysis has enabled us to make visible risks which may prevent an organization from achieving its purpose of virtualization. The impact of the capabilities we have itemized in this section is severe enough to justify management focus on each of them as a critical success factor for virtualization. Failure to explicitly address and manage the capabilities discussed in this chapter is likely to present a threat to any significant virtualization project. In the following chapter, we therefore summarize the lessons learned from our research in terms of these factors.

References

1. Ackermann F, Eden C, Cropper S Cognitive mapping: getting started with cognitive mapping. Retrieved 2 May 2006 from http://www.banxia.com/de-paper.html.
2. Gray CF, Larson EW (2003) Project management: the managerial process. McGraw-Hill, New York
3. Marwaha S, Wilmott P (2006, Fall) Managing IT for scale, speed, and innovation. McKinsey Quarterly, pp 14-21
4. Project Management Institute (2000) A guide to the project management body of knowledge (PMBOK guide). Project Management Institute, Newtown Square, PA
5. Rughase OG (2002) Linking content to process. In: Huff AS, Jenkins M (eds) Mapping strategic knowledge. Sage, London, pp 46–62
6. Schon DA (1983) The reflective practitioner. Basic Books, New York
7. Standards Australia (2005, March) Australian world-first ICT governance standard. Retrieved 10 June 2007 from http://www.standards.org.au/cat.asp?catid=66&ContentId=82&News=1
8. Ward J, Daniel E (2006) Benefits management: delivering value from IS & IT investments. John Wiley & Sons, Chichester
9. Weill P, Ross JW (2004) IT governance: how top performers manage IT decision rights for superior performance. Harvard Business School Press, Boston

13 Tools and Capabilities for Becoming Virtual

Paul Jackson and Jane Klobas

13.1 Introduction

In this book, we have introduced a framework for conceptualizing the process of virtualization and used it to study knowledge processes and virtualization in a single organization. In this chapter, we consider what we have learned from studying Unit 2 that can be of value to other organizations that are considering becoming virtual. Unit 2 did not achieve its goal of virtualization. But, as is often the case, breakdown reveals more about what is required for success than smooth traveling. The specific aspects of virtualization that the research team studied during the project provide additional insight into the risks of virtualization and the conditions and processes that might be adopted by successful virtualizing and virtual organization. We conclude this research by reviewing the lessons learnt from the individual research projects. We then draw on these, along with the analysis presented in Chap. 12, to summarize lessons for organizations planning to take advantage of network technologies to improve their ability to operate effectively across space, time and structure. Finally, we comment on the potential value for managers and researchers of the virtual alignment model (VAM) and the methods developed to track virtuality and capabilities in the study.

13.2 Virtualization and Knowledge Work

Even under optimal conditions, knowledge work is fragile, vague and poorly understood. In building new theory in Chap. 4, Jensen and Jackson suggested that the construct of social uncertainty may explain why staff did not contribute to or become involved in the Dialogue Forum or embrace virtualization. Uncertainty in the social arena, with its resulting focus on the individual and the in-group led to withdrawal of consent and participation, eroding social cohesion and reducing contribution to the larger social groups of TPC and Unit 2. This uncertainty is cognitive, not affective, and may not be noticeable as behavioral hesitancy or personal diffidence, but it will lead to reduced participation. It is a function of distance and space, but also of trust, identity, ontology, rate of change and power relations. If virtual work relations are not to lead to this withdrawal of participation in knowledge processes, then managers must attend to and enhance the other constituent elements: raise trust, work at maintaining shared meanings and ensure that clear lines of command and legitimation exist.

Communities of practice have been proposed as one method of maintaining knowledge sharing across spatial and legal boundaries, by providing group membership criteria such as common interest or purpose. In Chap. 5, Bernini and Klobas used social network analysis to investigate the effect of communities of practice on organizational commitment. They found that members of a strong community may indeed have a lower level of organizational commitment, preferring to place their loyalty with their community rather than the broader organization. Managers should be aware of this effect. Efforts to develop and encourage communities should be balanced and open, and managers should consider developing strategies of inclusion for the larger group.

In Chap. 6, Jackson developed a metadata description of the structure of organizational memory. This blueprint could be helpful in developing access to explicit or tacit content using directories, content management systems and ICT. This is potentially a practicable approach for supporting virtual knowledge work.

In Chap. 7, Jackson and Klobas extended the notion of transactive memory systems (TMS) to cover organizations, rather than small groups, and found that the maintenance and use of personal knowledge directories (who knows what, where to find something) play a significant part in knowledge work. TMS appear to increase in importance as staff become more distributed, particularly where knowledge is hard to codify and share using technology. Organizations that provide means and opportunities for the mutual maintenance and updating of these personal directories and facilitate communication between distributed staff when knowledge retrieval is required are likely to operate more effectively than those where these opportunities are limited. Virtualization provides a threat to TMS because working across distance and time limits these opportunities.

The importance of access to knowledge sharing technology, as well as its perceived value, was underlined by Renzi, Klobas and Jackson in Chap. 8. While systems must be perceived to be relevant, and the attitudes of managers and colleagues are important influences on intended use of a knowledge resource, these are of little value if the organization is unable to provide access to the systems to a significant group of people, such as the large proportion of Unit 2 staff outside HO.

A managerial view of virtual work was taken in Chap. 9 by Jackson, Klobas and Gharavi. One of the major reservations of managers under virtual conditions is that of monitoring and control. But the possible modes of influence over knowledge workers appear to be varied and numerous. This implies that managers do not need to focus on a single aspect of control, such as reporting or measurement, but can use several dimensions of influence such as inculcation with values and self-monitoring, observation by peers and customers, professional pride, procedures, auditing and so on.

Kjaer, the knowledge manager of Unit 2, revealed many insightful lessons learned from the perspective of a managerial participant in the process of implementing knowledge management systems for virtualization in Chap. 11. Proper scoping and planning, adequate budgeting, training, motivation and the development of champions, and the criticality of support systems for work processes. Above all, the message from Kjaer is that learning should never stop, and that reflection and honesty play a crucial role in ongoing improvement and the correction of glitches and hindrances.

13.3 Capabilities for Virtualization

Critical capabilities for successful virtualization are vision, leadership, management capability, staff capability, staff motivation, ICT, ICT governance, work processes, a communicative environment, the business case and planning. All these are important, but thoughtfulness and reflection are required to understand what they mean, how to weigh up their relative importance and how they should be approached. The following observations are derived from examining and extrapolating from the data gathered during this project, where appropriate, in relation to the experiences of other organizations and theorists as recorded in the literature. They are presented here not as a recipe for success or as the result of empirical testing, and readers must decide the relevance and significance of each observation to their own circumstances.

13.3.1 Vision

- Virtualization is not business as usual with a bit of technology thrown in. It is a change of mindset that requires careful planning, conviction and continual reinforcement.
- The vision needs to be clear, strategic and credible, using language and concepts understood by the staff. Credibility is gained through making the reasoning behind the strategy clear and compelling.
- The vision should relate to and consider the work processes and needs of the staff. It should be translated into objectives and tasks which guide each individual on the journey toward working with others in the virtual organization.
- The management team needs to be committed to the cause of virtualization and support the leader in promulgating the vision. Motivation of the management team requires a cooperative development of the vision, but on its own this is not a sufficient condition.

13.3.2 Leadership

- Leaders should demonstrate ongoing commitment to achieving the vision through hands-on action, conversation and communication. They should plan to allocate attention to virtualization even in the presence of other demands on their time.
- The vision requires continual communication and reinforcement by the whole management team.
- The motivation of managers to participate and to lead might be increased by specifically defining responsibilities for developing aspects of virtual working and linking achievement of specific goals to reporting and reward schemes.

13.3.3 Management Capability

- Policies and practices should be reviewed to take account of greater geographic dispersal, remote working and working under varying conditions and circumstances.
- Supervisors of virtual staff should be educated in the specifics of virtualization, managing business processes and performance, and communicating effectively using new tools with staff employed under new conditions and in different locations.

13.3.4 Staff Capabilities

- A catalogue of skills specifically required for virtual working should be developed and integrated into job descriptions and roles. This might include the use of specific technologies, personal time planning and management, e-mail management and business process knowledge.
- Competency levels should be reassessed to evaluate the level of independent work staff can undertake.
- Skills upgrade programs should be executed as required.
- Attention should be paid to maintaining and enhancing skills, even when employees may be out of sight and apparently performing well.
- Capabilities such as the ability to work independently, take decisions and accept responsibility, overcome isolation and make good judgments are very important. Existing and new employees should be assessed for these capabilities.

13.3.5 Staff Motivation

- The motivations of employees to adopt virtual modes of working should be understood: professionals and knowledge workers are often motivated by high degrees of freedom and autonomy, flexibility and responsibility. Work and role design for the virtual organization should address and enhance these motivations.
- The nature of identification with the company should be understood in order to maintain commitment as workers disperse. Putting resources and time into building a strong corporate culture or organizational commitment may be misplaced.
- If staff draw their motivation from a personal identity composed mostly of self-interest (such as professional progress and advancement, interesting and stimulating work or generous reimbursements) then these incentives should be maintained or developed.

13.3.6 Information and Communications Technology

- Any technology that is selected for virtual work must be functionally appropriate, useable and useful, and adequately support the business processes and communications necessary for virtual work.
- The infrastructure carrying the applications must be responsive, deliver acceptable performance at all points and be accessible to all members of the organization.

- Application access issues must be identified and problems resolved as early as possible. If ICT policies restrict access to certain functions beyond a firewall. for example, this will make virtual work impossible, ineffective or frustrating. Virtual work may require a rethink of what level of security is acceptable, trading off reduced security against the advantages of free information flow. Ensure that the appropriate level of business management makes these decisions – they should not be left to IT staff to decide.

13.3.7 ICT Governance

- It is not enough to acquire technology. Even good technology and useful applications can be squandered if the right management approaches are not used for implementation and exploitation. Proactive ICT governance is required to monitor planning, acquisition, installation, implementation and operation of the technology, ensure that issues are promptly resolved and that the technology is being used productively.
- Specific information systems (as distinct from information technology) knowledge is required to analyze the business processes, develop requirements and specifications for technology, identify weak spots and threats and resolve ICT issues.

13.3.8 Work Processes

- Virtualization requires a clear understanding of the organization's work processes, including secondary and support processes such as performance reporting and human resource management. Work processes should be analyzed to identify where changes are needed to enable and support work by a dispersed staff and staff employed under different contractual conditions.
- Work processes should be adapted to take advantage of virtualization. After a process analysis has been performed, process sequences and performance targets should be adapted to ensure that the potential advantages are actually realized.
- Issue resolution and escalation procedures should be reviewed to ensure that pathways are available for staff employed in diverse locations and under diverse conditions to receive attention for process exceptions or when they have grievances.

13.3.9 Communicative Environment

- Virtualization will mean that communication paths will become largely disembodied (or non face-to-face) and less frequently based on opportunistic meetings in the corridor or by the coffee machine. This will require adjustment of communication processes and conscious attention to communication media. Particularly during the process of becoming virtual, a feedback and communication mechanism must be put in place as the disruption of normal lines of communication may mean that important information regarding the impact of virtualization (among other things) may be lost.
- An authentic environment of communicative interaction is required to correct course and repair issues where necessary. Honest feedback is very important, offered within an environment in which criticism is taken as constructive and an opportunity to adapt and improve. Managers and staff need to be able to express their reservations about any aspect of virtualization such as the vision, the strategy, the mode of implementation and so on.

13.3.10 Business Case

- A sound business case is required in which the economics of virtualization are argued and the costs and benefits laid out. This will allow clear budgeting and commitment of funds and resources.
- A strong business case will contribute to the retention of management attention and commitment over the period of time during which the virtualization is taking place.

13.3.11 Planning

- Virtualization is, in many instances, a project: it is a one-off, unique undertaking with specific goals. As such, it requires planning, goal setting, measurement, milestones and budgets. All the accompanying aspects of a standard project should be considered.

13.4 Envisioning and Monitoring Virtuality

We now turn our attention to conclusions about the tools and methods we developed to track and assess progress towards the virtual organization.

We anticipate that this toolset can be used by both business managers and researchers.

Fig. 13.1 summarizes the overall approach we used. We developed three tools: the envisioning workshop, a virtuality dashboard accompanied by measures and methods for evaluating virtuality, and a capability dashboard also accompanied by measures and methods for evaluating capability. We comment further on each of the tools in the following sections. Application of each tool enabled us to develop, as an outcome, a concrete expression of vision (including drivers and goals), the level of virtuality and capability for virtualization. The dashboards enabled goals and progress to be reviewed at a glance. The VAM guided assessment of the extent of alignment between vision, level of virtuality and capabilities for virtualization, and identification of the consequences of misalignment. In the case of Unit 2, the misalignment between need for virtuality, actual virtuality and the capabilities indicated that action was required to raise capabilities if the level of virtuality was to be raised.

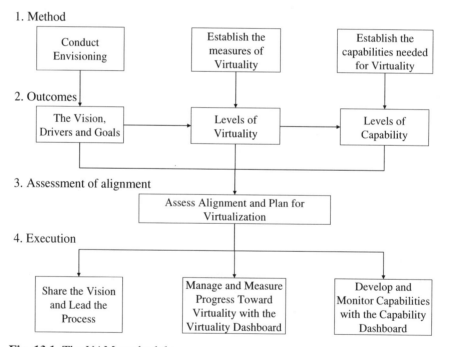

Fig. 13.1. The VAM methodology

13.4.1 Envisioning Workshop

Some form of envisioning process is required to develop a vision and strategy for virtualization. Ideally, this will be a collective and consensual undertaking in an authentic and honest communicative environment. The workshop described in Chap. 2 and Appendix 7 guided managers to identify the business reasons (environmental change, competitive pressure, staff needs, and efficiency goals) for virtualization and develop a clear vision for what virtualization means. This approach also enabled the vision to be phrased in such a way that attributes of virtuality could be defined and a desired level of virtuality established as a performance target for each attribute.

13.4.2 Virtuality Dashboard

The virtuality dashboard is a concise and yet informative source of insight for managers. In times when management attention is a scarce resource, the detail which is lost through abstraction can be compensated for by the immediacy of information. Our experience is that the virtuality dashboard is useful and accurate, but, as with all forms of performance measurement, "scores" and the dashboard need to be supported by quantitative or qualitative analysis or both, and be accompanied by qualitative explanation and analysis.

13.4.3 Capabilities Dashboard

The capabilities dashboard is a good starting point for understanding what must be done to achieve virtuality. It supports planning by identifying the capabilities required for virtualization and draws attention to which capabilities need to be developed and by how much. Like the virtuality dashboard, scores need to be supported by appropriate observation and accompanied by qualitative explanation and analysis. The capabilities dashboard also provides a platform for prediction of change, on its own or in conjunction with a tool such as the VAM.

13.4.4 Virtual Alignment Model

The results of our research present a convincing case for the importance of alignment and the usefulness of a tool like the VAM. The VAM provides a fairly simple method to organize information about the relationship between goals, current state and the capabilities needed to operate effectively in the envisioned state. Nevertheless, alignment is only useful if the goals one sets are worthwhile. One lesson we learned is that, although critical, alignment is only useful if the business goals are sound. Critical review of a strategy is required: is it important, worthwhile, realistic or meaningful? Only if they are, do the acquisition and positioning of capabilities to align with virtualization goals really make sense.

13.4.5 Using the VAM Methodology

The VAM methodology is based on an understanding that different organizations will need or want to take different virtual forms. Managers can use our toolset to envision the form of virtuality they need to meet their business goals in their business environment. The vision can be expressed in a set of attributes which characterize the required form of virtuality. An important aspect of our approach is that the defined attributes are not absolute or common to all organizations, but derived from the specific virtual form envisaged by a specific organization. Targets can be set and the gap between targets and the current position estimated using quantitative measures and qualitative observations. The capabilities required to achieve the targets can also be identified. The VAM provides a framework which guides planners to identify the extent to which capabilities need to be developed, or indeed if there is an excess of capability. Researchers may wish to use the toolset to examine specific phenomena or aspects of virtualization, such as social isolation, knowledge generation, employee satisfaction or market success, at one moment in time or over time.

13.5 Conclusion

The ability to mobilize networks of knowledge irrespective of boundaries of space, time and organization has become a critical competence for global and distributed organizations. The need for virtualization, whether it is directed towards telework, dispersed teams, remote projects, virtual supply chains and virtual corporations, networked collective intelligence or some other as yet not described organizational form, will continue. In large or complex organizations, one or several configurations of virtuality may exist. In this book we have described how we followed one organization pursuing a virtualization strategy and how we measured and observed progress towards their particular vision of virtual work. This journey will take different trajectories for different organizations, depending on their products, services, markets, technologies and preferences. But the need for envisioning, target setting, monitoring and measurement, analysis and development of capabilities is common to all. We hope therefore that the methods, tools and insights in this book will contribute to the understanding and development of virtual organizations for some time to come.

Appendix 1:
Virtuality Indicators

Jane Klobas

Introduction

This index describes how virtuality was measured in the study. Unless otherwise indicated, all survey items are measured on a five point scale:

1 – strongly disagree
2 – disagree
3 – neither agree nor disagree
4 – agree
5 – strongly agree

A sixth option, "I cannot answer this question" was also included in the survey form. Scores on the survey items could be mapped to the five levels of performance as a virtual organization described in Chap. 1. Thus, a score of 4.3 provided a preliminary indication that the organization was operating near the fourth level (standardized) on the dimension that the survey item was measuring. We did not, however, rely only on the survey items to assess level of virtuality. We also drew on organizational data and remarks made to us in meetings and interviews.

Virtual Staff

A single indicator, obtained from organizational records:

• Ratio of Contract to Permanent staff

Measured by counting the number of staff in each category and converting the result to a ratio, e.g., with 205 contract staff and 81 permanent staff, the measure of virtuality on this indicator is 2.5:1.

Dispersal of Staff

Two indicators obtained from organizational records:

- Ratio of HO-based staff to staff based outside HO
- Percentage of time permanent staff spend outside base location

One indicator obtained from staff survey:

- Communication patterns. In a non-virtual organization, there is an inverse relationship between frequency of communication and distance [1]. A different pattern of relationships would be expected in a virtual organization. Measured by asking:

    What percentage of the people you work with is located in each of the following locations? (Write the percentage to the left of each category. Please check that the total is 100.)

	The same floor in the same building where I work
	Different floor, same building
	Different building, same town
	Different town, same country
	Different country, same time zone as me
	Different country, different time zone to me

ICT for Virtual Work and Communication

One indicator obtained from organizational records:

- Percentage of authorized staff able to access the ICT provided or endorsed by the organization to support virtual work.

One indicator obtained from interviews with staff in representative locations:

- Reported ability to access ICT to support virtual work

One indicator obtained by survey:

- Staff perception of the ICT to support virtual work. Survey item:

    - I have access to all the information technology I need to work effectively in a virtualized organization[1]

---

[1] In an organization with a named virtualization project, "in a virtualized organization" should be replaced with the project name, e.g. "in the Global Network Organization".

Processes for Virtual Work and Communication

One indicator obtained from organizational records:

- Number and nature of formal work and communication procedures and practices changed in order to accommodate or promote virtual work

Two indicators obtained from interviews with staff in representative locations:

- Reviewers' assessment of attempts to ensure work and communication processes are suitable for a virtual organization
- Reviewers' assessment of the effectiveness of any attempts

Two survey items:

- My communications with other people in the organization are not constrained by where I work
- The work flows that are in place for my job are not constrained by where I work

Virtual Mindset

From interviews with staff in representative locations:

- Extent to which staff speak of the organization as a whole, i.e. without drawing attention to differences among different groups

Four survey items:

Which of the following is more important to you? (Choose just one by putting a mark in the box beside your choice.)

	The nature of the work that I do.
	The place where I work.

Which of the following best describes [organization name]?[2]

	We are a consulting organization based in [location of HO].
	We are an organization of consultants who work in developing countries throughout the world.

- The virtual organization is business as usual for me in my work for [organization name]
- I feel I am a part of [organization name] wherever I work

---

[2] The response statements for this question should be varied to describe the type of work and specific locations in which the organization works.

Innovation in Client Service

From organizational records:

- Services based on virtual working that are actually offered to clients

Shared Values

Extent of agreement with the organization's stated values expressed in the form of survey items. The items should be drawn from the organization's statement of values where such a statement exists. Senior managers' expressions of organizational values may be used to extend or to substitute a formal statement of values. While the average score is most important on other indicators, the variation in scores is important in this case: the less variation, the more a value is shared. All but the last two items listed below were drawn from TPC's formal statement of values and use the words of that statement. The last two items were drawn from the management workshop described in Chap. 2.

- My Unit 2 colleagues conduct themselves with integrity and credibility in every respect
- My Unit 2 colleagues have confidence and respect for me as a human being
- Decision making is predominantly consensual in Unit 2
- My Unit 2 colleagues always strive to maintain a high level of professional competence
- I have considerable freedom in every aspect of my work
- I work to meet Unit 2's quality demands
- In my situation, it is sometimes difficult to act in accordance with Unit 2's corporate values [reverse scored]

Shared Understanding of the Organization

Five survey items. The items have high internal consistency (Cronbach's alpha above .8) and can therefore be used to form a scale, i.e., to obtain a single score to represent shared understanding.

- I know what is going on in [the organization]
- I understand why things must be done a certain way in [the organization]
- There is a strong collective understanding of the goals of [the organization]
- There is a good cooperative spirit in [the organization]
- It is clear what is acceptable behavior in [the organization]

Identity

The Organizational Commitment Questionnaire described in Chap. 5 was used to measure organizational members' sense of belonging to the organization.

We also used the Twenty Statements Test (TST), a test commonly used in psychology to gauge the extent to which an indivual's identity is concerned with self, close relationships, and the collective or wider community [3; 5].

Trust

Trust was defined as the extent to which staff have positive expectations of the intentions or behavior of others irrespective of their ability to monitor or control the others [6]. We used two common items to measure general trust [4; 7]:

- Most people in [the organization] are willing to help if you need it
- In [the organization], one has to be alert or someone is likely to take advantage of you [reverse scored]

In addition, we used four items drawn from [8] to measure work completion trust (on a 5 point scale from 1–never to 5–frequently)

- How often do you need to check or ask if your colleagues have completed their tasks?
- How often do you wonder if your colleagues are contributing to the team?
- How often do you worry about your colleagues' work performance?
- How often do you check on your colleagues' progress on deliverables to clients or management?

The trust scale was administered twice (trust was not measured in the baseline survey). In both administrations, Cronbach's alpha was above .8.

Staff Satisfaction

We used one survey item, familiar to the staff and organization because it is used in the periodic organizational climate survey, to measure staff satisfaction:

- [The organization] is an attractive place to work.

Other organizations may prefer to use survey items that are familiar to their staff. Alternatively, staff satisfaction measurement scales are described in handbooks of organizational measurement such as [2].

Economic Effectiveness

Economic effectiveness should be measured against indicators established by the organization. If the virtual organization is managed as a project, for example, the organization might establish an expected return on investment (ROI). Progress toward that, or any other, measure of economic effectiveness will need to be measured throughout the project.

Overall Indicator of Perceived Level of Virtuality

At the end of the study period, we asked members of the organization to rate the level of virtuality using the scale that we used to rate the level of virtuality on each of the dimensions in the Virtuality Dashboard. The exact question was:

Overall Assessment of Unit 2 as a Virtual Organization

We would like you to give your evaluation of the actions that Unit 2 has taken toward operating as a virtual organization. Below, you will find a scale that is used to rate the performance of virtual organizations. Please put a mark beside the level that you think best describes Unit 2.

	None	No action taken
	Ad hoc	Effective only in HO and/or among senior staff
	Basic	HO and international staff have similar levels of performance but difficulties are still faced as a result of being virtual
	Standardized	Benefits of operating as a virtual organization outweigh the problems
	Optimizing	Effective for all staff in all locations at all times

References

1. Allen TJ (1977) Managing the flow of technology: technology transfer and the dissemination of technological information within the R&D organization. MIT Press, Cambridge, MA
2. Fields DL (2002) Taking the measure of work: a guide to validated scales for organizational research and diagnosis. Sage, Thousand Oaks, CA
3. Grace SL, Cramer KL (2003) The elusive nature of self-measurement: the self-construal scale versus the Twenty Statements Test. Journal of Social Psychology 143:649–668
4. Kramer RM, Cook KS (eds) Trust and distrust in organizations: dilemmas and approaches. Russell Sage Foundation, New York
5. Kuhn M, McPartland TS (1954) An empirical investigation of self-attitudes. American Sociological Review 19:68–76
6. Rousseau DM, Sitkin SB, Burt RR, Camerer C (1998) Not so different after all: a cross-discipline view of trust. Academy of Management Review 23:393–404
7. Zand DE (1972) Trust and managerial problem solving. Administrative Science Quarterly 17:229–239
8. Zolin R, Hinds PJ (2004) Trust in context: the development of interpersonal trust in geographically distributed work. In: Kramer RM, Cook KS (eds) Trust and distrust in organizations: dilemmas and approaches. Russell Sage Foundation, New York, pp 214–238

Appendix 2:
Baseline Virtuality at Unit 2

Jane Klobas

Virtual Staff

In December 2004, there were 81 permanent staff, of whom 22 were based in the field. An estimated 205 non-permanent ("freelance" or "contract") consultants were working in the field. There were, therefore, 2.5 non-permanent staff for every permanent staff member. No specific target has been set for the level of virtual staffing, although there is an expectation that the proportion of virtual staff will increase. We therefore consider virtual staffing to be **Standardized**.

Dispersal of Staff

There was 1 staff member based in HO for every 2.8 staff based in the field. At any one time, about 49% of permanent staff are outside HO. On average, permanent staff spend 22% of their time traveling. Most respondents worked primarily with people working on the same floor in the same building as them. The next highest dispersal rank was, however, with people working in a different country and different time zone; 70% of respondents reported working with people in this category, and it accounted for, on average (median), 20% of their contacts among other staff. Fig. A2.1 compares this pattern of communication with that expected in a non-virtual organization where the frequency of communication diminishes with distance. Dispersal of staff is business-as-usual the introduction of virtual teams of consultants has not yet been considered. The level of virtualization on this dimension is **Standardized**.

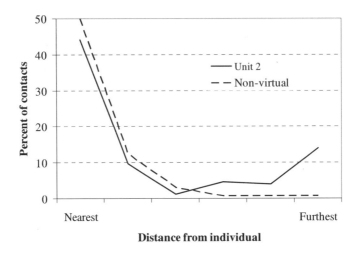

Fig. A1.1. Pattern of communication in Unit 2 compared with non-virtual firm

ICT for Virtual Work and Communication

The available information and communications technologies (ICT) are the telephone (terrestrial national and international carriers), Skype (for voice over IP), e-mail, and the Unit 2 intranet, the Development Information Portal (DIP). Administrative staff and consultants are not provided with corporate mobile phones.

Staff based in HO reported good access to e-mail both while in HO and while traveling, although some complained of slow lines while traveling. Several staff working outside HO reported having no access to e-mail while working in the field. These staff access e-mail when they are in population centers that provide access from a company office, or more usually, an Internet cafe or home. Predominantly, they use personal e-mail addresses and personal or public Internet service providers rather than those provided by the company.

Few staff were aware of the availability of Skype until a question was asked about it in the survey. Those staff who have tried to use Skype while traveling reported disappointing results.

The highest proportion of DIP users is among HO administrative staff (80%). Around 60% of consultants reported using the DIP. Respondents reported that access to the DIP was limited by the ICT infrastructure available to them outside of HO.

There are no collaborative work tools, although a company-wide project to select a corporate collaborative work platform during 2005 received strong Unit support and the Unit will participate in the pilot project.

The level of use of ICT to support the virtual organization is **Ad hoc**.

Processes for Virtual Work and Communication

No work methods, practices or practices or work flows have specifically been designed or modified to support virtual work. Existing practices for management of projects in the field operate smoothly. Those managers and staff responsible for bidding for contracts travel to those countries in which contracts are awarded. There has been no explicit evaluation of whether virtual working might offer alternative approaches to the bidding process.

Permanent staff in all categories perceived that work flow and communication are, to some degree, constrained by their place of work. Only international contract staff do not agree. For international contract staff, location does not constrain work flows and communication.

Level of virtualization of virtual work processes is between **Ad hoc** and **Basic**.

Virtual Mindset

Virtual mindset is an indicator of the degree to which virtual displacement effects staff's feeling of business as usual. Overall, there is a sense that working in the virtual organization is business as usual, with staff based outside of HO agreeing that this is the case more strongly than those based at HO. The virtual mindset of the Unit as a whole is classified between **Ad hoc** and **Basic**, reflecting the low scores of permanent consultants on the second question.

Innovation in Client Service

No services based on virtual organization were offered at the time of this survey.

Shared Values

Staff were asked, in the baseline survey to rate their level of agreement with ten values statements. These statements were drawn directly from company Statement of Values. Self-reported adherence to company values was high at a mean of 3.9. The level of virtualization on this dimension is **Standardized**.

Shared Understanding of the Organization

While management, HO administrative staff and international consultants on contract agreed with the statements associated with shared understanding and cooperative spirit (scores above the midpoint of the scale), scores for permanent consultants in all locations were below the midpoint of the scale. Unit 2 is rated **Basic** on this dimension, reflecting permanent consultants' relatively low scores and the difference between their scores and those of other staff.

Identity

Staff have a stronger sense of individual and interpersonal identity than identity with the company. The survey asked staff to describe their sense of belonging to four layers of the organization: TPC, Unit 2, the Market Area in which they work most often, and their professional community of peers. The lowest sense of belonging was to TPC while the highest overall score was for the community of peers. Although company identity is low relative to individual and interpersonal identity, there is a moderate to high sense of belonging to different layers of the organization. Overall, we assess the level of virtualization on this dimension as **Basic**.

Staff Satisfaction

Although all groups' mean staff satisfaction scores were above the midpoint of the scale, HO consultants' scores were low (3.2) relative to the others'. The relatively low score for HO consultants indicates that staff satisfaction is between **Basic** and **Standardized**.

Cost-effectiveness

Unit 2 has no financial indicators for measurement of progress toward the envisioned level of virtuality. Measurable investment to date has been the staff time invested in participating in the surveys and interviews described in this report. No training has been offered in use of ICT or in principles and practices of distance communication. There has been no review of work practices and procedures. A rating of **None** has been assigned to cost-effectiveness.

Appendix 3:
Virtuality After One Year

Jane Klobas

Virtual Staff

The ratio of contract to permanent staff remained much the same over the study period. At the beginning of the study it was 2.5:1. Six months later, it was 2.8:1, and at the end of the study, it was 2.7:1. Over this period, the number of permanent staff increased by 11%, while the number of contract staff increased by 19%. The level of virtualization on this dimension remained unchanged: **Standardized**.

Dispersal of Staff

The dispersal ratio of staff based outside HO to staff based in HO also remained much the same over the study period. The pattern of communication was similar in all periods, with most respondents communicating primarily with people working on the same floor in the same building as them, followed by people in a different country in a different time zone. The level of virtualization on this dimension remained **Standardized**.

ICT for Virtual Work and Communication

An electronic Dialogue Forum was launched in this period to provide a forum for online discussion and exchange of ideas. It had some use for the first two months after launch when there was a facilitator, the main topic for discussion was organizational strategy, and a project code was assigned for the strategy discussion. It had little use after that.

The DIP continued to be the primary tool for dissemination of information. Sixty percent of staff contacted in a Unit 2 survey of DIP access either did not have access or did not respond to efforts to contact them.

Remote and traveling staff continued to report problems gaining access to systems or, if access were available, with the speed of connections or security issues. Staff perception of the availability of ICT to support virtual work remains only moderate. The level of use of ICT to support the virtual organization remained **Ad hoc**.

Processes for Virtual Work and Communication

No specific actions to adapt processes for virtual work and communication were taken during the study period. There was no change in staff perception of the adequacy of processes to support virtual work. While project-related processes were mostly effective, other processes – including communication processes – were effective for less than half the staff responding to the survey. Virtuality of work processes remained between **Ad hoc** and **Basic**.

Virtual Mindset

A high proportion of staff (90%) reported that the nature of their work was more important to them than the place where they worked. There was a slightly stronger tendency to describe the organization as an international organization rather than an organization based in a particular city. These figures indicate that there was a stronger tendency toward a virtual mindset than a mindset based on geographical location. Managers and administrative staff, who dealt with staff in all locations, had a stronger sense of their remote colleagues than HO-based consultants. Consultants interviewed in HO admitted that they did not think of international colleagues much because their projects seldom intersect. Virtual mindset remained between **Ad hoc** and **Basic**.

Innovation in Client Service

No services based on virtual organization were offered during the study period. The level remained **None** throughout.

Shared Values

Both management and consultants based outside HO reported that it was harder at the end of the study period than at the beginning to act in accordance with corporate values. Consultants outside HO found it more difficult than managers. We re-evaluated this dimension as between **Basic** and **Standardized**.

Shared Understanding of the Organization

Understanding of the organization was unchanged for all groups except consultants based outside HO who reported lower scores at the end of the study. It appears that performance on this dimension may have slipped as outside consultants lost sight of the organization. We have downgraded the level of virtuality on this dimension to between **Ad hoc** and **Basic**.

Identity

In all periods, staff had a stronger sense of individual and interpersonal identity than identity with the organization or Market Area. As in other periods, sense of belonging was strongest to community and Market Area, and weakest to TPC. While sense of belonging scores suggested a level between Basic and Standardized, the fact that the original goal of improving sense of belonging through virtualization was not met led us to maintain the assessed level of virtuality on this dimension as **Basic**.

Trust

The level of trust was high for staff in all categories except consultants outside HO whose score was at the midpoint of the trust scale. This relatively low level of trust among key members of the virtual organization led us to rate trust between **Basic** and **Standardized**.

Staff Satisfaction

There was no significant change in staff satisfaction over the study period. Mean staff satisfaction at the end of the study was 3.8, between **Basic** and **Standardized**.

Cost-effectiveness

No financial indicators of cost-effectiveness were implemented and cost-effectiveness cannot be measured.

Appendix 4:
Capability Indicators

Jane Klobas

Introduction

Unless otherwise indicated, all capabilities were measured on a five point scale:

1 – very low (barely present)
2 – low
3 – medium (sufficient for normal performance in non-virtual organizations)
4 – high
5 – very high (sufficient for high performance in a virtual organization)

Vision

Vision was examined in interviews with the Director, a management group seminar, interviews with staff and the staff survey. Three questions were asked in the survey to estimate the extent to which the vision of virtualization is shared across the organization. Cronbach's alpha for this scale was .76.

- I understand what [the Director] means when he refers to "the virtual organization"[1]
- [The organization's] continued success depends on our ability to work effectively as a virtual organization
- [The organization's] customers will benefit from our ability to work more effectively as a virtual organization

---

[1] Items that used the generic form "in the virtual organization" should be replaced with the project name, e.g. "in the Global Network Organization" in an organization with a named virtualization project.

Leadership

Data about leadership for virtualization were obtained from interviews and seminars. Semi-structured interviews with the Director were a key source of information. The Director was provided with a list of aspects of leadership for virtualization taken from the literature reviewed in Chap. 1:

- Building and sharing a vision and purpose
- Implementing change management
- Building an environment of trust
- Developing management competencies
- Communication
- Rewarding staff
- Empowering staff
- Motivating knowledge workers

He was asked to describe what action he had taken on each of these fronts. An additional aspect of leadership emerged from the interviews:

- Ability to negotiate effectively with the wider organization

Management Capability

Information about management capabilities was obtained in meetings, seminars and interviews with management. In addition, staff perceptions of management capabilities were obtained from two survey items:

- My managers have all the knowledge and skills that they need to manage in the virtual organization
- I feel that my managers are well suited to work in the virtual organization

Staff Capabilities

Three indicators to measure staff capabilities were included in the survey. The first indicator measures their perception that they are suited to work in a virtual organization while the other two indicators measure access to organizational services to help with work in a virtual organization:

- I feel that I am well suited to work as a member of a virtual organization
- I have access to all the training that I need to work effectively in the virtual organization

- I have access to all the personal assistance that I need to work effectively in the virtual organization

ICT

Detailed analysis is required to understand and evaluate the ability of the ICT infrastructure to support a virtual organization. Evaluation needs to take place at at least two levels: the level of the provider and that of the user.

Interviews with ICT providers present the official view of what technologies are provided. If the organization also has architectural or infrastructure documents or other documents to guide planning, these documents can be consulted to gauge the extent to which virtual work is being taken into account. For our research, we met with Unit 2's information technology (IT) staff as well as with the staff of TPC's central IT Services Department.

The actual availability of ICT may differ from the theoretical provision. Users therefore need to be consulted. We asked users about the ICT infrastructure in all the locations where they worked, in seminars, interviews and surveys. In the survey, we listed the systems that management and IT staff considered systems for the virtual organization, and asked members of the organization to indicate how they obtained access to organizational systems (type and location of Internet and/or intranet connection), whether or not they could access each system and, if they could, how frequently they used it. We also asked them to explain their frequency of use. A generic indicator of user perceptions of the adequacy of ICT for virtual work was provided by a survey item:

- I have access to all the IT I need to work effectively in the virtual organization

Processes for Virtual Work and Communication

Evaluation of processes for virtual work and communication should consider both those processes directly associated with performing business activities, for example, project management in a project-based organization, and processes associated with communication or the "nutritional" [1] aspects of being in an organization.

Organizational documents describing procedures and processes can be scanned for evidence of the extent to which they support virtual work and communication. Interviews with staff can provide additional information.

One item was included in the survey to gauge staff perceptions of the adequacy of work practices:

- All the necessary work practices are in place to support the virtual organization

Business Case

If the organization has prepared a formal business analysis of a proposal to become virtual, it should be possible to gauge economic capability from that analysis. In the absence of a formal business analysis, other sources of information will be needed. These might include assessment of the adequacy of any budget set aside for virtualization, including development of capabilities along the dimensions described in this Appendix. If the organization does not assign a specific budget, the ability to use funds in other budget lines or draw on external sources of funds will need to be assessed.

Reference

1. Shapero A (1985) Managing professional people. Free Press, New York

Appendix 5:
Baseline Capabilities for Virtualization

Jane Klobas

Vision

The Director has a clear vision and an understanding of the implications of virtualization for organizational strategy, the staff and external consultants. The Management group understands this vision and appears to share it. External consultants, who work every day on the virtual boundaries of the organization, are aware of what working in a virtual organization entails, but HO-based consultants are less sure (their score on the Vision scale was 3.1, compared to 4.5 for the external consultants).

The *Vision* capability is **Medium**. This rating reflects the relatively low scores of HO consultants whose more confident buy-in to the vision is necessary before it can be considered to be shared, at which point it would be rated High.

Leadership

The Director articulated a vision and purpose for virtualization very clearly. He described the organization as virtual in terms of dispersal of staff and noted that the other dimensions of virtuality needed to be developed as an "add on" to what already exists. He is confident that he has shared the vision with HO administrative staff and that he has their support; the survey statistics for *Shared vision* support this confidence. He is concerned that some other staff feel that they will lose some of the "fabric" that keeps the organization together.

The Director's change management efforts have focused on incremental improvements associated with tools for virtualization (in particular Internet-based technologies), methods for disseminating information that is presented in meetings in HO to staff outside HO, structures to encourage dialogue between staff, and obtaining the understanding and commitment of senior management (Departmental managers) and HO administrative staff. These efforts have produced the DIP and a system for rapid publishing of the reports of weekly meetings. The DIP has been positively received, although staff hope for more from it. A new organizational structure in which a Departmental manager has been made responsible for briefing and debriefing is associated with efforts to improve dialogue.

The Director acknowledges that there is some resistance to virtualization. The scores of HO consultants on the virtuality dimensions suggest that there may be higher resistance among these staff than others. This is not surprising since consultants have not been as involved in change management as other categories of staff.

No specific action has been taken to build an environment of trust. The Director noted that some of his actions may even have reduced trust.

No specific action has been taken to develop management or staff competencies for the virtual organization. The Director recognizes the need to develop skills in online communication, but is unsure how to go about this.

The Director described the need to communicate with staff in all locations rather than giving staff in HO first priority. He acknowledged the importance of the language used to communicate about the process of virtualization and reiterated the need to emphasize that development along those dimensions of virtualization that have yet to be developed is an "add on" to the already partially virtualized organization. His espoused approach is to give a consistent message based on the idea rather than the tools.

The Unit's staff are seen to be empowered in relation to their project work. The Director sees confidence in use of tools for virtual communication as a necessary pre-condition for empowerment in the virtual organization; action has been taken to identify "e-tasks" and "e-skills".

The Director's preferred approach to motivating knowledge workers is to invite participation in the virtual organization, but he noted that Unit 2 does not yet have the operational or management culture to invite participation from staff who are not in HO. He sees actions taken in response to the most recent organizational climate survey as contributing to the motivation of staff to participate in the virtual organization.

Rewarding staff does not seem to have the same emphasis in European culture as in the primarily American literature which emphasizes its importance for virtualization. The Director's reflections on rewards emphasized the potential for an increased sense of belonging, increased participation and increased opportunities for management to listen to staff. Interviews with staff confirm that these are areas in which they would appreciate improvements.

The Director has taken specific action to represent Unit 2 and its needs for tools for virtualization to TPC.

Leadership capabilities are rated as **Medium**, recognizing that the Director has a clear vision and has taken some initial concrete steps toward change management, but that action still needs to be taken on several other leadership dimensions.

Management Capability

The mean response to the survey items that measure perceived capability was below the midpoint of the scale indicating that, overall, staff are not confident that management yet have the capabilities to manage in the virtual organization. Scores were particularly low for HO consultants and consultants seconded to projects abroad. The research team observed that no specific action has taken to develop management knowledge and skills to manage in the virtual organization. Management capability is evaluated as **Low** to **Medium**.

Staff Capabilities

Staff were confident about their suitability to work as members of the virtual organization, however only managers and permanent consultants on short-term mission reported that they had access to the training and support needed to work in the Global Network Organization. The score for all other groups of consultants were low. While staff are confident that they are suited to work in the virtual organization, we evaluated their capability to do so as **Low** to **Medium** because the support mechanisms for work in the virtual organization are not yet in place.

ICT

In interviews and seminars, staff who worked outside HO were highly critical of the communications infrastructure available to them. Communication and access difficulties were also prominent in survey responses. Most staff who did not use the DIP said they had access and communication problems. There is no CSCW software in place, and the proposed Dialogue Forum is not available. There is therefore no specialized software available to support teams or project work at a distance. ICT for the virtual organization is limited to e-mail and the DIP, and only for those who have access to sufficient secure Internet bandwidth to use these facilities. Because such a high percentage of staff have problems with access, ICT capability must be rated **Low**.

Processes for Virtual Work and Communication

Analysis of level of virtualization concluded it is between Ad hoc and Basic in terms of processes for virtual work and communication. The level of virtualization on this dimension also provides the platform of capabilities for future virtualization. We have therefore evaluated capabilities for virtual work and communication processes as between **Low** and **Medium**.

Business Case

Unit 2 has support from TPC for its virtualization initiative. Nonetheless, the project-based costing structure of Unit 2 puts constraints on the costing of a Unit-wide project from which returns may be intangible. Theoretically, virtualization will bring financial advantages in increased access to markets and consultants, and therefore to projects, but Unit 2 has not undertaken an analysis of the potential costs and benefits of virtualization. We were unable to rate accurately the economic capability of Unit 2 at the time of the baseline survey.

Appendix 6:
Capabilities After One Year

Jane Klobas

Vision

In their response to survey questions about their understanding of the Global Network Organization (GNO) strategy, respondents indicated that they understood the strategy. Furthermore, their responses suggested that were aware of the strategic benefits of working effectively as a GNO. The mean score of HO-based consultants was nearer to that of other staff in this period, rather than much lower as in the baseline study. On the other hand, managers' mean scores were lower than in the baseline study and, in interviews, several managers noted that the Director's vision for the GNO was not clear or that the case had not been made convincingly enough. Some consultants also criticized the focus on the virtual organization as hollow. On reflection, there seems to have been some confusion between GNO, virtual organization and the actions taken to support these organizational forms. Unit 2 had been reorganized as a GNO before the study began. The "global" in GNO referred to global dispersal, and the organization was to be improved by becoming "virtual" as well as "global", using Internet technologies to improve communication, collaboration, culture and business opportunities. Implementation of the "virtual" component rested on two information technologies: the DIP, which was to be improved, and the Dialogue Forum (DF), which was to be introduced to support asynchronous discussion. The vision did appear to promise more than improvement of an existing information resource and the introduction of a discussion forum, but actions were directed only toward the new and improved communication tools. On balance, given the lack of clarity, we continued to rate the *Vision* capability as **Medium**.

Leadership

Our comments on leadership at the end of the study period consider members of the Management Group as well as the Director. The Department Manager with responsibility for implementation of initiatives associated with the GNO invested considerable effort into improvements in communication, improvements in the DIP and access to it, and the implementation of the DF over the year. Her efforts were acknowledged by staff who spoke positively of changes in meeting structures, the communication leadership taken by this manager and the high quality of the DF implementation process. On the other hand, Market Area managers appeared to have hardened their attitude to virtualization, with generally negative attitudes expressed during interviews. Some staff reported that Market Area managers told them they did not approve of their participation in virtual organization activities. Without the support and leadership of this group of middle managers, the virtualization strategy was unlikely to succeed, regardless of the efforts of more senior managers. We revised capability on this dimension downward to between **Low** and **Medium**.

Management Capability

Staff perceptions of management capabilities for the virtual organization increased from low to medium to medium over the period, probably reflecting the work of the manager charged with implementation of the GNO. No other actions were taken to assess or to improve management capability. Nonetheless, the impact of the Department Manager was significant, and management capability was upgraded to **Medium**.

Staff Capabilities

Staff perceptions of their own capabilities to work as members of the GNO were slightly lower at the end of the study period, but still moderately high (mean of 3.8). Their perception of the availability of training, support and technology for working in the GNO remained low. We continued to rate employee capability as **Low** to **Medium**.

ICT

Despite attempts to diagnose and improve infrastructure for access to Unit 2 systems, 60% of staff outside HO remained unconnected because of problems with Internet access or authentication, or could not be contacted. The addition of another ICT tool for communications (the DF) increased ICT capability, but continued poor access from outside HO acted as a severe constraint. There was no significant change in staff response to the item, "I have access to all the IT I need to work effectively in the Global Network Organization", and staff based outside HO continued to report even lower satisfaction with access to IT. Nonetheless, some improvements had been made. We therefore upgraded ICT capability slightly from Low to **Low to Medium**.

Processes for Virtual Work and Communication

The introduction of the DF created the potential for improved processes for virtual work and communication. We suspect that one problem with introduction of the DF may have been limited attention to the work processes that surrounded use of the tool. While a facilitator was appointed for the first two months and a job number was issued for participation in the DF discussion on organizational strategy, no initiatives were taken to socialize staff to communication in an online environment in which one's statements are permanently recorded for all (from peers to managers at all levels) to see, and little attention was paid to educating potential users to the ways in which online discussion forums could be incorporated in their work to improve communication processes.

Staff did not perceive any significant improvement in the processes for virtual work and communication. Their responses to the item, "All the necessary work practices are in place to support the Global Network Organization" remained low and were substantially unchanged from December 2004. We rated process capabilities for virtual work and communication processes at the end of the period as **Medium**, reflecting the high quality of project management processes, but process capabilities for virtual communication outside the project arena remain nearer Low than Medium.

Business Case

In spite of the potential for support from TPC, Unit 2 was constrained in its efforts to become a virtual organization by the financial limitations of being a project-based organization. Much of the cost incurred during the study period were indirect opportunity costs, specifically the cost of a senior manager investing her time in the GNO project rather than other activities and the cost of administrative staff studying access to the DIP. Little direct cost was incurred during the period, although the appointment of an IT support person will incur direct costs in the year subsequent to the study. The junior nature of this appointment reflects the low direct investment that the organization has been able to put into its virtualization strategy. We do not expect this appointment to have a significant effect on the critical IT infrastructure and process capabilities; to have such an effect, the appointment of a senior information systems professional would have been required. Inability to invest in staff of the required level led us to rate economic capability as **Low to Medium**.

Appendix 7:
Exercises for an Envisioning Workshop

Paul Jackson

Exercise 1: The Shape of Virtualization in Unit 2

The first exercise is to develop a formal definition of virtualization (WHAT is virtualization – what form will it take in Unit 2?), e.g.:

Virtualization at TPC Unit 2 is _____?

Each manager will present the view of virtualization from a different perspective. Each will have a hat which is the identity of an anonymous colleague known to them:

- A CEO hat
- A Manager at Unit 2 hat
- A Project Manager hat
- A Consultant's hat
- An Administrative Employee hat
- A Union Representative hat
- A Support Specialist hat

Each manager will present a definition of virtualization based upon the hat they are wearing and state what it means to them.

- What does virtualization mean to me in my job?
- What work is done virtually to make my job different to now?
- What must be done face-to-face?
- Who communicates with whom and how?
- What is the effect of virtualization on "my hat" and the people I deal with?

Exercise 2: The Objective of Virtualization

The second exercise will develop goal statements for "virtualization" at TPC (HOW will it help?).

The objective of the virtualization process can be expressed in the form "**TO** achieve business goal xyz **BY** providing certain facilities, capabilities and conditions for Unit 2 staff, e.g.:

- TO assist _____ BY_____

- TO improve _____ BY_____

- TO gain _____ BY_____

These statements will be constructed as follows:

1. The first half of the statement (TO) will be brainstormed by the team and, where possible, will include metrics for measuring the improvement.

2. The second half will be completed by specifying for each goal:

   "To achieve success in goal XYZ we **need** the following resources and capabilities…"

   Each response will be written on RESOURCE post-its and linked to each point.

3. Then the group will consider each RESOURCE post-it and write ISSUE post-its of a different color which represent issues, problems or hindrances in the provision of that resource. These will be linked on the white board to the RESOURCE post its.

Exercise 3: Virtualization Case Studies

The following vignettes are challenging scenarios which describe virtualization in progress or the results of virtualization. The main groups of factors which influence the success of introducing virtual organizing are seen to be:

- Leadership and management
- Business process effectiveness and elegance
- Employee capability and motivation
- Technology enablement

Each participant will be assigned a case and report back to the group what that case means to them. The questions following each scenario are intended to stimulate thought processes, but please do not feel restricted to answering only those questions

Leadership

The organization experiences demanding times. The business environment is difficult and a general feeling of negativity has taken over the staff. Sick days are up, morale is down and rumors are flying. Layoffs may be required, but there may be some light at the end of the tunnel because after the troubles are over, there are great opportunities for the Unit. But many of the staff are external and seldom seen. The Unit HO is empty. There is no-one to meet, no-one to talk to. You call a meeting to discuss the situation but only 10 people turn up. You broadcast an announcement on the Website, but have no idea who read it, how they reacted or what it meant to them. You want to improve the climate through motivating, optimizing business processes and empowering staff. You want to let everyone know where things are going and that you have a plan for change. But where do you start?

- How do you feel about this?
- Does TPC have the leadership skills to make the company work in this environment? If not, what must change?
- Could you give clear, inspiring messages to build a vision and unity of purpose?
- How will you make it work?

Business Process

There is a project commencing, upon which the organization depends. It will mean follow on work and be a great reference in difficult times. You believe your project manager and staff are competent, but some are new, and some (although excellent) have a reputation for occasional lapses. They are spread out all over the globe and have never worked as a team together before. The support specialists are also distributed and work from home in different cities and even countries. Some also report to other managers. You rarely see them. You are worried, will they know how to perform, will they understand their roles and obligations and how they depend upon each other? The timelines and milestones seem to be clear – at least to you...

- How do you feel about this?
- How can you be confident that the team really understands the importance of this particular project and its priorities?
- How can you trust them to pursue TPC's interests?
- How will you control progress, identify and repair problems before it too late?
- How will you ensure the team members (and other managers) really know their own roles?
- How will you monitor team cohesion?
- How will you make it work?

Employees

TPC wins a lot of business and you need to expand quickly. You need new project managers and administrative staff. You advertise and the best candidates live overseas. You interview them through videoconferencing, employ them and commence induction through the Internet. They are assigned to projects and some travel to their site for months at a time and have their base at home. Every six months they come to HO and you meet them and at six monthly intervals thereafter. They rarely meet other staff, even when they are in HO. You find it hard to assess their performance and contribution. Similarly, some tell you at intervals they don't feel valued by the organization and wonder how their great efforts are to be recognized if you don't even really understand how hard they are working and how difficult it is to overcome working alone and without someone to talk to. Meanwhile, the staff who are mostly at the office wonder what on earth the remote people are up to...

- How do you feel about this?
- Describe the particular problems in this scenario and how you would deal with them.
- Do you have the people management processes to deal with this? What is missing?

Management Without Face-to-Face Contact

You are a senior manager of Unit 2. You are absent from the office for 150 days per year. You do not stop managing or delegate your role when you are on the road: you conduct net-meetings, use e-mail and videoconferencing to communicate with your staff. Your laptop has Internet Voice and

Video Phone: you can view all financials, record, correspondence, human resource information and project management systems from the single screen. But you cannot stop in the hallway, just have conversations with staff, and invite people for a beer...

- How do you feel about this?
- Is it realistic? Could you work like this and be a good manager?
- Most of your staff are on the road. Does it matter you are too?
- How can you imagine this working? What needs to change?

Technology

Your office is in cyberspace. You log on and the world and the organization are at your fingertips. You feel at home when you see the screen, with the TPC logo, all your tools, and all your information. You can link to anyone through a skills database, electronic forums (for specializations and projects), talking into the laptop microphone, you have videoconferencing. All your information systems (finance, HR, project tracking) are available at high speed, from anywhere. There are bulletin boards for special issues, projects and there are well laid out sources for all information you need to do your work. Everyone in TPC has this capability and actually uses it: you post a query and within minutes it is answered by someone, because everyone is online

- Can your technology group ever provide this?
- Are you aware of technologies which can give you the global networking you require?
- Will this ever happen? If not, why not? What could prevent it?
- It will be great to be like this... won't it ...?
- Why do you need an office?
- What will you miss? Are you just being sentimental?

Appendix 8:
Questions for Exploring TMS

Jane Klobas and Paul Jackson

Uncovering TMS – Interview Questions

1. What do you think constitutes the information and knowledge which makes your Department effective or even special?
2. Where is information and knowledge regarding roles, procedures and work-related advice usually kept (technology, paper, people's heads)? How is this information and knowledge usually found? Are there any issues in accessing this information and knowledge?
3. Are there any things in your work environment which you feel influence your capability or motivation to express your knowledge to others?
4. Are there any things in your work environment which you feel influence your capability or motivation to absorb new knowledge?
5. Do you think the organization learns from your experiences? Describe the processes of how the organization learns from the experiences of the staff. How does it make this available to others who might need it?

Evaluating TMS – Questionnaire Items

Questionnaire item
I have a map in my head of who knows what in the [organization]
My map of "who knows what" in the [organization] includes people outside Head Office as well those within Head Office
I keep my knowledge of what others in the [organization] know up to date

Questionnaire item
It is difficult for me to keep up to date with who knows what in the [organization]*
My colleagues in the [organization] contribute little to the knowledge I need to complete my tasks*
My personal map of "who knows what" is an effective way of finding knowledge in the [organization] when I need it
The structure of the [organization] makes it difficult for me to get knowledge and information from the people who have it*

*Reverse scored item

Appendix 9:
Measuring ICT Value and Accessibility

Jane Klobas

The following items were used to measure attitudes to use of the DF (Value), perceived control of use (Accessibility) and intentions to use the DF in the future[1]. Note that the bold headings were not included in the survey form and the Value and Accessibility items were randomly intersorted. In this study, Cronbach's alpha for the Values scale was .85. For the Accessibility scale, it was .78. Principal axis factoring was used to demonstrate discriminant validity. The scale can be adapted for other systems by changing the name of the system and the organization. Items associated with the published goals of the system or specific attempts to optimize accessibility might be added according to the needs of the organization.

Items to Measure Value and Accessibility

Even if you have not used the Dialogue Forum, please give us your impression of it:

	I cannot answer this question	strongly dis-agree	dis-agree	neither agree nor dis-agree	agree	strongly agree
Items used to measure attitudes to using the Dialogue Forum (Value)						
Using the Dialogue Forum is important for my work						

---

[1] Validated in several other studies including Klobas JE, Clyde LA (1998) Learning to use the Internet in a developing country: validation of a user model. Libri, 48:163-175

	I cannot answer this question	strongly disagree	disagree	neither agree nor disagree	agree	strongly agree
I am not interested in using the Dialogue Forum*						
The Dialogue Forum helps me to keep up to date with what is happening in Unit 2*						
Using the Dialogue Forum, I can make a contribution to Unit 2						
The Dialogue Forum is not relevant to me*						
I appreciate the interaction with others that the Dialogue Forum provides						
I enjoy/would enjoy using the Dialogue Forum						
Items used to measure perceived control of use (Accessibility)						
I do not know very much about the Dialogue Forum*						
I know how to use the Dialogue Forum						
It is/would be frustrating to use the Dialogue Forum from my current place of work*						
I have no time to use the Dialogue Forum						
I have access to all the help I need to enable me to use the Dialogue Forum						

Please answer the following questions by marking the point between 1 and 5 that best represents your response.

	I cannot answer this question	1 not at all	2	3	4	5 frequently
I intend to participate in discussions in the Dialogue Forum during the next three months						
During the next three months, I intend to read what others say in the Dialogue Forum						

Appendix 10:
TPC Network Infrastructure

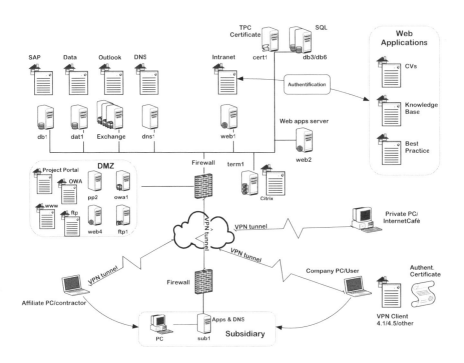

Becoming virtual :
 knowledge management and
      c2008.

2008 01 09

Printing: Krips bv, Meppel
Binding: Stürtz, Würzburg